BEATING THE U-BOATS

REAR-ADMIRAL JOHN PHILIP ROLLESTON, D.S.O.
Who played a conspicuous part during the First World War in destroying the U-boats.

BEATING THE U-BOATS

By
E. KEBLE CHATTERTON
(*Author of "The Epic of Dunkirk"*)

The Naval & Military Press Ltd

Illustrated

Published by

The Naval & Military Press Ltd
Unit 5 Riverside, Brambleside
Bellbrook Industrial Estate
Uckfield, East Sussex
TN22 1QQ England

Tel: +44 (0)1825 749494

www.naval-military-press.com
www.nmarchive.com

In reprinting in facsimile from the original, any imperfections are inevitably reproduced and the quality may fall short of modern type and cartographic standards.

PREFACE

In *Fighting the U-Boats* I told the detailed story of the period covering the years 1914-1916, examining one by one how, where, and why each enemy submarine was sunk.

In *Beating the U-Boats* I have in the same manner completed the story of 1917 and 1918, showing the means and methods by which the Germans' U-boat menace was utterly defeated after many difficult months that called forth our supreme effort on the sea. Together these two volumes cover one of the most thrilling periods in our history. But whilst *Fighting the U-Boats* and *Beating the U-Boats* embrace the entire adventurous epoch of those four years in which we met, and finally smashed the enemy's cunning, the reader who is interested in these exciting duels will find all the glamour that belongs to some of the finest marine episodes in our time.

This book may therefore be read by those who delight in first-class yarns quite independent of their historical setting. The lessons to be obtained in our contests with U-boats during this critical period of our existence are available in perusing the following chapters.

E. KEBLE CHATTERTON.

CONTENTS

CHAPTER		PAGE
I.	GERMAN MINELAYING	7
II.	PURSUING THE U-BOATS	12
III.	PERISCOPES AND TORPEDOES	19
IV.	FOULING THE FAIRWAY	27
V.	THE GERMAN MENACE	32
VI.	"WASSER BOMS"	37
VII.	SUBMARINES VERSUS DESTROYERS	40
VIII.	U-BOAT ADVENTURES	43
IX.	MEDITERRANEAN DRIFTERS	47
X.	SLOOPS AND SUBMARINES	55
XI.	TURN OF THE TIDE	63
XII.	U-BOATS' HAZARDS	69
XIII.	SUBMARINE CAPTURED BY SOLDIERS	74
XIV.	GERMAN MORALE	80
XV.	THE U-BOAT'S TERROR	85
XVI.	WAYLAYING THE ENEMY	93
XVII.	UB-81 GOES TO HER DOOM	99
XVIII.	OUT OF THE DEPTHS	108
XIX.	THE "CLOVER BANK" II	115
XX.	GERMANY CRACKS	120
XXI.	THE VICTORIOUS "ZUBIAN"	124
XXII.	YACHTS VERSUS SUBMARINES	128
XXIII.	THE SUBMARINES WEAKEN	132
XXIV.	WEEKLY SINKINGS	138
XXV.	WAYLAYING THE LINER	144
XXVI.	GERMANY BEATEN	149
	APPENDIX—THE CAPABILITIES OF A U-BOAT	153
	INDEX	161

LIST OF ILLUSTRATIONS

Rear-Admiral John Philip Rolleston, D.S.O.	*Frontispiece*
	FACING PAGE
In the Otranto Straits	16
H.M.S. *Partridge II*	17
British submarine	32
British submarine after coming to surface	33
British E-class submarine	48
Dropping a depth charge	49
The biter bit	64
U-103 photographed in Heligoland Harbour	65
Commander Rucker, one of the most notorious U-boat captains	80
The torpedoed Q-ship *Zylpha* is about to sink	81
U-boat victims	96
Submarine's torpedo does her damnedest	97
H.M. Yacht *Lorna*	128
Salving the German UC-44	129

MAPS

	PAGE
How the patrol areas were eventually assigned as America was entering the war	57
How the U-48 was shelled and sank	103
Closing the Sea. How the Anglo-American minefields closed the North Sea against German U-boats	143

CHAPTER I

GERMAN MINELAYING

IF the period 1914–16 was that in which we were startled by German submarines, which surprised not only us but themselves by such attainments, the next two years witnessed a gradual success in grappling with a vast menace till in April 1917 the peak of sinkings had been reached and thence—with certain modifications—the national danger to the British food supplies became less and less until the sea grew safer and safer by November 1918.

In *Fighting the U-Boats* we had a story to tell which can be compared only with *Beating the U-Boats* for the grandeur and immensity of its subject. For until then never had the realm been so endangered. Despite all our naval strength we were threatened so severely by the mine and submarine, that the possibility of becoming starved was no idle boast of the Germans but a severe threat. Though we had not lost the Battle of Jutland, we had to realize how inventions had so quickly moved that no longer could naval history be written in terms of the surface ship. Explosives had become so magnified in their power, and the ship could be navigated below the surface with such facility on her warlike occasions, that the very nature of Anglo-German drama became transformed. There was one rivalry of stalwart armed and armoured deep-draught ships, but though Jutland shewed them performing a full dress rehearsal, another war-within-war had to be decided in respect of the under-water vessels. And we shall now apply our minds to watch this exciting contest which engaged a stupendous effort of money, courage, and seamanship.

Our aim, then, is to shew every German and Austrian submarine loss which occurred between January 14, 1917, and the signing of the Armistice on November 11, 1918. It is a great story, a mighty theme of terrific endeavour and tragedy, the clashing of great passions, the varying spectacle of uncertain results pending. We want to examine every one of these submarine sinkings—whether of U-boat, UB-boat, or UC-boat—and learn for ourselves exactly what was the great task, how we overcame what seemed a hopeless undertaking; whilst not omitting to fill in the background of our picture with colourful details that will make the picture more vivid though not less authentic.

The rise and fall of the German submarine menace in itself means a most entertaining campaign. As a phase of the recent past it is also an illuminating study suggestive of comparison with the U-boat activities of the Second Great War that began in 1939. Though Hitler sought to benefit from the mistakes of 1914–1918, and to make the Second War little else than a more savage and brutal continuation of the First, he failed at the outset to appreciate that because of our sea supremacy the U-boat peril in the long run must finally be defeated. And Germany never has got over the shock of sinking her Fleet in Scapa, though Hitler's mind does not envisage what it means to this day.

As the year 1916 receded and 1917 shaped itself more definitely, it became more certain than ever that Jutland would not be repeated but that German hostility on sea would be under two headings: (*a*) Mines; (*b*) Submarines. Now that naval warfare, confined to the operations of small ships, emphasized this must be different from any preceding section of history, the trend of events was fast being moulded in a unique direction so that a fresh emphasis was given to certain expressions. Sea power and naval might no longer could be confused; 'control of the sea' required very exact definition. Mines and U-boats might be more dangerous than lasting.

But the initial months of 1917 by answering the instant demands showed in which direction we must expect enemy pressure to proceed and whence it would originate. Thus, notwithstanding existing resources, the Admiralty commissioned 30 small paddlers, 18 Scottish motor drifters, and a large number of steam drifters. The intention therefore was to employ shallow craft for minesweeping but use the trawlers for anti-submarine work. There would now also be 100 new twin-screw sloops, and 300 drifters. At the same time more German submarine minelayers were becoming available.

The number of German mines went on increasing until April 1917 when we swept up 515, but with some exceptions there was a fall onwards till the end of the year. The fact that during 1917 practically every important portion of the British Isles was mined along the coast—excepting that area between Humber and Cromer which the enemy had intentionally left clear because he probably was contemplating raids or invasion at that part—is hardly surprising when we bear in mind that the total number of mines laid during 1917 was double the number of 1916. Nevertheless the greater minesweeping experience combined with higher training of personnel and the use of M.L.s for scouting at low water for these dark 'eggs' had much to do with a gradual reduction in the loss of minesweeping vessels. Similarly there were fewer losses of mercantile ships partly because traffic was better controlled and the use of 'otter' gear became more general during the latter half of this period.

What was the 'otter' gear?

It was an affair attached to the merchant ship's bows somewhat similar to the device used in the Navy known as a 'paravane'. Crudely expressed, we may state that the 'otter' gear resembled two great whiskers which coming in contact with the moorings of a mine cut them adrift and enabled the mine to be sunk. Thus this mine having been thrust aside from the ship's line of progress, she is enabled to carry on her course.

It is extremely interesting to study how this form of warfare was being carried on. The old days of sending out such German war vessels for this duty as the *Königin Luise*, the *Albatross* and *Stuttgart*, were gone. With the exception of the raiders *Mowe* and (later) the *Wolf*, the task of minelaying had passed to the submarines. In the first part of 1917 the enemy concentrated on the south and south-west coasts of Ireland thinking thereby to destroy much of the Anglo-American traffic which was becoming quite considerable though more would develop presently because of the notable political international change that would shortly come about. As I was personally concerned for many months in sweeping these tares off the two specified parts from Ireland, I happen to retain vivid recollections.

At first—that is to say in the early weeks after the submarine's arrival from Germany—she would unload the entire cargo of mines in one batch off some notable headland such as Galley Head, Mizzen Head, or the Old Head of Kinsale (where in each case there was a lighthouse which stood convenient for giving the submarine a 'fix' during her work); but by the end of the year the enemy used to study more closely our minesweeping organization. That is to say he would carefully note the channels swept, presently again foul the cleared passage and even torpedo the sweepers. The aim was to disorganize our efforts and intensify the offensive value of the minelayers.

Against such efforts we managed by diligent clearance of any suspected area to make the best use of fast, light-draught vessels which could do their job of sweeping with speed and handiness. In the Mediterranean these mines were specially laid off such places as Malta, Lemnos, Candia, Salonica, Port Said and Alexandria to entrap our transports. The problem was to obtain more vessels, so trawlers and M.L.s which had been hitherto employed hunting submarines or escorting merchant shipping were now fitted with sweeping gear.

Coming down to precise details with regard to British coastal area, mines were discovered off Dover, the Owers Lightship (near Selsey Bill), off Portland Bill, Lowestoft, Harwich, Aberdeen and the Tay. *UC*-43 deposited 18 mines in groups between Flamborough Head and Whitby in an exposed and difficult area to sweep but there was always so much traffic steaming along this coast. *UC*-43 was approaching the end of her tether and we shall presently note what was her fate. So also *UC*-32 who laid mines off the Tyne and Sunderland both on December 30, 1916, again laid mines off this N.E. coast on January 25 and 26, 1917, but then betook herself N.E. along the coast though she too was shortly about to come to a sticky end.

The German mind differs from ours basically and is so ardently warlike, that the collateral duties of navigation by him are regarded rather as something extraneous—which can be carried out easily by what we should call 'a Reserve Officer' who has been brought up in the Mercantile Marine. German commanding officers were surprisingly ignorant of navigation and pilotage, and shewed little enough interest in the subject. They aspired to fighting and left the work of fixing their sea positions to their navigating Warrant Officers who had come from some Hamburg-Amerika liner or other merchant vessel. Consequently it was hardly surprising sometimes these submarines made such serious mistakes. Presently we shall find *UC*-32 coming to grief for that very reason. But I well recollect seeing one of our own merchantmen getting ashore by a piece of bad luck during a winter's night. It was January 2, 1917, at 3.40 in the early hours of morning. There happened to be no light at the western end of Cape Clear and she was just skirting the first bit of land after crossing the Atlantic. She was keeping well inshore to avoid any possibility of mines and submarines, for both dangers had been quite close to this rocky bit of coast. The vessel was the S.S. *Nestorian*, with a valuable cargo of cotton, and had crashed on to the rocks so firmly that it needed no prophet to guess the result. Fortunately H.M.S. *Iris* (one of the sloops which at one time would be minesweeping and presently hunting submarines) was in the neighbourhood and she managed to rescue the crew. But this corner of Cape Clear is ever opposed to the surge of the sea and full blast of the wild Atlantic winds: so very shortly the wreck slipped back into the deep and was swallowed up. But for days the waves sported with bales of cotton which made fine salvage for the local islanders.

These German minelayers used to come over to the most out-of-the-way spots if only they could lay an ambush such as would waylay a vessel coming in to be examined for dodging the Blockade. Kirkwall was an examination port for this purpose. So, too, was Lerwick. Within the first week of the New Year five mines were found off Kirkwall and six were laid half a mile from Kirkabister Lighthouse by the entrance to Lerwick. Seven were also discovered in Shapinsay Sound (approach to Kirkwall). But the Orkneys were not the only bits of Scotland thus to be startled out of complacency: for off Tarbet Ness was revealed a very nasty group. Nine were deposited in the vicinity of Fifeness, the N. Carr Lightship being used as a convenient bearing. It was H.M. Yacht *Agatha* which found the first only a few hours after it had been laid.

It must not be reckoned that mines in places never known to have been so visited were suddenly revealed by some chance bit of luck. On the contrary, it was because persistent daily sweeping disclosed the danger only after monotonous dull days. One of our armed whalers sighted a small mine on the north side of the River Tay channel on January 7. It seemed very surprising, but the object had certainly come out of a submarine and was destroyed next day. Sweeping then commenced, and at the end of war the Germans confessed that here they had laid eight in the Tay.

Yet vigilance could not always bring about success. When the fishing trawler *Cygnet* reported having sighted a mine three-quarters of a mile east of Aberdeen, H.M. Yacht *Nairn* was sent to investigate and she soon located the mine which could not be sunk owing to the heavy sea, though another attempt the following day succeeded. Further down the coast an episode illustrated how narrow were some of the minesweepers' escapes.

It happened off Harwich, where the visitations of UC-boats were anything but rare and we used to lay nets sometimes to catch them. One of our naval drifters named the *Cape Colony* had been at anchor on the night of January 7–8 watching the moored nets. Owing to the bad weather she dragged considerably but at daylight she began to weigh. The cable was being wound up and there was no submarine in the nets, but something bad enough could be seen. Suddenly up came the anchor; between the fluke and the shank was seen jammed a mine. At once they stopped the revolving capstan, then the *Cape Colony* pitched her bows to the sea. And that did it.

With a terrifying detonation the mine exploded. And though no lives—marvellous to relate—were lost, yet the crew were in the water for a considerable time wrestling for their lives against the heavy sea running.

Victories over U-boats were not restricted to occasions when the submarines had been sent to the bottom by destroyers' depth-charges or guns. Those narrow escapes from annihilation by our vigilant patrols, or by our measures of defence, were quite capable of ruining the German commanding officer's enterprise and the spirit of his crew for all time. Often enough some surprise action, a sudden unforeseen complication, would have such a deadening effect as to transform a submarine of promise into an ultra-cautious unit concerned only for its safety.

Especially was this the case when arrogant and conceited young captains, with more self-reliance than experience, learned reluctantly that the British Navy knows a few tricks of its own.

In the last war some of our retired admirals, with splendid patriotism and self-effacement, returned to their old Service but with the temporary rank of Captain R.N.R. and were given command of such vessels as armed yachts or Q-ships. The idea worked extremely well, despite the strange anomaly when these more ancient mariners received their orders from commanders-in-chief who a few years previously had been junior to those newly come back. Sometimes, also, when an ex-admiral pretending to be Skipper of a tramp steamer found it difficult to forget the authoritative manner of one accustomed to handling squadrons, there would develop some amusing incidents with such officials as harbourmasters, pilots, and the like.

Now one of the most charming and zealous of these former flag-officers was Admiral J. L. Marx, who passed away not very long ago. For a time he went looking for the enemy from aboard H.M. Armed Yacht *Beryl*, owned by Lord Inverclyde. Then he took over Q-13, which was really the converted sloop *Aubrietia*. At least one boat-load of seafarers had reason to thank this old gentleman for their lives. Their ship had been torpedoed in the Atlantic and disappeared for two hours they were rowing about anxiously in boisterous weather across a heavy sea. Then they caught sight of what seemed to be a tramp steamer not much over 1000 tons, so they hoisted sail, ran down to her, were picked up, and found her to be *Aubrietia*. The latter then searched the ocean and within two hours rescued some more survivors on rafts, followed presently by three other boat-loads. Never were a shipwrecked crew more pleased with their unexpected luck.

But it was on January 12, 1917, that *Aubrietia* happened to be steaming in the Channel Islands area. Time 10.30 a.m. Exact position eight miles N.W.¼N. of the Casquets. Ambling along like one of many a cargo steamer, Q-13 of 1250 tons pretended to be the Danish S.S. *Kai* of 1391 tons, which was near enough for size in case a doubting German cared to turn up *Lloyd's Register*. But this Q-ship, which looked so ordinary, was well armed with one 4-inch and two 12-pounder guns, plus a small 3-pounder.

Quite a match for any U-boat!

As if from nowhere, a submarine appeared and without hesitation at 10.38 fired a shell which passed over the ship, and another missile came whizzing immediately after. Then began the usual tactics on both sides. The Admiral stopped engines, the 'tramp' blew off large quantities of steam, and in answer to the German's signal made her number as the *Kai*. He was next ordered by the enemy to send a boat alongside, and this instruction seemingly was being obeyed, though to gain time and tempt the submarine nearer, the well-rehearsed British crew were not hurrying themselves.

This greatly annoyed the impatient Hun, who now fired one more shell to hasten matters. That occurred at 11 a.m.; ten minutes later the boat got away, pulled to leeward over a very heavy sea, and now already the submarine from her windward position rapidly approached on the surface towards *Aubrietia's* port beam.

The Admiral waited till 'Fritz' got within 300 yards at 11.23, decided this to be the ripe moment, pressed the buzzer, guns swung into action, and the fight commenced. Remarkably short and sharp it lasted. A 12-pounder shell hit the conning-tower with an immense explosion, blowing the conning-tower clean out of existence, scattering the four men who had been standing there. This unusually shattering burst was caused not wholly by impact of missile against steel but by reason of the enemy's over-confidence. Anxious to make a quick job of destroying the little steamer without wasting a costly torpedo on her, the German captain had intended to proceed as follows:

The *Kai's* boat would fetch across a demolition party with a bag of bombs to be placed aboard the steamer, and up *Kai* would go before descending as splintered metal. Then the German would be rowed back aboard, and the British crew cast adrift in the rough sea. But it didn't work out like that.

The shell indeed detonated those bombs which had been brought up from below, and now a second shot hit the hull just forward of where the conning-tower used to be, whilst a 3-pounder smote her in the same locality. The German waited for no more, submerged quickly, up welled oil and bubbles which covered the sea; *Aubrietia* dropped a couple of depth-charges, but never sighted this enemy again.

On the facts presented you might have felt convinced the enemy had been destroyed. Such, however, was not the case and at a later date the German official account proved that the enemy did get home. Yet you can imagine the lesson for life which every member of that submarine's crew today learned. If ever they regained their self-reliance, always would they be jittery, always timid in the presence of a steamer, and certainly not aggressive.

CHAPTER II

PURSUING THE U-BOATS

YEARS after the war we got to know that Admiral Marx's opponent this day had been *UB*-23 (Lieut.-Commander Voigt) who had a very narrow escape. It was really a contest between two distinctive types; the one a clever but retired British Admiral of the old school—breezy, hearty, with a short torpedo beard; a live wire, and sailorman from cap to boots—opposed to a very modern young Hun brought up amid new gadgets but never suspecting this poor old steam tramp which the German despised. I used to meet Admiral Marx when he came ashore from his anti-submarine trips, but you would never have suspected him of being such a clever warrior. The *Aubrietia* originally was one of the sloops and she had been altered and painted to resemble a merchant ship. When this Q-ship hoisted her pretended number it was that of the S.S. *Kai*, a

Danish vessel of 1391 tons. Subsequently the real *Kai* was sunk off S.W. Spain on November 5, 1917. But *Q*-13 was of 1250 tons, so when the German submarine commander on the bridge turned over the pages of *Lloyd's* and looked up the stranger's dimensions, he could well believe the figures. So the elder sailor fooled the German at the outset.

Voigt was less astute than just fortunate. He had set out from Zeebrugge confident of himself, yet those surprising shells from *Aubrietia* had hit him seriously though Admiral Marx's depth-charges failed in their effect. *UB*-23 in running back towards Zeebrugge managed to get ashore on the Goodwins, which can hardly be termed clever, and in that perilous position she remained ignominiously till she got off after one and a half days. Again she set out from Zeebrugge, went down the Bay of Biscay, but once more into trouble, for on July 30, 1917, Voigt limped into Corunna in such a condition that he had to be interned 'for the duration' and probably it was safer that Voigt should incur no more risks.

I wish old Admiral Marx could have met Voigt after the war. These incidents would have taken some narrating!

This was the stage of hostilities when the submarine was meeting her match in the stealth and disguise of the Q-ship. All sorts of sailing ships and steamers were employed in that great adventure, but success came to a limited few.

Did you ever hear the yarn of the *Mary B. Mitchell* ?

She was quite a comely little vessel, only 129 feet long, built of steel, 210 tons (gross), with three masts, being rigged as a topsail schooner; and something about her graceful lines, her miniature poop deck, always filled the eye of any old shell-back. For, in some respects *Mary B. Mitchell* suggested a small edition of the bygone clipper sailing ships.

Built at Carrickfergus way back in 1892, registered at Beaumaris, and owned by Lord Penrhyn, she came into Falmouth with a cargo of china clay and attracted the naval authorities' attention. That was in mid-April, 1916, when German submarines instead of operating close to the land had begun to assault shipping at the English Channel's widest part, and in the Atlantic.

Why not discharge this schooner's cargo, pay off the crew, fit her up with concealed guns, sign on a specially selected personnel, and send her to roam the sea as a new sort of decoy?

This was soon decided upon, her name officially changed to *Q*-9 (though she altered her alias, the colour of her hull, and her pretended nationality just as often as convenient), and with great secrecy she became a cleverly disguised man-of-war. They gave her one 12-pounder gun concealed in a dummy collapsible deckhouse on the poop; two 6-pounders hidden one under each hatch; all three with swinging pedestals. Besides these were a couple of Lewis guns plus small arms and Mills hand-grenades. By the time her new crew had learnt the routine, it was possible to throw off all disguise and bring every gun into action under three seconds.

Q-9 was a marvel of compactness; from her hidden wireless in the rigging to the gymnastic apparatus carried for keeping the men physically fit. And when she first sailed out of Falmouth on June 26, 1916, she bore a plate with *Mary B. Mitchell* thereon till, having gained the open seas, she removed this inscription and allowed her name to be read as the *Mary Y. Jose* of the port Vigo. The yellow streak and black hull made her resemble one of those Spanish neutrals often met with at sea.

During this first shake-down cruise she sailed about between Ushant, Ireland, and Milford, practising her guns at night away from inquisitive strangers. When her captain had pressed the bell for 'Action Stations', hatches slid smoothly off, guns swung into position, and only now were the crew (other than a few ordinary seamen) allowed to show themselves on deck.

So successful was her disguise that several British transports sighting her in the Bay of Biscay took her for a U-boat's depot-ship and altered course away. When *Q-9* at the end of four weeks was returning to the Cornish coast she so deceived the Falmouth patrols that they boarded this 'Spanish' schooner and needed a lot of convincing. During other trips in the Channel Isles district she impersonated the French *Jeannette* of 226 tons registered at La Houle; sometimes she would be the *Brine* of St. Malo, or the *Neptun* of Riga, or the *Marie Thérèse* of Cette.

It was not till December 2, 1916, that she first came in contact with the enemy south of the Lizard. Under all sail, with a nice south-east breeze, she was bowling along to the north-west, the hour being 10.25 a.m. Her complement consisted of Lieut. M. Armstrong, R.N.R. (captain), Lieut. J. Lawrie, R.N.R. (navigator), Sub-Lieut. J. Kerr, R.N.R., and 21 men.

Away on the starboard bow, distant about two miles, Armstrong now observed several objects: a submarine towing two ship's lifeboats, also a Brixham fishing smack, a steam trawler, and another submarine. Five minutes later, without any warning, the first submarine opened fire at *Q-9*. After casting off the lifeboats she hoisted the International Code signal 'Abandon Ship', whereupon *Mitchell's* well-drilled 'panic party' busied themselves launching their boats.

Nearer and nearer, still on the surface, motored the enemy, who fired two more shells and got within 800 yards. Armstrong with binoculars focused on the U-boat was watching every item carefully, waiting for the next development, when . . .

"What's she up to now?"

For the German sailorman, who had just been firing the gun, was seen to clamp it in a fore-and-aft position, then run towards the conning-tower, whilst the U-boat began turning away and prepared to submerge.

That was the schooner's opportunity. Now, or never!

Just at that critical moment the 12-pounder's lanyard most unfortunately carried away, but the 6-pounders boomed forth, nine rounds were speedily loosed off, and two hits were distinctly observed before the U-boat could hide below water. So hurried was her crash dive that she disappeared with ensign still flying and the unfortunate gunner still not able to get inside the conning-tower. It was at the base of this latter that a shell had been seen to burst, then she listed over to port heavily, righted herself, before disappearing in a column of water.

Presently the Q-ship, cruising about, spoke the two boatloads who were Norwegians from the S.S. *Skjoldulf* that had just been sunk and were being towed towards the Cornish coast when this duel suddenly occurred. So close were they, indeed, that they saw everything. The

Scandinavian Master insisted that the schooner had demolished part of the conning tower, and the Second Mate confirming this statement added that it was the second British shell which did the job.

What caused the U-boat to take fright and change her attitude to the defensive? If the former had not spotted some small detail suggestive of a 'trap ship', then she did not like the look of the steam trawler which was bearing down on her and turned out to be the armed patrol *Rosetta*.

But Armstrong left her to pick up the Norwegians, whilst his attention became fixed on another development. The first enemy evidently went off home seriously, though not mortally, damaged. But the second U-boat now came along. At 10.45 her periscope was visible on the schooner's starboard quarter, which meant that the German was about to get into position. Five minutes later Armstrong perceived the torpedo approaching, and surely no human agency could prevent . . .

"Hard astarboard! Hard over!"

The wheel was spun round hurriedly, and the missile barely passed clear, avoiding the stern by five yards.

That ended an exciting occasion, and finally the *Mitchell* proceeded into St. Mary's, the principal island of the Scillies; for a doctor was required to attend Sub-Lieut. Kerr, who during the action had fallen down the cabin-hatch, injuring his ribs. And this delay would afford opportunity to paint a new disguise over the hull.

When next this three-master came out of Falmouth, there had been a slight change in personnel, Lieut. Armstrong having gone to another ship, so Lieut. Lawrie became captain, and he was to undergo a most trying experience.

On the evening of January 7, 1917, *Q*-9 found herself off Berry Head, east of Dartmouth, when bad weather strengthened into a real winter's gale, and the ship began the most alarming trial. Run into port for shelter? Impossible! Her presence would lead to awkward questions, and her essential secret character be divulged. At all costs, she must keep out at sea.

Worse and worse rose wind and wave, a heavy strain on gear was being borne, but next night shortly after 9.30 down crashed foremast and spars over the side, followed by mainmast also. Splendidly the crew toiled in the dark to clear up the wreckage, and she lay-to under close-reefed mizzen topsail. On the foremast stump a jurymast was rigged and a reefed staysail set, the wind having veered from west through north-west to north-east.

Sailors are not wont to exaggerate conditions, but Lawrie described the waves as 'mountainous'. During the 9th she was being driven south-west down Channel in the direction of that dreaded Ushant area with its strong tides, pyramidal seas, and pinnacles of rocks. Little hope of surviving, if she got thereabouts in her present maimed condition.

About 9.15 a.m. she saw a large cargo steamer loom up, made signals asking for a tow, and the stranger tried to comply with the request, but in that weather all efforts failed. "Impossible" the steamer finally had to signal, and the picture of this vessel proceeding on her way up the English Channel was scarcely pleasing to the *Mitchell's* men. Moreover, by this time the schooner lay only ten miles north of Ushant, and the north-east gale showing no sign of easing.

The afternoon faded into darkness, death was just to leeward, the crippled vessel began making signals of distress in a vain hope. Would she drift clear of Ushant? She might just do it. And she might not. A gun was being fired every few minutes for help, rockets were sent up and flares kept burning; yet from the shore never an answering signal.

"We're for it, this time," was on the lips of everybody, and now the rocks, against which monstrous seas beat mercilessly, seemed forlornly near.

So passed a few more anxious hours.

At 9.30 that night the first act of this drama had ended. The *Mitchell*, marvellous to relate, did not hit anything, and now the Norwegian S.S. *Sardinia* in response to the signals bore down. In the wind and blackness she could do nothing, but stood by all night till seven o'clock next morning, by which time the schooner was out in the Bay of Biscay, some ten miles west of Ushant's north-west corner, where the tide runs at seven knots.

As the dawn broke, *Sardinia* threw over a buoy with a small line attached, which the Q-ship now picked up and to it bent a tow-rope, so that by 9 a.m. the steamer with sailing vessel began slowly to claw to windward. Provided the rope didn't break, little risk of being wrecked now remained.

Yes, of course there would be a salvage claim, but what about Q-9's secret character being revealed? And to a neutral? That was what worried Lieut. Lawrie. He must think out some solution, but the dilemma did not look easy.

The time ticked on, two more hours passed, and at 11.15 they were abreast Les Pierres Lighthouse, when a French torpedo-boat on patrol came to have a look at this jury-rigged ship. To set the ally at ease, Lawrie hoisted the Red Ensign, but longed to do more than this. Grateful as the schooner's captain was to *Sardinia*, willing to comply with any suitable information for salvage recompense, he still must hide from the Norwegian that *Mitchell* was a man-of-war.

But how? Such a problem needed some thinking. And the right moment for solution.

The British Captain was alert, and then about noon when the torpedo-boat steamed into a suitable position Lawrie got the chance he wanted. Cautiously displaying the White Ensign over *Mitchell's* stern, but in such a manner that *Sardinia* could not see it from ahead, the former by the least bit of play-acting conveyed the idea.

Quick on the uptake, the French commander immediately 'savvied', sped towards the Norwegian and signalled:

"I will take over the tow. Please cast off."

Aboard the *Sardinia* would be a copy of *Lloyd's Register of Shipping*, with the details of ship's name, tonnage, port of registry, owner, and so on. All that the schooner now required to announce was:

"*Mary B. Mitchell*, Beaumaris. Falmouth for Bristol Channel with general cargo."

The tow-warp having been transferred to the Frenchman, the steamer resumed her voyage, and the battered sailing vessel was brought safely into Brest. Thus, despite every anxiety and danger, Q-9 had won through. A mere phase in her adventurous life had been experienced.

IN THE OTRANTO STRAITS

Cape Santa Maria di Leuca—a favourite landmark for German U-boats coming up the Straits returning to Cattaro.

H.M.S. PARTRIDGE II
Photograph taken at Genoa.

She was now repaired, remasted, and given an auxiliary motor—to be used only by night, or in absolute necessity. Forth she sailed looking for more trouble in her old areas but under fresh disguises; sometimes as the *Eider* of St. Malo, the *Cancalais* of La Youle, or the *Arius* of Riga.

Like a magnet for submarines seemed this little schooner. By the appearance of such helpless innocence she always attracted any U-boat which chanced to be about, and of course those masts, yards and canvas made a prominent picture on the horizon. Yet never was any combat more difficult than for one of these vessels relying on the wind whilst fighting such an extremely mobile creature as could move in any direction, alter speed, and dive out of sight.

Imagine *Q*-9 going into action whilst heeling over to the wind, with lee deck awash and the gunners trying to keep on the target. Not even in the days of Nelson or Drake did British seamen have such a hard task. At least the Q-steamers (converted 'tramps', colliers, and the like) afforded fairly steady gun-platforms.

On June 20, 1917, five months after having escaped shipwreck, the *Mitchell* was cruising in the Bay of Biscay some miles seaward of France's north-west coast when another submarine appeared on the surface. The latter had been sent there for a special purpose and was idling along to the westward, waiting. Meanwhile the sight of this three-master became a sufficient temptation. What a U-boat captain liked was to return home, at the end of his four weeks, with a long string of flags flying (after the manner of a victorious racing yacht), showing that he had sunk so many British steamers.

Especially he hated entering port without any success achieved. Thus rather than have nothing better to boast about, he would not hesitate to destroy small coastal craft. So the *Mitchell*, three miles away, looked good enough for shelling just now.

Lawrie was quite ready for him, began the customary preliminary pantomime of 'panic', launched the small boat and pretended to abandon ship. But by this date there had been so many successful and nearly successful Q-ship incidents that the Germans had been taught to be wary.

"Have a good look round before approaching too close. Make sure she is not another of those confounded 'trap-ships'!"

Cautiously the submarine crept towards the prey, scanned the deck for any likely concealment of guns, looked critically for any possible crack or crevice of hinges. Today the German appeared doubtful, hesitant, refused to be lured inside 800 yards, waited to make up his mind, whilst the unseen British fighting crew with suppressed excitement longed for action to start.

Lawrie, realizing his enemy's obstinate shyness, decided to begin; pressed the bell, then down folded poop deckhouse, guns and men appeared from nowhere, up fluttered White Ensign, and the 12-pounder's first shot at once hit the stranger abaft the conning-tower making a fierce explosion. Then the battle was on.

Sixteen more shells whizzed across in rapid succession, seven being direct hits, the last striking just below the enemy's foredeck, midway between conning-tower and bows. This time the explosion was much greater, up rose a column of sea and vapour 20 feet high. Either the

'Fritz' had been so stunned as to become reckless, or his crew were a poor lot; for, though the latter fired 20 rounds at this conspicuous tall target, not one was a hit. Every shot merely burst uncomfortably close overhead.

The submarine disappeared.

That same evening, however, shortly after six o'clock another U-boat hurried over the surface, overtook the *Mitchell*, performed the same cautious tactics, and awaited developments at 800 yards. Typical German drill-book procedure! And this was the summer when the Huns had lost so many of their boats and crews that indifferently trained personnel were being sent to sea no longer as volunteers.

Still more on the defensive, and not quite convinced, the submarine's captain now dived to periscope depth, made a careful inspection through his lens, and at last decided the sailing ship was what she purported to be. But, rather than waste a £1000 torpedo on such small tonnage, he would despatch her by gunfire.

Thus did he begin rising to the surface, and all this while Lawrie watched, whilst the schooner's men with disciplined patience remained hidden behind bulwarks.

Slowly the periscope rose taller, then appeared the rim of the chariot-shaped conning-tower. Lawrie waited till two feet of hull showed up. Then he pressed the bell. And things happened of a heap.

The British crew also knew something about drill. Into action swung the after 6-pounder, its shell smote the hull some three feet below the conning-tower and a foot above water, creating a large blue flash and sending out a volume of yellow smoke.

Almost simultaneously the 12-pounder's missile crashed into the submarine's bows, causing yellow-black smoke mingled with steam and spray. Then the U-boat gave a convulsive lurch forward, became down by the head, listed drunkenly to port, and submerged with a loud, gurgling, hissing noise, whilst oil, large bubbles, and much eddying manifested themselves in place of what once was a submarine.

But note the curious sequence.

Next day was June 21, the afternoon being clear and sunny. Round the corner past Ushant, and the scene is the western end of the English Channel. A dozen genuine cargo ships under sail had come out of Falmouth bound across to the French port of Morlaix, escorted by the 179-tons brigantine *Probus*—alias *Thirza*, alias *Q-30*. For she was another of these little 'mystery' vessels. On the horizon she could not quite understand a ketch-rigged craft which seemed to be moving too quickly.

All doubts were banished when the 'ketch' started shelling the convoy, and showed herself to be a U-boat. *Probus* therefore chased after her, shelled the object, and with the fourth shot sent the German's sails with mast tumbling over the side. That surprise was enough. The German scurried away to the north-east to lick his wounds.

Five days later yet another 'mystery' sailing vessel *Gaelic* (alias *Q-22*), 174 tons, barquentine-rigged, also had a duel with a submarine, and likewise at the Channel's western end.

Now what did these activities of June 20–26 signify? Why so many U-boats hereabouts?

The answer is that German spies in America had given warning that the first contingent of United States troops were expected to reach Europe somewhere around this period. Actually these soldiers landed at a west French port on June 26.

And which of the 'mystery' sailing ships definitely sank a submarine? That is the biggest mystery of all, and will never be solved beyond dispute. But we do know that during this month of June, somehow, somewhere, *UB*-36 with all hands disappeared. Not even Germany ever learned how, and why.

Personally I have little doubt that she received her fatal punishment on June 20 from the *Mary B. Mitchell* in the Bay of Biscay, so that a small schooner saved the lives of some thousands of American soldiers.

CHAPTER III

PERISCOPES AND TORPEDOES

IT is possible that the reader will have remembered my *Fighting the U-Boats* (which appeared in 1942), and that therein we gave a diagram of Commander F. H. Grenfell, R.N. (retd.) aboard his Q-ship *Penshurst* sinking *UB*-19 on November 30, 1916, in the Channel Islands area, having only the previous day engaged (but unsuccessfully) another submarine almost at the same spot. It is therefore very remarkable when Admiral Marx had his brush with *UB*-23 on January 12, 1917, that incident occurred only eight miles N.W. of the Casquets. The inference is that for some reason the German submarines had instructions to frequent this neighbourhood.

For what reason?

Well, it might have been because the cross-Channel steamers from Weymouth to the Channel Islands were still running to Guernsey. Anyway, notwithstanding that our Q-ships had already in this vicinity sunk two submarines and damaged another couple, yet on January 14, 1917, also slightly north of the Casquets, Commander Grenfell in his *Q*-7 was cruising about between Alderney and the Isle of Wight looking for trouble. He found what he wanted at ten minutes to four that afternoon.

The *Penshurst* was the real name of *Q*-7 and she was the kind of steamer that no one would waste a second glance on her appearance. She looked a very ordinary little vessel of 1191 gross tons, built with engines and a fairly high funnel aft but the bridge about midships. She might be some old coaster such as you would pass along the English Channel any day of the week. But to make her look the part, she would be seen slovenly with some of the crew's washing hanging on a derrick to dry. She could disguise herself easily, so after one encounter the *Penshurst* could be quickly transformed to alter her appearance. Thus one day she might have two masts and a black funnel: another day she would have three masts and the funnel a white band at the top. But always concealed on either side of the lower bridge were two 6-pounders. Also inside a dummy boat mounted on the main hatch just forward of the funnel was a 12-pounder whilst a couple of 3-pounders were concealed in the after deck-house. Depth-charges could be released through the counter.

Another of the Flanders submarines, which suddenly appeared 3000 yards away, fired a shell which flopped short, whereupon the *Penshurst* stopped engines, pretended that she was frightened and sent away her boats with an 'abandon ship' party. Captain Grenfell was a quiet, courteous officer whom his men greatly respected, efficient, high-principled; but he suggested nothing of the hot-blooded fire-eater.

As the *Penshurst* fell off to port in the Channel swell and lay with her head about W.N.W. the submarine closed rapidly off the steamer's starboard bow. She was firing at intervals, and when a distance of 700 yards off turned as if to cross ahead of the steamer, stopped, quickened her rate of fire, and twice in rapid succession hit *Q-7*. The first shell broke an awning ridge pole on the bridge, the second cut the engine-room telegraph connections, killing two of the 6-pounder gun's crew and wounding a couple of other sailors.

Commander Grenfell at first withheld his fire, but at 4.24 p.m. began with a lyddite shell from the 12-pounder. It was an ideal effort for the shell burst violently at the base of the conning-tower which ceased to exist, large portions being scattered and a great volume of black smoke arose. The second shot from this gun hit just abaft this spot, making further injuries. The starboard 3-pounder hit the lower portion of that conning-tower at least four times, after which the dazed enemy sank by the stern: whereupon *Penshurst* steamed ahead and dropped three depth-charges, of which two exploded right over the spot where the enemy sank. Thus was destroyed *UB*-37 with all hands; so there was nothing else for the Q-ship to do other than pick up the 'panic' boats, and steam across Channel, where she entered Portland and discharged her wounded to the Naval hospital.

Germany still believed in laying mines along traffic routes even in distant seas, for she had late in 1917 sent the steamship *Wolf* across the oceans as a raider. This vessel had laid mines off the Cape of Good Hope which caused the loss of several merchant ships. Altogether about 16 mines were accounted for including one exploded by a whale: in fact, these dangers were not cleared away by the next year. Mines were laid also off Aden; Bombay, where four steamers were destroyed and the P. & O. *Mongolia* damaged. But another batch was laid 10 miles S.W. of Colombo. Several ships thus blew up, at least 25 of their mines were presently swept though one drifted 180 miles west of Colombo before striking another British steamer. But Captain Nerger, who took this German raider all over the world, was so ambitious that he steamed forth with no less than 458 of these mines, which gave our local sweepers considerable trouble. Some mines were eventually discovered off the Australian coast and in New Zealand waters. But some were found after the Armistice in the South China Sea. Of the 458 that this raider brought out, we finally found 258 mines. The *Wolf* had an adventurous cruise in which she captured a number of mercantile vessels whose crews she kept on board for a considerable time.

Among the latter was one British Master Mariner who periodically used to throw overboard into the sea bottles containing information of the cruise. Of course we have heard so many tales—mostly lies and fanciful stories—concerning such mystery voyages, but at least two of these bottles were picked up many thousands of miles apart. Thus one was found by natives of Toli Toli (Celebes) on December 9, 1917, and eventually reached the Consul-General at Batavia who informed the British Commander-in-Chief, China, and it was this means which went a long way towards recording *Wolf's* remarkable voyage.

The second bottle was thrown overboard whilst the *Wolf* was approaching Germany on her return voyage. The message was dated February 10, 1918, and was washed up on the coast of Norway.

Despite the record of men killed and good ships thus lost by these mines scattered promiscuously around the world, there remains one amusing episode. The explosives which were laid off South Africa were swept up by four hired whalers. The number of these explosives deposited here was 25. One, as we have seen, was exploded by a monstrous whale, but for some reason the mine—probably by means of the tidal currents and boisterous winds—broke adrift and came ashore. Not till a year after the minefield had been laid did a Mr. Abraham Louw, a Boer farmer, and his son Girt on January 26, 1918, discover near Elands Bay, S. Africa, something on the beach which resembled a large cast iron receptacle.

What could it be?

Inspired by curiosity they fetched their cart, unscrewed part of the 'receptacle', rolled it into the sea, filled it with salt water, screwed up again the brass cap and now lifted the thing on to their cart. It was noticed that a brown tar-like substance was beginning to trickle out. Actually this substance was the mine's T.N.T. softened by the sun, but the two Boers were ignorant of such matters. Playfully they decided to light this trickle with a match, but it sent up a flame 200 feet high which so frightened them that they forsook the cart and went to tell the police. The flame also terrified the inhabitants of this area that the more cautious sought refuge in the hills whilst others hid under their beds.

Next arrived on the scene Constable Reader, but the mechanism of the 'receptacle' so little intrigued him that he rolled it under some bushes, covered it with reeds and departed. At last arrived a naval officer from the Admiral's flagship, and he endeavoured to collect the various parts, but the two farmers had thoroughly if not carefully dismantled the *Wolf's* mine. The primer had apparently been opened unskilfully with a tin-opener. Some bits of the horns had been distributed between the two farmers and their friends, but when the latter had been persuaded to disgorge their souvenirs it was found that these had been separated from the 'receptacle' by means of a hammer and cold chisel. Mr. Louw finally had to admit that, after all, this had been a German mine whereas he had taken the 'receptacle' for a new kind of boiler used 'in the manufacture of wireless telegraphy'.

And meanwhile the enemy was laying his mines off parts of England as Whitby, the Tees, and other portions of the N.E. coast such as Flamborough, the Tyne, Sunderland; S.W. of Dartmouth and Portland Bill. No wonder our minesweeping vessels were in such urgent demand. But the worst had yet to come.

The reader will doubtless remember how we related* that at 8.50 a.m. on October 26, 1914, early in the last war H.M.S. *Audacious* struck a mine and foundered outside Lough Swilly, 18 miles N.E. of Tory Island. On October 25 the British merchant ship *Manchester Commerce* also

---

*Fighting the U-Boats, p. 34.

struck one of these mines and went down though the news was not passed on till October 27, 1914. Now the enemy was ever mindful of this North Irish area since he remembered till the end of hostilities that some important ships of the Atlantic to Liverpool traffic passed this way. Therefore it was well worth laying some more mines. On January 21 a Hull steam trawler passing this coast noticed that about 40 miles N.W. by N. from Inishtrahull a German submarine was busy sinking some of our other trawlers. For what purpose? Probably in order that these fishermen might not afterwards report the presence of a U-boat about here: for the enemy was sowing tares.

Collating all the facts as we now know them, a German submarine laid half a dozen mines at 2.8 metres (Low Water Ordinary Springs) in Lat. 55.19 N., Long. 7.32 W. This spot was off Fanad Head at the eastern approach of Lough Swilly and on Thursday evening January 25, 1917, H.M. Armed Merchant Cruiser *Laurentic* which had been hired from the White Star Line and was now serving under the White Ensign, steamed straight into tragedy at this exact spot. The following vivid account* will be found interesting:

> "Tuesday, Jan. 30th. . . . Met . . . Captain Norton, whose ship the *Laurentic* was sunk off Lough Swilly last Thursday evening. He thinks it was due to two mines which struck his ship at an interval of thirty seconds. He was steaming out of harbour at full speed without lights to escape submarines, but one of these pests must have laid mines outside, probably moored 20 feet below the surface, and as he went out at low tide he ran the worst risk. . . . There was a strong easterly wind . . . fifteen boats got clear, but only seven were saved; the others were swamped or blown out to sea, and the men died from exhaustion. . . . the trawlers came out and saved him but could not find the other boats in the dark."

It was not till February 9 that sweepers from Buncrana located the *Laurentic's* wreck about two miles N.E. by E. from Fanad Head lying in 20 fathoms. All vessels of the Auxiliary Patrol from Buncrana were ordered to search for missing boats with the result that 121 survivors and 73 bodies were picked up. Three days later H.M. Yacht *Surf* also picked up a lifeboat two miles N.W. of Green Head and in it were found 14 dead bodies. This part of the world is notorious for bad weather and atrocious seas, as the minesweepers who had been sent to clear up the Tory Island minefield that sank H.M.S. *Audacious* could testify: but the deaths, which totalled over 300, were largely due to the exposure off this wild coast. From a viewpoint of finance the disaster to *Laurentic* was a serious blow since she went down with 6½ millions of gold and other valuables which she was just taking across to New York. Later on patient salvage work resulted in winning back from the sea much that had been consigned to the deep.

Just as in the later war we were heavily concerned in forcing munitions through to Northern Russia during 1942, so in 1917 we were intensely busy in such work. Despite the intense cold the Germans made all sorts of efforts to interfere with these merchant craft. Gales of wind, snow and

---

The First World War, by Lieut.-Colonel Repington, Vol. i., p. 446.

ce were bad enough for that bleak journey past Hammerfest along the Norwegian coast to the White Sea, but German minefields and German submarines made the rounding of certain headlands a desperate adventure. However, we lent the Russians some trawlers and the Russians themselves supplied a few. One day certain of the latter came in contact with U-76 and the German submarine received such heavy knocks that she simply could endure no more. It was a toss up as to whether U-76 could carry on down the coast and make Germany, or whether she would have to submit to fate. She rounded North Cape and was making for the Norwegian shore off Hammerfest when things became so bad that U-76 had to send up distress rockets. Out went a local motor-boat which managed to rescue 35 officers and men. Only the engineer failed to be taken off, but that frequently was inevitable with the Germans, for when a submarine had to be sunk he was the last man to leave and open the Kingston valves. So whilst U-76 ended her days in the approaches to Hammerfest, 35 Huns were landed and allowed to journey back to war and Germany.

We have already brought to the reader's attention the fact that in a German UC-boat on an expedition for minelaying it was the Warrant Navigating Officer (frequently one who had been serving aboard a Hamburg-American steamer) that took charge when fixing the submarine's position at sea or when laying his mines off the land. Picture him, then, as one of the personnel in UC-32 when Lieut.-Commander Breyer was skipper during the early days of 1917. This craft had already laid one lot of mines off the Tyne and Sunderland also on December 30, 1916; and on January 22, 1917, again left Heligoland for the Tyne. This Warrant Officer's name was Bernhard Haack. Sometimes when crossing the North Sea, sights were not possible and UC-32 was frequently chivvied about by our patrols, so navigation was often largely a matter of guesswork. Headlands, a lighthouse, a church spire, a windmill or pier, would help to make the position of mines laid inshore less inaccurate. But the commanding officer was not keen on the risks of carrying so many explosives and much preferred the independent cruises of a U or UB-boat which could keep in deep water and rely on torpedoes. It must be understood, then, that UC-32 was not altogether a happy ship.

And she was one of those based not on Bruges. She headed north for the excellent landmark of Horn's Reef, then cut across the North Sea for the Tyne and sank a Swedish steamer on January 24. Twice in his life had Haack as Mate of a German mercantile vessel been to the Tyne and for this reason was reckoned in the German Submarine Service as expert war pilot of the district. But the truth is that, since Haack's knowledge of the Tyne's approaches was very slight and that of Breyer slighter still, it was the old story of a one-eyed man leading a man that was wholly blind. We can prophesy the result.

On the evening of January 25 Haack succeeded in laying four[*] mines off the Tyne. Next day he laid another 14 off Souter Point and near Seaham. Evidently Breyer now yearned for greater freedom, so proceeded N.E. to return along the Scandinavian trade route with a view of sinking shipping by less indirect methods. During the forenoon of Sunday, January 28, the tempo of life was about to undergo modifica-

[*] UC-32 laid mines at dusk off the Tyne on January 25 at High Water.

tion. The Grimsby steam trawler *G.Y.-60* (*Alexandra*), Skipper J. A. Ives, was who on her way home after a successful fishing voyage, had now been steaming for about an hour and was at present some 45 miles E. by N. from the Longstone. She was steering to pick up the Farne Islands when she suddenly sighted *UC*-32 on the opposite course. *Alexandra* bore away more southerly so as to give the German a wide berth. The distance between the two seemed about a mile and the submarine who lay just to the westward opened fire, her shots falling very close. It was calm weather, very clear, and the *Alexandra* realized that it were useless to argue with a UC-boat, so Ives launched the trawler's small boat and proceeded to row away. UC-32 then resumed firing, motored up alongside the fishermen's rowing boat.

"Eh," called Breyer to attract attention. "Have you perhaps wireless?"

"No," replied Ives bluntly. "We're only a fishing steamer."

Breyer next ordered Ives and the trawler's engineer to come aboard the submarine, after which three Germans stepped into that boat, brought some bombs with them and were towed by the submarine towards *Alexandra* where the three Huns having placed the bombs in position returned. But when they exploded, the *Alexandra* did not founder, so the U-boat had to sink her by shells at short range. And what about these Grimsby prisoners? Breyer had no desire to be crowded so he stopped a Norwegian steamer named *Stirling* which was bound for Newcastle and put the fishermen aboard—all, that is to say, except Ives. The hours dragged on and presently the latter fell asleep. It was strange to be cruising over the same North Sea but aboard a German!

Suddenly something occurred. What was that? Oh yes . . . a foreigner addressing him. But in English.

"All right, Hans. I savvy. Tell the Captain I'll obey his request and come at once. . . . Oh, in the conning-tower, is he? Well, I won't waste a minute."

It was in the early hours of the morning, still dark and dreary as any other January middle watch in the North Sea. He found that the submarine was motoring along the surface spooning up a bow wave, having during the last few hours still kept on a N.E. course. Sixty feet away on the starboard side he sighted a trawler with fishing lights, and a little further on four more trawlers.

The U-boat captain wanted information.

"Fishing ships? Yes? Dat is goot."

But Breyer wanted to know something else. Were these minesweepers? Or perhaps patrol trawlers?

Was that all the German officer wanted? Was that the reason for interrupting a man's deep slumber? Minesweepers or patrols? How the hell could anyone answer such a question on a dark night like this? Wherefore Ives merely replied:

"More'n I can say, sir. In a manner of speaking . . . I don't rightly know."

Willingly or unwillingly Ives was telling the Germans nothing. They sent him down below again. The submarine waited for daylight.

At 7 a.m. the German craft deemed it prudent with the first streaks of dawn to go down beneath the waves for an hour or so till at eight o'clock he dived to 37 feet when he came to the surface. He was now some 140 miles N.E. by E. of the Tyne and could discern three fishing trawlers: the *Thistle*, the *Petrel* and *Mayfly*. Across the bows of the first Breyer fired his gun, after which the fishing crews of all three thought it was time to launch their boats and shove off. Breyer called *Petrel's* boat alongside and ordered Warrant Officer Haack to jump in, and the latter took with him some bombs, a revolver and a bandolier. But *Thistle* was the first to be sunk by gunfire and the bombs. Haack next proceeded a couple of miles S.E. to the *Mayfly* when the Germans suffered a great surprise. For suddenly on to this morning scene appeared H.M. Armed Trawler *Speedwell II*, of Granton. So surprised was Breyer at this development, so little had he counted on any armed resistance, that he sounded the alarm signal (corresponding to our 'Klaxon'), all the Germans rushed to their assigned stations and the conning-tower hatch was closed with a bang. *UC*-32 submerged to 113 feet.

It was a great change from the protection of night, and Breyer wasted no consideration on Haack. Typically German, the enemy always left any of his colleagues in the lurch if so inclined; but the Warrant Officer was not happy about it. In fact he was feeling desperately frightened at being left in the hands of these fishermen. What would they do to him? He could only assume they would behave like Huns.

What a hurry Breyer had displayed! In his zeal to dive, that commanding officer must have put the submarine's helm hard over, for she dived with a heavy list. Too bad for Haack to find himself with a bag full of bombs being rowed about the North Sea. The humour of the situation had not yet become apparent to him, but the Humber trawlermen are usually less dull to sense the ludicrous. In the distance coming over the sea was a Scandinavian steamer, and Haack thought how nice it would be if the kind fishermen would row him alongside.

Evidently the *Thistle's* Skipper did not appreciate that idea. Having just been robbed of his ship, the Grimsby man was not feeling particularly fond of Germans but rowed alongside one of the other trawlers and was deciding what should be done. Haack was in such a dilemma that no way out seemed practicable: if those bombs were not so blatantly obvious, he might have saved his skin by clever lying. But the revolver and bandolier only emphasized matters. How could he succeed in fooling these simple Englishmen?

Haack was the first to leap out of the boat on board the trawler and hurried down below. But the Grimsby Skipper rapidly followed him. Just in time to find the German surrendering bombs, revolver, bandolier. The day was still young so there could be no necessity for excessive haste. Haack would not be back in Germany for quite a while. Noon passed, those Yorkshire fishermen invited Haack to have a 'bite' with them, and at 4 p.m. before the darkness settled down again transferred the homeless Warrant Officer to a patrol vessel which brought Haack into port as a prisoner-of-war. And the latter, having been not too happy when he served in *UC*-32, was now glad to talk freely. Presently he could congratulate himself on having been cast adrift.

But what did happen to Breyer and the rest of the ship's company?

UC-32 could not easily get over the shock of *Speedwell's* appearance. Little consolation just now in hiding under the waves, for depth-charges began to explode all round. These were becoming so dangerously near that the German submarine hardly dared exist. Breyer forbade any of his crew even to speak, and then came such a terrific explosion that the submarine seemed to strain and rattle like a toy. It was as if every bolt in her hull was being forcefully withdrawn. A second lot of electric globes were smashed, one big electric fitting under the deck descended with a horrible clatter and broke in pieces. Water began pouring where there had been rivets and dripped on to the engines, though they stopped this calamity before it was too late. All the same the last explosion had damaged the port engine.

Breyer then took his craft down to over 160 feet. "The minefishers," he remarked unhappily, "have sent down a wasser-bomb." But at this depth the submarine still cruised about for another couple of hours, when the batteries became weak and made it necessary to return to the surface.

By afternoon *UC*-32 thus reached a position 115 miles N.N.E. of the Longstone. She remained cruising about the surface in much the same area for the rest of that day and then went back across the North Sea till about 7.30 p.m. she sighted Horn's Reef and lay on the sea bed in 94 feet. She reached Heligoland on the surface about 3 p.m. on January 31 and 24 hours later was back in Wilhelmshaven. If she was to report that she had come home minus Haack, the crew had to tell their friends all about the experience of those depth-charges and how as they groped about the ship in darkness they were undergoing mental tortures. No Germans ever forgot such nervous strains.

Before the end of that month Breyer must again carry on his mine-laying routine and with Haack's successor aboard once more crossed the North Sea to lay his mines off the N.E. English coast. It may have been that the successor was hardly an experienced 'pilot' this cruise. Or perhaps it was just negligent carelessness. Anyway the latter arranged to lay the mines on February 23 at 6.30 p.m. whilst *UC*-32 was still on the surface. The position ordered was half a mile S.80 E. from Roker Pier Lighthouse. The latter is the northern breakwater that protects the entrance to Sunderland, around which winds from S.W. or E. lash up a boisterous sea. It so happened that without Haack's presence *UC*-32 had just begun her task when in the twinkling of an eye something went seriously wrong. A flash, a vibrant rumbling, and the submarine was blown up. Fortunately for the Germans the Sunderland Examination Vessel was about this spot on duty. Three men they sighted struggling in the chilly water. They were the German captain and a couple of others; but 22 were never seen again. *UC*-32 had at last terminated her trips for sowing destruction along the path of our busy steamers.

The final scene of this incident occurred on February 24. A diving party was sent down to investigate. They located the wreck of *UC*-32 900 yards eastward of the Roker Pier Lighthouse, discovering the submarine's conning-tower with the fore hatch still open. The diver likewise revealed the gun, its mounting, and the submarine's periscopes. One torpedo was salved with warhead and pistol complete, whilst about 14 mines were still in their tubes.

CHAPTER V

FOULING THE FAIRWAY

It was on the first day of February 1917 that Germany began her Unrestricted Submarine Campaign. Her intentions were indicated when issuing orders to the U-boat captains. She was reminding herself that having so far lost 50 of these craft, she still had not won the war.

"This form of warfare," Germany informed her naval officers, "is to force England to make peace and thereby to decide the whole war. Energetic action is required, but above all rapidity of action. . . . Our object is to cut England off from traffic by sea, and not to achieve occasional results at far-distant points. As far as possible, therefore, stations must be taken up near the English coasts where routes converge."

Evidently the enemy was not doing as well as he had hoped. Therefore also U-boats as a rule were to proceed via the English Channel, both to shorten the cruise and the time spent in dockyard hands, "for the heavy strain on the boats of the North Sea and Atlantic" always necessitated considerable repairs. The fact is that our enemies were beginning to feel something of our defensive measures. For instance, any passage of a submarine through the English Channel was calculated to scare the stoutest heart. On this selfsame February 1 *UC*-17 whilst working her way through the Dover net barrage close to the S.W. end of the Goodwins between Buoys No. 1 and 2 got a bad fright by becoming badly entangled. Some 54 yards of wire netting still clung to her bows and if only one of our patrols with gun and depth-charges had just then steamed on to the spot, *UC*-17 might have become a loss, but only by desperately working her engines was it that she managed to shake herself free.

It was noticed that the increased U-boat activity synchronized with that of coastal minelaying. Between August 4, 1914, and February, 1917 the greatest number of German mines destroyed was in the following areas: Grimsby 838 mines, Lowestoft 674, Sheerness 628, Dover 511, Harwich 318. Thus along our shores bordering the North Sea were the chief dangers as compared with the Devonport area (37), Portsmouth (38) and Queenstown (34). Yet figures showed that submarines were making extended voyages and sinking our shipping not merely off the South-West approaches, in the S. and W. regions off Ireland, but also in the Bay of Biscay and Mediterranean. In fact 256,394 tons of merchant shipping were sunk this month, but serious as that amount seemed to us, the German authorities were far from satisfied. The U-boat commanders were urged especially to look out for making attacks by night, not to waste time in boat communication, to pass Dover if possible by night, and suspect every ship, including sailing vessels.

Germany, however, made the mistake of instituting this Unrestricted Campaign with too few a number of submarines. Actually on February 1, 1917, she possessed 109,* of which not less than 25 and not more than 44 could be in active service. We mentioned in *Fighting the U-Boats*† how East Coast fishing smacks were being secretly armed, commissioned, and sent out from Lowestoft as decoys, but in the spring of 1917 the device

---
*But see p. 29.   †P. 142.

was again resumed. Those fishermen, apart from being superb seamen, shewed that as fighters they were cool, resourceful, indomitable. Let me give two instances.

On this first of February the armed smack *Boy Alfred* (Skipper W. S. Wharton, R.N.R.) was operating about 17 miles S.E. of Southwold together with another smack named *I'll Try* (Skipper T. S. Crisp) when a submarine appeared within 300 yards of the *Boy Alfred* and waved a flag for the smack to approach closer. Simultaneously the German fired either a machine-gun or rifle, hitting the smack in many places. It was really a game of bluff played between a young, fair-haired, self-confident swaggering German full of his own conceit, and a stalwart North Sea mariner who despite his rugged personality and his ketch-rigged craft with the brown sails was no fool. The *Boy Alfred* had no fear of any Hun but even launched his small boat over the side and awaited events. The submarine had got within a hundred yards when the German commanding officer emerged from the conning-tower ordering Wharton to abandon ship. "I'm going to torpedo you," he threatened.

What the Skipper answered does not matter, though you may guess.

"And fire that there gun at 'im" needed no further emphasis.

The submarine was on the smack's port beam.

Bang went the shell of a 12-pounder. Another followed promptly. And a third.

The aim was excellent. At short range the missile hit the U-boat plump, just before the conning-tower, and burst. The Germans had never expected anything like this, but did not stop to argue the point. That impact and bursting of a shell came as such a surprise that when a fourth arrived and penetrated the conning-tower the dazed German had received quite enough and disappeared.

Meanwhile a second submarine, who obviously was co-operating but waiting his chance, had gone to the eastward of the smacks. She was cruising around with only periscope showing but Skipper Crisp in *I'll Try* cleverly kept altering course—for he had just started up the motor with which his vessel was fitted as an auxiliary—and endeavoured to bring the periscope ahead whenever seen. Several times the enemy submerged but finally the whole of the upper deck and conning-tower were visible 200 yards off the starboard bow. Perceiving his chance, Crisp quickly put his helm hard over so as to bring the submarine off the smack's broadside. The smack fired one shot, but it was a beauty. Smiting the base of the conning-tower, she caused an explosion which blew pieces of the submarine into the sea. A torpedo then passed under the stern of *I'll Try*, missing her by about 10 feet; and this 'silver fish' then came to the surface, ran along the top for a while but eventually sank. As to the submarine, she also was not seen again.

It was indeed nothing but a short, sharp conflict between two pairs of foes. Skipper Wharton already had been in three engagements with submarines off the East Anglian coast and was in possession of the D.S.C. For a long time it was believed that Crisp of *I'll Try* had severely damaged the foe submarine, wherefore he was awarded a bar to his D.S.C.*
The Admiralty believed that *Boy Alfred* had definitely sunk his submarine,

---

*In the following August Crisp was awarded posthumously a V.C. for another occasion.

so to Skipper Wharton there came also a bar to his D.S.C. The sum of £1000 was likewise awarded to *Boy Alfred*.

But gallant as were both these fishermen, whose example to other Lowestoft men was a real tonic, yet it is only fair to state that of the submarines neither received fatal damage. Sweeping operations were undertaken in the vicinity but no obstruction discovered. It was afterwards believed that both enemies managed to get back home, so we must regard the incident off Southwold as proving nothing further than the fishermen's boldness.

In Scheer's *Germany's High Sea Fleet in the World War** the Admiral remarks: "The large amount of technical apparatus in a U-boat required very careful handling and repair on her return from an expedition; also the damage due to the voyage or to enemy attacks had to be repaired. Generally speaking, after four weeks at sea a boat would need to lie in the dockyard for the same length of time for repairs." It may well be assumed that these two submarines which had come over towards Southwold were certainly prevented from making a second visit for at least several weeks. Incidentally Scheer also slightly differs as to the number of German U-boats operating on February 1, 1917. He gives the latter as amounting to 103: viz 57 already in the North Sea, eight in the Baltic and 38 in Flanders. Of the Mediterranean submarines he says the Germans at this date possessed 31.

The year 1917, as it drew towards springtide, saw the enthusiasm of German s a warfare attaining its offensive height and British anti-submarine warfare getting very near to its peak. By reason of the War Channel, which was kept daily swept for mines but always well patrolled for submarines between Dover Straits and those busy ports of Durham and Northumberland, we kept the German submarine much concerned with his own existence. That is to say he might venture some daring efforts, but he would have to be careful for his own safety. However ardently U-boats might endeavour to obey the instructions of February 1, our destroyers, our steel-stemmed trawlers and fast-darting M.L.s, were too alert off this East coast to give the enemy much respite. The Yorkshire littoral with its wild wintry weather and precious few practicable harbours continued a bleak area alike for hunters and hunted; but the passage of so many seaborne cargoes bound beyond Flamborough Head exercised a powerful attraction for submarines. It was on February 7 that H.M. Trawler *Swallow* (Lieut. J. Dixon, R.N.R.), together with H.M.T. *Pigeon*, whilst maintaining a keen watch off Whitby observed at 10 a.m. a vessel which appeared to be sinking, so they steamed at full speed to investigate. The stranger was the *Corsican Prince*, a steamer of 2776 tons. On getting closer they sighted another steamer slightly larger, named *St. Ninian*, also stopped about three miles from the coast, with boat tackles over the side and several boats lowered. Both ships had been torpedoed without warning and 15 lives had been lost from the *St. Ninian* including that of the Master.

Just then the *Swallow* caught sight of a periscope a little to the east of *St. Ninian*, whose two boats were full of sailors. Shouting to the latter that they were to remain in the boats till picked up, Dixon proceeded at full speed for the periscope and rammed the submarine so close to the

*P. 260.

conning-tower and with such impact that the *Swallow's* bow was knocked violently to starboard, though the submarine now passed along the side several feet away. The *Swallow* then turned and at 10.30 dropped a depth-charge, but took the precaution to buoy the spot since considerable oil was welling up to the surface. Was the enemy caught unawares? At any rate, just in the moment of ramming, this U-boat was occupied with firing another torpedo at the *St. Ninian* 300 yards away, and the missile took effect so that the steamer, like the *Corsican Prince*, sank in a few seconds.

But the U-boat submerged so rapidly that her bows rose five or six feet in the air and she dived stern first. Meanwhile the steamer's boats were picked up by the *Pigeon* and the survivors landed in Whitby. But what about the U-boat? Had she been sunk by *Swallow's* stem? No, she had not. But the *Swallow* after waiting a while bleated on her wireless at 11.30 a.m., and this summons for help was intercepted by two destroyers, H.M.S. *Doon* and *Waveney*, who were seven miles to the southeastward. They proceeded to the scene at 20 knots, so were not long in arriving and at once began to hunt.

It was at noon that H.M.S. *Waveney* caught sight of a periscope cutting through the water in a southerly direction, and the pursuit seemed rather like a terrier chasing a wily rat. Once the German became quite close, but the *Waveney* passed right over her without touching. Then the U-boat partially rose and the destroyer began firing from the fo'c'sle gun, one shell not quite hitting but bursting near the periscope. The 'rat' was being given a lively hunt, for at 12.20 p.m. her periscope was again seen cutting through the water but this time in a S.W. direction. Quick as a greyhound, the *Waveney* was on her new course at full speed. She made now to ram, though the manœuvre has ever been difficult from the time when in classical days Mediterranean galleys thrust their warlike beaks into a rival's planking.

The submarine was certainly struck and was felt to bump her side against the *Waveney*, but even now it was just another indecisive blow. It may be asserted that the Hun captain at the periscope never spent such a thrilling period, chased from wave to wave and all the time pursued by a sharp steel forefoot. The 'rat', however, was twisting and turning, rushing and doubling, till the shorter craft could seek invisibility beneath the sea in a series of narrow escapes. How much longer could she carry on? The hour must soon come when batteries would be getting low and the submarine compelled to regain the surface. From the following evidence this is clearly confirmed.

For about this time naval wireless again called across the North Sea. H.M.S. *Nith* received a signal that the two other destroyers were chasing the enemy, whereupon the *Nith* steered to cut the submarine's track and at 1.15 p.m. espied the German. The marauder was heading S.W. But slowly. She must have only just risen to the surface, and begun running on her oil engines, when she caught a glimpse of the *Nith* and again dived. That destroyer promptly dropped a depth-charge and one and a half minutes later up rose a large patch of oil.

Daylight was beginning to fade, sunset being due at 5 p.m. It was now 4.30 when the *Swallow* observed a disturbance in the water and oil extending in a N.W. by N. direction. The *Pigeon* dropped a depth-charge

FOULING THE FAIRWAY

but darkness set in, and it became impossible to see the result. Still our commercial shipping off the coast had been harried and the route temporarily endangered. But what happened to the submarine?

How she eluded all the vessels which pursued her is just one excitement after another. But a change was coming next day. That difficult enemy was *UC*-39, which had been running around like a wild bull. She may have been partially injured by the various attacks, but evidently during the night of February 7–8 this *UC*-39 proceeded further south. On the 8th she captured and sank by bombs the S.S. *Hanna Larsen* (1311 tons) 20 miles E.¾N. of the Spurn, but on the same day when molesting another ship in a position Lat. 53, 36, 10, Long. 0.6 E. she was surprised by yet another destroyer, H.M.S. *Thrasher*. This time at last she had to surrender and her captain was killed. Most of her crew were taken captives, but after a lapse of sixteen months a satisfactory postscript wrote itself, since H.M.S. *Quail* on June 7, 1918, chanced in the course of her duties to discern some small bubbles risen to the surface. These were traced to the above position, which was buoyed. Three depth-charges were dropped on this occasion, divers were sent down and the wreck of *UC*-39 was still found to be emitting (after all this period) both oil as well as bubbles.

So far, then, only three enemy submarines had been sunk this year: *UB*-37, *U*-76 and *UC*-39, but a fourth must be added to the date of February 8. It was a day of dramatic happenings, since the destroyer *Ghurka*, which on March 4, 1915 had shared the glory with H.M.S. *Maori* for sinking the submarine *U*-8 in the English Channel near Dover, was patrolling on February 8, 1917, off Dungeness. The *Ghurka* unfortunately was unaware that one of the enemy's submarines had recently laid eight mines off that spot, so *Ghurka* foundered not so very far from where she had previously won fame.

Patrolling in the Dover defile was indeed ever something of an adventure, since anything might happen all of a sudden. It might be a submarine kill, an ambush of mines, the running of a torpedo, even an inquisitive German aeroplane, or German destroyers engaged on a raid. But in the early hours of February 8, 1917, H.M. Destroyer *Liberty* happened to be patrolling on a W.S.W. course towards No. 7A buoy of the Dover Barrage. She had altered course from E.N.E. only at 2.50 a.m. when half a mile from No. 7A. It was now 3.9 a.m. when a large submarine was seen to break surface and lying almost at right angles to the *Liberty*, slightly off the destroyer's starboard bow but right in the centre of the moon's rays. The enemy had evidently just come through this obstacle at a favourite jumping spot, but the 'policeman' on duty was there waiting. Straight for the conning-tower under the full moon the *Liberty* steered at full speed, firing one round. Unfortunately this shot fell wide, and the flash from the gun blinded those on the bridge.

The Captain (Lieut.-Commander P. W. S. King, R.N.) therefore determined not to waste time but ram the German. Travelling at a speed of 24 knots, the destroyer hit the enemy a magnificent blow only two feet forward of the conning-tower. You can imagine what the effect of such speed and weight of steel were like, meeting 420 German tons: in fact the latter's dull weight momentarily stopped the destroyer dead. Not put off by that, Lieut.-Commander King began dropping depth-charges, which of course exploded to some purpose, and the fate of *UC*-46 was rapidly settled. It was discovered that the destroyer was beginning to leak quickly, but presently, when she was taken round to Chatham and docked, it was established beyond all doubt that she must have cut through the submarine to a depth of at least four feet. Lieut.-Commander King was awarded a D.S.O. for his neat performance.

The truth simply is this: Within the Narrow Seas there had been found no more terrible enemy to the U-boat than a cleverly-handled destroyer with her depth-charges.

CHAPTER V

THE GERMAN MENACE

ONE result of the German threat of this Unrestricted Campaign was for us to employ all sorts of vessels—sail and steam—as decoys. Some were less successful than others, but of the sail-driven ships (often fitted with auxiliary motors) there were commissioned the 220-tons lugger *Bayard*, the topsail schooner *Result*, the 122-tons three-masted schooner *Prize*, the ketch *Sarah Colebrooke*, the brigantine *Dargle*; and the yacht *Brown Mouse*, built on the lines of a Brixham trawler. The *Result* came from Barnstaple but was fitted out at Lowestoft during February, being armed both with 12-pounders and torpedo-tubes. She was, however, slow, unhandy, and would lie no closer to the wind than five and a half points. One day in the middle of March, raw and cold, in a rising wind she had an engagement with *UC*-45 who was crossing the North Sea having most probably just concluded a minelaying excursion.

The most successful naval officer to fight submarines was Gordon Campbell, who from the decoy S.S. *Farnborough* on March 22, 1916, had sunk *U*-68 off S.W. Ireland, and on February 17, 1917, also off S.W. Ireland, destroyed *U*-83. Not yet had German commanding officers learned the importance of suspecting intentionally dismal, unkempt steamers and sailing craft that really were ingenious traps. Huns and British mutually were trying by every sort of clever guile to deceive each other, but sometimes the submarine found the obstacles alarming. For instance, one day (February 12, 1917) when Steinbrinck of the Flanders Flotilla was hovering about the Irish Sea he found that his *UC*-65 was veritably surrounded by drifters with their nets. They seemed to bar the whole area between the Smalls and Tuskar. Finally he escaped only by diving to 197 feet and going at slow speed: but the craft was delayed merely a few months* from being sunk altogether.

There seemed a good deal of luck in this game both fortunate and ill-fated: since it was a risky matter for any German commanding officer to brag. Take the voyaging of *UC*-44 who used to come across the North Sea from Heligoland first to operate off our north-east coast. Tebbenjohanns† was her captain. On February 11 when 130 miles N.E. by N. from Shields he sank a local steam trawler and made the skipper his prisoner. Then steering north, he sank the steam trawler *Dale* next day 42 miles south of the Orkneys, but again came south and

*See below.   †See his fate in a later chapter.

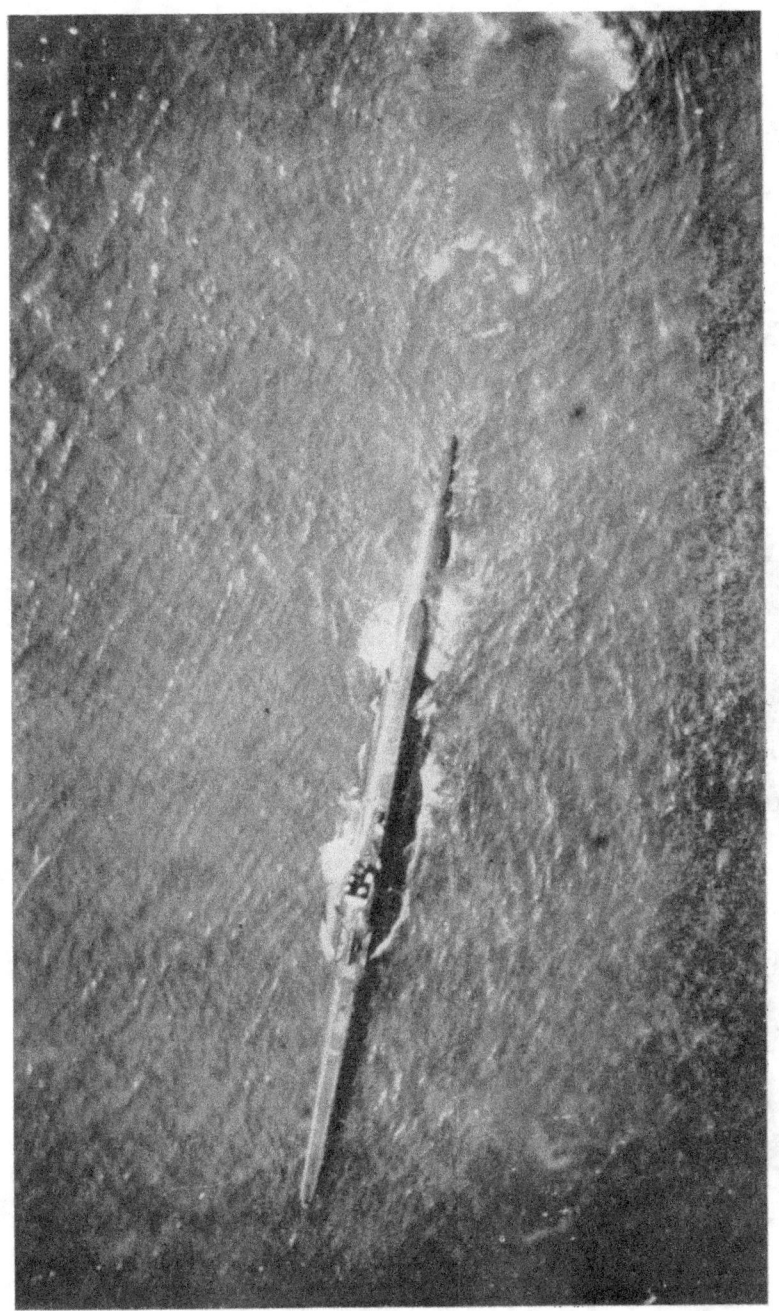

BRITISH SUBMARINE

Ready to dive. This photograph was taken from an aeroplane and shows the smallness of the target.

BRITISH SUBMARINE AFTER COMING TO SURFACE
Notice sailor about to place telescopic sight in position.

sank the steam trawler *King Alfred* on the 13th 75 miles S. of Fair Isle, doing the same thing to other trawlers including the *Mary Bell* on the 14th 50 miles east of Aberdeen; and having taken five trawler skippers as prisoners he went across on the 16th to Heligoland and landed them.

But off Scotland about eleven o'clock on the 15th he was thoroughly shaken up both metaphorically and literally for he had the ill chance to be sighted by a couple of our destroyers who depth-charged him so heartily that all the electric fittings were destroyed and the crew groped about in darkness beneath the waves. Tebbenjohanns pretended that his craft was 'done in' (by ejecting from the after torpedo tube some oil and bits of chairs). Smart idea, and the trawler skippers' captives were impressed, but six months later we had the last laugh, and officers have often told me the story.

One of the devices which our people at this time used in the North Sea was to employ a seaplane with dummy figures which resembled an exhausted pilot and observer, but one of our submarines co-operated in readiness to pounce upon any U-boat that might essay picking them up. The old trick of replacing certain buoys by certain of our submarines had some disadvantages. It was a bright idea to replace the Smith's Knoll buoy with a submarine on the surface, but the conning-tower was covered with a canvas structure resembling a buoy, though the difficulty was to have the submarine maintaining a steady depth and heel over as a buoy does in a tideway. And there was always the risk that the enemy might penetrate the disguise, and fire a torpedo at it.

The regular traffic in mines from Flanders to our East Coast was rather a nuisance, but in the middle of February 1917 one evening at dusk a dummy Shipwash Lightship was placed in a new position between the Shipwash and Bawdsey Banks and the real Shipwash Lightship next morning at daylight brought into Harwich Harbour. Unattended indicator nets were moored east of the Shipwash shoal, and we know that such wiliness did worry a German submarine's navigation. For example, when the dummy Sunk Lightship was moored in a certain position and lit, a group of mines was afterwards found near the dummy which the enemy had evidently assumed to be the real article.

Recently a decoy steamer named the *Lady Olive* (alias Q-18) had been fitted out to lure submarines, but she was armed with one 4-inch and four 12-pounder guns. The former was cruising at the south-western end of the English Channel at 6.54 a.m. of February 19 when she was attacked by a submarine who was coming up firing from three miles astern. German shells were falling but at first it could not be certain exactly whence the shots were being directed. Evidently the enemy had been hovering off the Devonshire coast during the previous day; for at 1.45 a.m. on February 18 something had seemed to happen. At that early hour the weather was thick and H.M. *ML.*461 was patrolling three miles to the eastward of Berry Head when the officer-of-the-watch heard a splashing sound 150 yards off the starboard bow. Nothing, however, could be heard on the hydrophone, but presently both the officer-of-the-watch and two of the hands whilst again listening by this hydrophone distinctly heard noises. Once more the instrument revealed a sound like the starting of a heavy motor engine and immediately through the fog loomed a large submarine which now made off to the southward at about 15 knots.

c

When the German commanding officer came on deck, the submarine's engines were still audible and forthwith the *Lady Olive* gave chase, but nothing more was discerned in the fog. Just exactly whither the enemy now ventured cannot further be decided: yet it looks pretty certain that the U-boat had evidently cut across from West Bay and had begun cruising not far from the Channel Islands area (where the Q-ship *Penshurst* had sunk *UB*-19 on November 30, 1916, as detailed on p. 205 of my *Fighting the U-Boats*). Since *Penshurst* encountered two such craft within a few days and H.M. Q-ship *Aubrietia** exchanged shots with another submarine, we have plenty of evidence that the German enemy was wont to lie in wait hereabouts.

Just before 7 a.m. Lieut. F. A. Frank, R.N.R., *Lady Olive*'s captain, sent away his 'panic parties' in two boats and they began pulling to the southward, but all the rest on board concealed themselves. Ten minutes later the submarine came close under *Lady Olive*'s stern to read her name. And now the Q-ship, finding that the enemy bore only 100 yards off, opened fire. The first two shots hit the base of the conning-tower, but a third put the Hun's gun out of action, killing the German gunlayer. Six more shots took effect below the base of the conning-tower, killing the man standing therein.

Large volumes of vapour issued from the holes below the latter and the submarine listed to starboard, gradually settling down and sank. Frank thereupon rang down for full speed with the intention of going ahead to drop a depth-charge over the spot.

No answer was made to the telegraph, so he waited . . . and waited . . . Then rang again. . . . Still no answer.

Frank hurried from the bridge to the engine-room, where he found the place full of steam with sea-water rapidly rising, the dynamo out of action, and the steampipe burst. What then had happened?

In truth the submarine had fired two shots into this part of the Q-ship's hull, and it was found impossible to use the wireless.

The morning waxed on, things were becoming undeniably worse. Two and a half hours brought no aid. At 9.30 a.m., *Lady Olive* being doomed, the ship's boats and rafts were provisioned and Frank saw that the steel chest containing confidential documents was thrown overboard. Taking to the three boats and two rafts, they proceeded in single line whilst the sea filled engine-room, stoke-hold and after 'tween deck.

Fortunately the weather was fine, but this homeless band of men decided to make for the French coast. After sixty minutes Frank sent one of his officers with half a dozen men in one of the boats seeking assistance, and about 5 p.m. Frank decided to leave the rafts but remove from them the other men into two of the boats; for some were commencing to faint and headway could not be made since the rafts were drifting to leeward. Twenty-three men in each boat crowded a space intended for 17, so they continued to row southward, Frank's craft leading the course.

Slowly, heavily, they toiled over the tide until about 9 p.m. they sighted a French light, but shortly afterwards everything was blotted out by mist and rain. After an hour they sighted another light but lost the loom of the accompanying craft. Then about 11 p.m. they espied a bright light on the mainland to which they made. The damp thickness settled down

*See Chapter I.

once more and they rowed ever onward. Surely with dawn the French coast would be clearly seen with relief?

But daylight broke and no land was visible. The men were very tired, very sleepy, and miserably downhearted with the wind freshening from south-west; the sea rising and curling in an ugly fashion. Frank put the boat's head to sea, helped all he could to cheer up the men and insisted that there was land ahead. All of them did their turn at pulling except the sub-lieutenant, the sergeant-major, and coxswain, who steered in turn. About noon of February 20 the wind eased up and the swell began to moderate. Lieut. Frank determined to have a good talk with his crew, telling them that their only chance of making land was to put their backs into the job. Surely that night they would reach the shore?

So they all resolved to do their best despite their overcrowding and their increasing weakness . . . when . . . yes . . . something . . . what was that? A destroyer? And at the stern she was wearing the tri-colour, but . . .

Suddenly the French destroyer turned westward . . . she was not approaching the boat . . . then she altered to the eastward and now she was circling towards the Englishmen. Why? A very good reason. The destroyer had observed there was a submarine following the boat.

The French vessel came closer and the distressed mariners recognized the name on the quarter. "D-U-N-O-I-S" they spelled out the word. "*Dunois!*" they shouted, but the Frenchmen were all excitement and in a great hurry.

"Come aboard," cried the Gallic captain. "Yes, but please be quick." Some hoisted themselves out of the boat, took a jump, climbed to the deck.

"Wait a minute!" Then the *Dunois* was off again as the propellers churned up the froth. At six o'clock she swept close once more, 16 men again raised themselves, but now the *Dunois* was firing at the submarine and suddenly spurted full speed ahead. The port propeller guard crashed into the side of the boat, ripping its starboard side right out and forthwith that wooden craft filled with water though seven men still remained. *Dunois* approached yet again, when her cutter was lowered and picked up the rest. Taking them into Cherbourg, the destroyer landed the Englishmen, and next day met a trawler with on board the boatload that had been missing.

So the episode concluded without loss, though the Q-ship had gone down to the depths. Assuredly the submarine had been severely damaged, but got back home in spite of the *Lady Olive's* direct hits and those two shell holes received in return.

If this time the *Lady Olive's* people had not been victorious, at least their ally had saved them from wind and tide.

The fresh development of submarine warfare had during February 1917 risen decidedly. There were 35 ships sunk in January 1917 and 86 in February, which actually rose to 103 in March and 155 in April; and that was the highest submarine activity during the whole war; so that in May the figures of sinkings dropped to 106 ships. In our previous volume we called attention to the success of Hersing who journeyed in *U*-21 from Germany in April 1915; but in February 1917 he left the Mediterranean again for home. He made an uneventful passage until February 22 when he came across eight Dutch steamers off the Scillies. Unaware that his Government had granted this convoy a safe conduct, he promptly sank six of these vessels. Then Hersing carried on to Wilhelmshaven, and finally Germany agreed to compensate Holland for the injuries.

The enemy was still being thwarted by these obstructions in the Dover Straits and his U-boats on coming home were continuously reporting harrowing stories of being entangled by netting. Finally an attempt to clear the Dover Straits for an unimpeded and free passage of submarines was made by sending a nocturnal raid by destroyers against our drifters on March 25. It is true that as a result of the raid of October 26, 1916, the Dover Patrol had been gradually strengthened by vessels from the Grand Fleet Flotillas as well as by destroyers from the Harwich force stationed at Dover to assist the 6th Flotilla. Drifters were also withdrawn from the Dover barrage at night, and their places taken by four or five destroyers which patrolled S.W. for five miles from these barrage light-buoys at Nos. 5A, 7A, 9A, 11A, and 13A. Two light cruisers and a division of destroyers were stationed at anchor off Deal, one monitor off Ramsgate and another also off Deal. In addition there were the Ramsgate Armed Drifters and one torpedo-boat patrolling the northern approach to the Downs.

So we come to this night of March 25, 1917, when the weather was fine but overcast, the moon four days old and obscured by clouds. Some would say that the conditions were ideal for a raid.

At 10.30 p.m. one destroyer, *Laverock*, when three and a half miles S.W. of No. 11A buoy and steering to the north-east sighted a strange destroyer on her port bow steaming S.W. Immediately afterwards that German burned a red flare, and a heavy fire was opened on *Laverock* by four or six destroyers. Two enemy torpedoes were also aimed, of which one hit the *Laverock* but did not explode. The enemy altered course northward and retired across the barrage. The Ramsgate Drifters were spread along the line between the North Foreland and North Goodwin, and the nearest drifter inshore was about a mile from the North Foreland. She was the *John Lincoln* and after 11 p.m. three destroyers were observed half a mile seaward steering N. along the coast. A few minutes later these three opened fire towards the land, whereupon the *John Lincoln* at once released a green rocket which was the signal for an attack by surface vessels. The first shots of the enemy were fired at the North Foreland, the second towards Margate, causing some slight damage to house property, killing one woman and two children, but the enemy escaped to the eastward.

So, however much the Germans tried to clear a passage for their underwater craft this adventure availed very little. Probably the real intention was to get minelaying submarines through the Straits.

It was the Yorkshire coast which was often enough sufficiently cruel in the prevailing weather but sometimes even worse when the submarines lurked about the region. One of our naval submarines during the afternoon of March 10, 1917, surprised the enemy off Muckle Flugga just before four o'clock. *UC*-43 was sighted barely six miles away, and a keen contest began, the British submarine *G*-13 manœuvring cleverly to gain the perfect position. When *G*-13 at last fired both bow torpedoes at 2300 yards the enemy having dived below the surface, was hit just forward of the conning-tower and disappeared immediately, but behind him was left nothing else than a square mile of oil fuel and pieces of planking. Down sank the German and not a survivor existed.

CHAPTER VI

"WASSER BOMS"

TOWARDS the end of this last war the word 'paravane' was introduced to signify an apparatus invented for use on either bow or stern for the destruction of a floating mine. Originally it was devised and developed by Commander Burney, but the very word 'paravane' was for a long while considered too confidential for actual mention. When used for merchant shipping the device could be spoken of as an 'otter'.

About the time when hostilities were terminating the safest thing for a U-boat was for her to dive to about 200 feet and remain still at that depth. As finally developed, the explosive paravane was given a torpedo-shaped body. The 'otter' department was started only at the beginning of 1917 but its work could before long be continued at the principal ports of the United Kingdom and Mediterranean: in fact 3000 commercial vessels were so fitted for installation. Reports soon began to accumulate from warships and 48 out of 52 proved that naval units were cutting moored mines adrift. When hospital ships tested the 'otter' gear, it was realized that a ship could go through a minefield by daylight with impunity, the mines being then cut off and released to the surface. In fact having got among such dangers the best thing was to steer a straight course at full speed. It was finally reckoned that 200 million pounds' worth of ships and cargoes were thus saved.

The number of German mines gradually increased until April, when 515 were accounted for. It is notable that there was a considerable fall during May, but again the increase was a steady diminution in most weeks between June and December. It is further significant that the total number of mines for 1917 was double that of 1916. Why? Probably because more minelaying submarine losses were wiped out; or perhaps greater minesweeping experience was being developed among the personnel, or because M.L.s were being used at Low Water in scouting for mines.

At first the enemy concentrated on the south and south-west coasts of Ireland, then off the principal convoy ports. At one time the Hun dropped all his mines in one cargo after reaching the operational area but later he would lay his explosives off headlands and other seamarks; while after carefully studying our minesweeping tactics his methods became more particular. For instance, *UC*-43 laid 18 mines during January between Flamborough Head and Whitby.

The time now arrived when H.M. Yacht *Rovenska* at the beginning of the year reached Falmouth escorting from the Mediterranean eight of our drifters, but the ninth (H.M.D. *Ativern*) had foundered in the English

Channel through bad weather. Altogether during February and March no fewer than 24 skippers and 177 ratings of those who had served about two years in the Mediterranean were sent home.

And not without stealth these minelaying submarines continued to do their job off our coasts. Eighteen mines about the end of December 1916 had been laid S.E. of Montrose. Granton sweepers, having been first warned by the Montrose fishermen, began sweeping and discovered these traps during February 1917 but it was during the latter part of this month.

It is of *UC*-44 that we are able to present two aspects and I think the reader will agree that regarded as a whole they make an extraordinary narrative. Few series of episodes can ever indeed outrival such a sequence of events. Consider *UC*-44 as the villain of this yarn and the date wholly confined to the year 1917, yet even then it all reads more like a fairy tale than blunt fact.

Already we have noted at once the energy of our patrols such as against submarines sent from Germany to lay mines off north-eastern as well as against ports or headlands; and the alertness of steam yachts, steam trawlers and our own destroyers. Neither side could afford to be unvigilant, for shells and depth-charges seemed ever to be whizzing past one's ears. There was a German named Tebbenjohanns in command, who had crossed the North Sea more than once and knew well enough how to pretend. On February 11 when 130 miles N.E. by N. from Shields he stopped the steam trawler *Ashwold* also of Shields, and took her skipper as prisoner. Next day *UC*-44 apparently altered course to North and sank the steam trawler *Dale* 42 miles S. by E. from Ronaldshay in the Orkneys. Soon afterwards *UC*-44 came south once more, for on February 13 she sank the steam trawler *King Alfred* 75 miles short of Fair Isle. Now on February 14 she sank some steam trawlers (as for example the *Belvoir Castle*) 15 miles S.E. of Buchan Ness, and the *Mary Bell* 50 miles off Aberdeen. On February 14 *UC*-44 got back to Heligoland having in all cases taken the trawler skipper captive.

It is remarkable to note that Skipper Hall, late of *Mary Bell*, said on February 15 that while a prisoner in *UC*-44 this submarine about 11 a.m. was attacked by depth-charges from two British destroyers, smashing all the electric light fittings and placing the submarine in darkness. Tebbenjohanns then ordered oil to be placed in the after torpedo-tube, also some chairs. Thus was discharged something that would feign partial destruction. *UC*-44 not merely returned to Germany this middle of February but five months later had won so much technical and navigational knowledge that she pretended to have been quite undamaged and would suffer nothing further.

But Tebbenjohanns became overconfident. The commands issued ordered him to visit the south-east of Ireland and to lay his 18 mines by a certain mark off the coast of Waterford. It was night-time, the hour about 10 p.m., and arrangements had been made to release the cargo . . . when something on the anniversary of August 4 occurred. Something intensely dramatic. The force of this terrible tragedy was created because one of the Huns had been a muddle-headed fool, for no sooner had some of the new cargo made a dangerous explosion on the same spot where the original mines had been left by the first visitor, than this second minefield exploded on top of the other. Tebbenjohanns was shot out of the conning-tower, and afterwards divers were sent down, who found the conning-tower hatch open with half her mines still in the tubes. Salvage operations followed, and examination of her log-book yielded further information that this vessel could negotiate Dover Straits whenever desirable.

Yet on February 17 at 9.45 a.m. a certain decoy vessel known as *Q*-5 under Commander Gordon Campbell was in 51.34 N., 11.23 W., jilling along at seven knots when a torpedo was seen approaching and it became evident that the torpedo would hit the ship. Helm was put hard aport to try and avoid such a happening but the missile struck the ship in No. 3 hold wounding an Engineer Sub-Lieut. R.N.R. In the meantime 'Action Stations' had been sounded, and none was kept on board except where men were specially required. The Chief Engineer reported that his engine-room was filling but he was ordered to hang on as long as possible and then hide.

This was done, and meanwhile the submarine was observed off the starboard quarter till she came past the ship only 10 yards away. "The temptation," reasoned Commander Campbell, "to open fire was almost unbearable." The enemy having passed close across the bows and broken surface, Commander Campbell pretended he was torpedoed; but when the German manœuvred till she got on the only bearing that would allow, off went all *Q*-5's guns at point-blank range. It was a terrific moment: the first shot (from the 6-pounder) hit the submarine's conning-tower and carried away the Hun captain's head. The surprise was such that the German boat never recovered, and for the time remained on the surface while the S.S. *Lodorer* (*Q*-5) remained on the surface with a disreputable hull astreak of white paint, a black funnel and looking anything except smart.

But the work being performed was superfine: the enemy's conning-tower was hit continually, some of these shells going clean through; that is to say at least 45 besides the Maxim bullets. Finally the U-boat sank with conning-tower open and at least eight men having leapt into the sea, but one of our lifeboats from the *Lodorer* managed to save a German officer and a man. It was a ghastly sight, for the water was thick in oil and blood with air-bubbles very conspicuous. Boats were then recalled to the ship, which was certainly rapidly filling and sinking by the stern. Commander Campbell therefore signalled for assistance. Nearly all hands he placed in the boat, but a few men he kept on board giving them orders to destroy all confidential books. Before noon a destroyer arrived on the scene and all the crew transferred to her as she was now getting worse. Then H.M. Sloop *Buttercup* arrived to take the *Lodorer* in tow but the tow-rope parted, and by 5 p.m. the Q-ship was hard to steer with the swell breaking over the after deck.

Presently arrived too H.M. Sloop *Laburnum*, but suddenly the *Lodorer* exploded a depth-charge. At first the *Buttercup* took this detonation to be that of a torpedo and slipped the tow. Finally *Laburnum* brought the Q-ship to Berehaven, the stern being nearly eight feet under water. *Lodorer* was able to win for Commander Campbell the coveted Victoria Cross, and even when she lay beached on her side at Mill Cove, well up in Berehaven, no sailorman ever passed this spot without remembering that

17th of February. For *U*-83 had been sunk by the Commander who was to become the king of all Q-ships.

As to the minelaying submarine *UC*-18, there remains a little mystery, but some of our vessels which used their explosive sweeps in the Dover Straits were possibly responsible for this sort of vengeance, and it may be that H.M.S. *Medea*, a very modern type of fast destroyer, travelling at 22 knots towing a paravane, accounted for *UC*-17: for there have happened instances where the difference between fact and not-quite actuality has barely existed. It is also not quite clear exactly how and when the Q-ship *Privet* was sunk. The probability is that on March 12 *U*-85 was destroyed off the western mouth of the English Channel almost simultaneously with the destruction of *Q*-19 (otherwise the *Privet*). It happened in mid-March that the Germans were unlucky enough for *UB*-6 to get ashore off Hellevoetsluis, where the tide runs strongly, and she was finally interned. The exact place of *UB*-6's stranding was off the Maas on the Hinder Ribbon.

Another near instance at this time occurred on March 10. The Elders and Fyffe S.S. *Aracataca* was steering N.47 E. from a position in Lat. 51.19 N., Long. 16.3 W., when a submarine burst out of the sea, killing one man; but the liner replied and claimed to have hit the submarine twice. On to the scene appeared H.M. Destroyer *Parthian*, but the liner's Master behaved so gallantly that he was able to save his ship and go into Berehaven. The mining by the enemy was not haphazard. He was endeavouring so to foul the area near the shore that he would force shipping to pass outside territorial waters. The paravane was recently justifying itself, and during March mines were found off the entrance to Cromarty Firth near the Whistle Buoy around which they laid half a dozen buoys.

CHAPTER VII

SUBMARINES VERSUS DESTROYERS

THERE was no question as to the enemy's mining determination. Such dangerous missiles were found also both north and south of Wick, off Elie Ness (Firth of Forth); off Berwick-on-Tweed; Flamborough Head; in the Lowestoft and Harwich areas; off the Sunk and Tongue Lightships; off Queenstown and the Old Head of Kinsale; off the south and north entrance to Lerwick; and elsewhere such as the English Channel. But the harbour entrances were especially notorious, the Germans now using a type of delay release which might last as long as 13 days. During the month of March *UC*-55 laid no fewer than 18 mines off the Orkneys, and in being strongly impressed by our patrols off Kirkwall the Germans remarked that "the promptness of the counter-measures taken immediately on sighting the submarine was astounding. Within $1\frac{1}{2}$ to 2 hours there arrived on the spot 12 destroyers, one submarine chaser, and 10 sweepers." The enemy submarines were also much impressed by the utility of the smoke-screens made from merchant steamers. "Trawlers are encountered all over the place—under the land and up to 30 miles away from it."

About March a fresh flotilla of British submarines with H.M.S. *Vulcan* as mother ship and placed under the orders of Admiral Bayly, began to operate against U-boats on their passage down the west coast of Ireland en route for their respective areas along the southern trade-routes. Eventually our flotilla amounted to six of the E-class, six of the D-class and two of the H-class types. In April 1917 *Vulcan* with eight submarines went to Lough Swilly whilst H.M.S. *Platypus* with six submarines was stationed at Killybegs. Meanwhile the amount of British merchant shipping tonnage sunk by U-boats amounted to 283,647 tons plus 3586 tons of fishing vessels. Seeing that German submarines this March sank shipping in such different places as the Bristol and English Channels, west coast of Ireland, in the Atlantic, North Sea, Bay of Biscay and Mediterranean, one could indeed regard the U-boat menace as pretty well universal.

Yet another instance of how nearly the submarine escaped on March 9 (1917) may now be mentioned. It happened at 2.5 a.m. that H.M. Trawler *Westward Ho* caught sight of a U-boat at 57.55 N. Long., 3.28 W., when on the port quarter about 700 yards away the trawler's skipper immediately sent his crew to 'Action Stations' and rang down 'Full Speed'. At a range of about 600 yards the submarine was hit with the third, fourth and sixth shots. It was a very bright cloudless night with a full moon and after being first sighted the enemy was just coming to the surface. When the *Westward Ho* fired red rockets it brought H.M.S. *Osprey* and other vessels. Search was made in the locality and hydrophones used, but nothing further could be seen and there seemed little certainty of a kill having been effected. But U-boats always hoped to sink a fishing vessel whenever an opportunity presented: for instance, out of a large number, no fewer than 11 smacks were sunk about 25 miles N.W. of Trevose Head, Cornwall, between March 11 and 12.

It was on February 25, you will recollect, that the Germans with their destroyers attempted another quick nocturnal raid on the Dover Straits, 'the object, of course, being so to frighten away our destroyers, trawlers, drifters and any other craft that might harass the German submarines going up or down Channel. After the raid of February 25 the disposition of our Dover forces by night then remained much the same. During the night of March 17-18, however, the moon in its last quarter was above the horizon only in the early morning. It may be mentioned that it was Low Water off Dover on March 18 at 12.12 a.m., the tides being at Neaps, the weather calm and clear.

Now the Northern approach to the Downs was being watched at night by six armed drifters that were based on Ramsgate. Spread out between Broadstairs Knoll Buoy and the North Sand Head, they were supported by *T.B.*-4 which cruised to the southward, and it so happened that two days previously the S.S. *Greypoint* bound north had been forced by an engine breakdown to anchor about a mile east of the Broadstairs Knoll Buoy. It was past midnight—precisely 12.35 a.m.—of March 18 when H.M. Drifter *Paramount* sighted three or four German destroyers coming from the N.E. and passing close to the eastward of *Greypoint*. The drifter fired a green rocket as a warning that they had sighted the enemy, but the latter replied by firing on the drifters and torpedoing the *Greypoint* at 12.40 a.m.

The enemy then appears to have carried on for about a mile S.W. and next altered course to N.E.; but on their return journey they continued to fire at the drifters, and at the *Greypoint*; bombarding also Ramsgate and Broadstairs. H.M. Drifter *Redwald* was so seriously damaged that she had to be beached. The Torpedo Boat No. 4 near the Gull Lightship sighted the enemy and at once proceeded towards the firing at 15 knots; but the latter had a much higher speed and by 1 a.m. the Germans had finished their adventure already.

Looking back on events in their mingled sequence we must bear in mind that at 10.50 p.m. on March 17 we had H.M.S. *Paragon* and three other destroyers covering the Dover Straits Barrage Patrol which was about three miles S.W. of 11A Buoy. She was steering N.E. when she sighted three or four Hun destroyers steaming in from the eastward, when the enemy suddenly altered course to the S.W. The *Paragon* was then torpedoed and was heavily fired on at close range, but presently broke in two and sank, her depth-charges exploding and killing many of the men in the water. No officers were saved in this tragedy, and only 10 men. At full speed H.M.S. *Laforey* was on the scene about 11 p.m. burning her searchlight. Then something happened. Whilst she was thus illuminating the scene to pick up survivors, the destroyer *Llewellyn* was stopped close to her, but at about 11.15 p.m. *Llewellyn* had just switched on her lights when she was struck by a torpedo, though by good luck was able to steam stern first and reach Dover.

Evidently after sinking *Paragon* the enemy steamed south, and on their return journey sighted *Laforey's* searchlight and fired one or more torpedoes. The entire crew of *Greypoint* were rescued near the Broadstairs Knoll Buoy by the *Paramount* and simultaneously heard the sound of a pea-whistle, so at once extinguished all lights. Somewhere between 1 a.m. and 1.45 a.m. six M.L.s were sent out from Dover, picking up eight survivors and five bodies from the *Paragon*. But how little good had been all this speed, this excitement, this loss of life! Whom could the enemy have profited, since Dover still remained the most difficult of all defiles? Whether the enemy released his mines by submarines off the headlands or made a surprise attack by surface ships with other weapons it mattered little enough in the great contest; but what stood out conspicuously was his determination to register all the damage possible as we sought by every means to maintain a stout anti-submarine defence. So many incidents were happening along the north-east British coast that the Admiralty issued orders for British, Allied, and neutral vessels to be given escorts all the way from Lerwick to Stornoway.

In the early hours of March 29 there happened a sudden, rapid, and heavy gunfire which began S.E. of the harbour entrance to Great Yarmouth. German forces played their searchlights on a merchant steamer which they shelled. The latter was of only 674 tons and a Hun destroyer sank her eight miles east of Lowestoft, taking seven prisoners; but after a quarter of an hour the raid was all over. Brightly were the enemy keeping a smart lookout just now for the things which were happening; since once again Commander F. H. Grenfell had yet another engagement with a submarine in Lat. 50.28 N., Long. 0.12 W. Neither vessel was sunk, but the *Penshurst*, though holed, still managed to reach port again. That the enemy nearly always was in the Channel Islands neighbourhood was still further confirmed on March 31 when the British transport *Queen*

Louise was torpedoed three miles north of Cape Barfleur; yet after having been abandoned, the Master and seven men returned on board and got her into Havre.

Again the Huns would vary life by some more minelaying. They did this, for instance, at the entrance to the Mersey towards the end of March and the beginning of April, two channels being swept in the approaches to the port, viz. from Lynas Point to the Bar Lightship, and then north of this. German submarine officers in making their efforts to rush through Dover Straits were, however, very conscious sooner or later of being caught in the nets. For a U-boat usually intending to pass between Buoys 1 and 2 this was a favourite place; and in her report of February 1, 1917, *UC*-17 mentions that she got caught in one of our nets between such buoys. It was only by bursting her way through the net with 54 yards still hanging to the submarine's hull and occasionally going astern with her engines that at last *UC*-17 managed to clear herself. You can well understand how the enemy hated our watchful vessels and obstructions that they delighted in making a Dover raid between the North Foreland and Dungeness.

Some of the cruelty which so frequently has manifested itself under Hitler was not altogether unknown to the Kaiser regime. For instance, seafarers were shocked on Lady Day 1917 when one U-boat had the audacity to send a party and climb aboard the South Arklow Lightship and sink her by bombs. To what reason? Possibly the lightship was making signals to the S.S. *Annan* (who was coming south) that the position of the U-boat had best be regarded as a warning.

CHAPTER VIII

U-BOAT ADVENTURES

AMONG the 'star-turns' or submarine 'aces' Lieut. Commander Moraht was long remembered for his skill, daring, and (till the close of his career) good luck. Germany during the First World War regarded him as so able that they delighted in giving him the order 'Pour le Mérite' because it corresponded to our Victoria Cross; yet his fame did not rival that of such captains as von Arnauld de la Perière who with the sinking of 400,000 shipping tons, or Max Valentiner with 300,000 tons, or Rücker with 170,000, won distinction.

Still, Moraht with 130,000 tons to his credit was always considered an unusually successful practitioner. In command of *U*-64 he used to operate off Flamborough Head during 1916 and in the North Sea, though he gained no distinction when trying to waylay some of our British units that took part in the Battle of Jutland. *U*-64, all the same, was of convenient size, displacing 810 tons on the surface but 930 tons when submerged. Like certain other selected commanding officers after the summer of 1916 he was finally sent with his craft to wage war in the Mediterranean. She carried two torpedo-tubes in the bow, another couple in the stern, one gun on deck and had a speed of 16 knots whilst motoring along on the surface, and nine knots whilst under water. Her voyage to the Adriatic base at Cattaro was to be a long one. Rather than risk the obstacles in Dover Straits, she proceeded via the Orkneys and Shetlands, but at economical speed she carried oil-fuel for 6000 miles. Certainly this was not the time of year for choosing the Bay of Biscay's gales or trying to get sights from a cloudy sky. Sometimes the waves were so hammer-like in their blows that he dodged them by submerging and steering 'blind' during 40 hours.

It seemed to his three officers and 35 men more than worth it, if they could exchange the North Sea fogs and cold for Mediterranean sunshine. Moreover, argued some, the Middle Sea would provide easier targets with less risk. For, during that summer, whilst returning to Emden after one of her cruises, *U-64* only just escaped disaster. A British submarine on the alert sighted her, aimed and fired a torpedo which should have been a certain hit. In those days our 'silver fish' sometimes did odd things: this one made a sort of side-slip, struck a sandy shoal and exploded itself there. But Moraht's crew were shaken up badly, and never forgot the incident.

Arrived in southern waters, Moraht settled down to his new work, one of his first prizes being the Norwegian S.S. *Tripel*, for in those days, as in the present hostilities, Germany paid no respect to neutral shipping. The capture of any steamer meant unlimited fresh food instead of tinned meats; and the occasional rendezvous with another U-boat provided opportunity for swapping yarns or obtaining the latest news. Not a bad life, thereafter, coming out from Cattaro for three to four weeks at a time, and altogether *U-64* made eight successful cruises in the Middle Sea.

Certainly for a time it did seem as if Robert Moraht was one of those mortals who have all the luck. On leaving Wilhelmshaven he was aged 32, had been 15 years in the German Navy, yet this was his first year in the submarine service. And already a commanding officer after only 11 months. But that indicated how badly in need of submarine personnel our enemies had soon become.

Now on March 19, 1917, fate handed him a wonderful gift. Destiny with a curious magnetism was drawing two steel vessels from opposite directions into the same picture. During that forenoon *U-64* was steering to the north-west, bound for the treacherous Gulf of Lion, and already the south-west corner of Sardinia could be discerned. Below, in his miniature cabin, Moraht sat reading when the voice-pipe whistled and he was summoned to the conning-tower by his officer-of-the-watch. In the distance, coming towards them but zigzagging, was a strange large ship of unordinary features.

Six years previously France had built that massive, somewhat ugly battleship *Danton* of 18,027 tons and 20 knots speed. Her five funnels, of course, with the wide gap between numbers three and four, made her unique in the world's navies: no matter in which of the Seven Seas she might be sighted, her peculiar features would always identify her as the one and only man-of-war which a few miles away looked more like a factory. Escorting this battleship was the French destroyer *Massue*. The *Danton* had just concluded a four-months' refit in Toulon and was bound for Corfu.

Several miles still separated when Moraht gave orders to dive and made preparations for attack. Unseen, he took up a position so that the battleship should be ahead of his bow tubes. Then at noon two short orders sufficed.

"First tube . . . fire! . . . Second tube . . . fire!"

Too late the French sighted the missiles. Too late helm was put over to avoid them. Both struck the target, the ship took a heavy list, in vain *Massue* hurried to the scene and dropped depth-charges. Moraht had dived hurriedly into safety. Three-quarters of an hour later *Danton* likewise disappeared below the surface but for all time. Purely by chance, two French trawlers happened to be in the vicinity and they together with *Massue* managed to rescue 806 survivors, though 296 others (including the captain) perished. Two days later, still hovering about here, Moraht picked up from the water a sailor's ditty-box. In it were letters which confirmed *Danton's* identification.

Oh yes! Robert Moraht again had been lucky. But, as French naval officers in other parts of the Mediterranean agreed, *Danton* ought never to have crossed that danger zone in daylight and with only a single escort. Although the destroyer *Massue* and two French *chalutiers* were present, more by chance than design, Moraht was contending with a great ship that was crossing a zone in daylight which robbed her of protection. Even French naval officers criticized the careless routeing of an unmistakable vessel. Admittedly for miles she had been shadowed. So when this unusual French design was located on the afternoon of March 19, 1917, Moraht found it necessary only to confirm the appearance by looking up facts in the identification book. The floating box of letters confirmed that *U-64*'s target was the victim which had indeed been that of Moraht. Two German torpedoes sufficed, the five-funnelled warship listed and finally capsized.

But as hostilities progressed it was mine warfare which in one way or another became a terror to Germany's submarines. The public has scarcely appreciated how formidable a reply we made to the enemy's minelaying cruises. Sometimes, also, Teutonic inefficiency assisted our strategy.

For example, two days after *UC-26* ended her chequered life, *UC-76*, which had only just been built, was in Heligoland taking aboard her cargo of 18 black 'eggs' destined for British waters when . . . an awful bang shook the harbour.

One of these round objects exploded, set the others off likewise, sank the submarine, and with her perished Ober-Leutnant Barten.

Four days later—though Barten's boat was afterwards salved—a tragic sequence of happenings impressed the German Navy most alarmingly.

Aware that our destroyers had been fairly active in and around Heligoland Bight, the enemy failed to appreciate how thoroughly our daring vessels had plastered the approaches with hidden dangers.

In fact, H.M. Destroyers *Abdiel*, *Blanche* and *Royalist* laid a minefield fifteen miles south of Horn's Reef light buoy and got away without being seen.

This extensive obstruction, moreover, was deposited to form an ingenious pattern that it would be most difficult for the sweeping trawlers to locate.

For a month it remained neither discovered nor suspected, but on May

14 Kapitain-Leutnant von Firks was coming out to sea in *U*-59 escorted by a minesweeper *Fulda* and other vessels.

Personal reasons have always embittered me towards Firks, because about six o'clock on the evening of October 23, 1916, he sent my friend, Lieut.-Commander John White, R.N., together with most of a fine British crew, to their deaths, whilst only a dozen men were miraculously picked up in the Atlantic 18 hours later after a gale of exceptional severity had set in.

H.M.S. *Genista* went to her grave protecting the S.S. *Alexandrian* from a similar disaster.

The steamer, with a valuable cargo of machinery, escaped, but two of *U*-59's torpedoes caused 73 of *Genista's* people, including all officers, to be robbed of life.

Von Firks was a callous fellow, but seven months later his punishment came about with perfect vengeance. May 14 was foggy, and the cavalcade failed to pick up their marks. Into our minefield blundered *U*-59, and she carried von Firks to his doom as quickly as he had wiped out *Genista*.

Nor was that all.

The *Fulda* also fouled the mines and sank. Likewise vanished another of the escort. Two days later the Germans sent their sweeper *M*-14 to locate the wreck of *U*-59 and, during the search, *M*-14 struck another mine, so down she went. Torpedo Boat No. 78 rushed to her aid. She hit yet another mine, blew up, and disappeared.

That self-same night *U*-86 was outward bound from the Ems, and had to be escorted through what the Germans imagined to be a safe channel, but again one of the accompanying steamers knocked against a mine and perished, so that the submarine and rest of the convoy must needs turn away and anchor in Borkum Roads.

As to the barrage in which *U*-59 succumbed, this still harassed the Germans even during the following year.

Why? Because, thanks to British persistence, German minesweeping operations had to cover an immense area which extended 180 miles north and 140 miles west of the River Jade .

To send sweepers out so far from land became such a risky business, and invited annihilation at the hands of British cruisers, that strong supporting forces from Wilhelmshaven were essential.

One need waste no sympathy for the submarine commanders, whose unscrupulous behaviour has been rivalled only by their successors in the present war, yet where the most experienced U-boat captains in the last war learned to proceed with caution, newly promoted officers dashed recklessly into the most foolish situations till finally and too late they sacrificed their own lives and those of their crew.

Thus it was with Ober-Leutnant J. Ries, in charge of *UC*-77, which left Germany late in May 1917 to shell Aberdeen. Our destroyers foiled her, made her dive, and she laid her mines off the Forth.

At midnight of June 3-4, when five miles east of Girdleness, Ries sighted the Grimsby trawler *Virgilia*, which was not armed but on her way to the Humber with a full catch of fish from the Faroes.

Ries behaved abominably, sank the ship by bombs, took Skipper Alfred Rawlings prisoner, left the crew to fend for themselves in their small boat—after the German had thrown overboard both mast and sail.

Fortunately these fishermen were picked up by an M.L. a few hours later.

Next night *UC-77* was off Hartlepool, when she attacked another vessel with 22-pounder shells.

This time, however, things happened differently; the stranger turned out to be a patrol vessel with good guns and better gunners than the submarine owned. The first British shots damaged the U-boat, Ries just escaping death when a shell passed over his head. Several of the crew, injured, rushed aft, their hands and faces covered with blood.

Ries then precipitately dived, but the deluge of depth-charges began, the first striking the submarine aft, giving her such a violent shake-up that all hands thought it was the end.

A second explosive burst one of the oil-tanks, so that 15 tons of fuel were lost, and then a third just missed her ahead. Ries, not content with these narrow escapes, a few minutes later got foul of nets, though he managed to slide out of a tight corner by using his engines ahead and astern.

He sank five more ships, cruised along the coast disguised with a lug-sail hoisted at the conning-tower so that the U-boat resembled in the distance a motor fishing craft, and finally got back to Heligoland on June 10.

A most fortunate, if undeserving, fellow.

Destiny awaited him. A year later he had not yet learned to be cautious, and on the evening of July 10, 1918, he was trying to steal through the Dover Straits, where our defences against submarines were now so thorough, and many *U*-boats had foundered, that Ries should have been critical of his procedure.

Actually he neglected to note that *UC-77* was leaving astern a track of oil and bubbles.

But the drifter *Kessingland* observed these, followed up the track, unloaded a lot of depth-charges, so did the *Golden Grain*. Heavy explosions despatched submarine, Ries and his raw crew, to regions whence there is no return.

The penalty had been paid at last.

CHAPTER IX

MEDITERRANEAN DRIFTERS

OF all walks in life which could in the long run suddenly be altered it is to the submariners that sudden changes must belong.

Serving in that adventurous Flemish Flotilla was a man named Degetau who commanded *UC-68*. He was another of those self-confident youngsters. In fact, covered by the darkness of night in the early nocturnal hours as he got nearer to Zeebrugge, he had every reason to be looking forward towards those boisterous expressions of recreation when . . . Bang! burst! a British torpedo was awaiting him and the hull was shattered this fifth of April. Another fortnight and once more trouble was coming in the same area. On April 19, 1917, *UC*-30 struck one of those North Sea mines which so often he had laid. This time the German, barely outside his own doorstep, came to eternal grief.

But apart from these direct incidents we had to take note of the decay which within a couple of years manifested itself on the wooden hulls of fishing drifters that we had sent out from Poole and sundry ports round our coasts. Many of these had originated with Scottish crews, who toiled manfully and faced the Austrian shells not less than the torpedoes. But it was the teredo worm which was just about as destructive. When, for example, a bunch of 15 drifters from the Mediterranean came again into Poole towards the end of March, practically every one was leaking, for the worm had very badly holed the bottom planking on the water-line and just below.

Few raw Scottish fishermen ever expected that the skipper, or his relatives who made up the crew, and the vessel itself which came straight from a normal job to hoist the White Ensign, would mount perhaps one gun whilst in the hold would be carried yards of nets. From the different families these drifters would usually work their way southward, gathering large numbers at such places as Milford in Wales or Poole in Dorset. The next stoppage at Gibraltar and Italy was to be a final call, but in some cases the Aegean was their operation area, making themselves a great terror among the islands. The first units organized to hunt with the aid of hydrophones were the Aegean drifters which began so to work this month.

They were organized in divisions of seven, the leader being in the centre. Each division was moved according to the direction of the drifters who heard the submarine: the aim being to keep the submarine within the periphery of the division and eventually force the enemy to the surface within range of the drifters.

During April the Adriatic drifters instead of netting a fixed line so operated that since the position was changed every week the enemy would never know where the nets had been placed. On the average there would be about 70 drifters on duty. It was therefore an impossible job trying to make 44 miles of sea impenetrable. Bad weather compelled them to haul their nets and scatter. Eight steel drifters reached the Adriatic from England early in February 1917, but about that time some of our M.L.s arrived via the French inland waterways, and along the Mediterranean past Italy to Mudros, after calling at Taranto.

The fact is that Britain was sending out to the Mediterranean almost every kind of warship—light cruisers, destroyers, trawlers, drifters, presently some of our H-class submarines, M.L.s, and even a few Q-ships. Of the latter we may mention the *Margit*, the *Werribee* otherwise known as the *Thornhill*, *Wellholme* or the *Wonganella*. It was on March 11, 1917, when she was under command of Lieut.-Commander J. D. B. Guy, R.N., coming from Malta to England via Gibraltar, that she was shelled by one of those German submarines who had come south. Although the Q-ship's 'panic party' did the usual bit of play-acting and pretended to get out the boats, one German shell wounded an officer and several of the crew in the starboard lifeboat. Another shell crashed

BRITISH E-CLASS SUBMARINE
Going on patrol.

DROPPING A DEPTH CHARGE
From the stern of a destroyer.

through the bulwarks of the ship, wounding some of the men and burst the winch's steampipe.

An indescribable din consisted of the roaring of *Wonganella's* steam blowing off from the boiler. Then were the Q-ship's guns opening fire. It was a marine medley as *Wonganella* barely avoided by 10 feet the enemy's torpedo. No more was seen of the Hun who had shot away the Q-ship's signal yards, so the ensign had to be carried up the rigging and secured thereto. At dusk a doctor was obtained from H.M. Yacht *Iolanda* and thus when the *Wonganella* reached Gibraltar on March 13 it was possible to save the lives of nine men who were badly wounded.

In April, too, began the sweeping of the coastal tracks off the western coasts of Italy and Sicily. The Germans had inaugurated in the Mediterranean that Northern habit of laying mines in groups, and we have seen the UC-boats thus busily employed. So also here in the Middle Sea they laid their groups of explosives off headlands or in such positions as the Straits of Bonifacio and Messina.

On an earlier page we mentioned Lieut.-Commander Arnauld de la Periere. The story of this man is a strange one. His father belonged to one of the oldest French families, to whom tradition and the feudal system have always meant something very real. Only deeply-rooted wars such as the Franco-Prussian hostilities or the Hitler nonsense could interfere with the traditional ebb and flow. Now during the war of 1870 a certain member of his family was taken prisoner by the Germans. But when at length peace returned this French officer decided to remain in Germany. Later he became naturalized and wished to marry a German lady. The son of that family grew up, was educated in the rising Navy of the Kaiser, and developed great zeal. As Lothar von Arnauld de la Periere grew up, he had to bear a good deal of chaff from his contemporaries because of his French name, but in time gained a reputation of his own, and won popularity among his fellow officers as a good sportsman, with the result that even before last war this Lieut.-Commander with the clear eyes and firm mouth had become adjutant to Admiral von Pohl, Chief of the Admiralty staff. Lothar had the reputation for being very reserved towards his men, but very solicitous of their health and believed not so much in torpedoes as in relying on long-distance gunnery.

His great reputation was when he commanded *U-35* in the Mediterranean. Usually he opened action with his 22-pounder at 6000 yards, then gradually closing to half that distance. When the war ended, and he headed the list of sinkings with 400,000 tons, it had been achieved chiefly in the Mediterranean. One of the most notable duels occurred on March 1, 1916. He was 120 miles south of Cape Matapan when began the contest with H.M.S. *Primula*, one of those vessels which as a sloop had been constructed on the principles of a merchant ship and only lightly armed. Named after a flower, this particular warrior was a most doughty fighter when Arnauld de la Periere had to use his torpedoes—one at 3 p.m. and another at 5 p.m. This happened in the neighbourhood of Port Said. Only after great doggedness were the *Primula's* bows blown away. With consummate determination the *Primula* tried to ram the enemy by going astern. So two rivals were well met. After the Kaiser's war ended and Hitler grew to power, Arnauld de la Periere like so many of our own officers was rising to high promotion. In fact he was Vice-

Admiral when our aeroplanes happened to bomb Northern France, and thus it chanced that at long last the Ace of Aces was laid low and perished by British explosives from the sky.

Not without interest can we compare our activities of White Sea minesweeping during the present with those of the past war. In the Kaiser's day minesweeping was carried out whenever weather was suitable and there had been no ice prevailing, and German submarines still persisted in depositing their mines at the entrance to Kola inlet. During June, July and August shipping for Archangel were assembled in convoys and were swept through every 48 hours.

At the Admiralty was a 'Special Construction' section which arranged for the disguises of certain vessels and the selection of personnel. About 180 different vessels (which included 34 convoy sloops and 12 brigs in the Mediterranean) were specially equipped. But besides these numbers were employed ferry- and passenger-steamers, merchantmen, trawlers and drifters; the size of any particular ship ranging from 200 to 4000 tons at the early part of 1917. Both our Q-ships and the enemy's submarines were about at the height of their utility. During the war our Q-ships sank 11 German U-boats—all by gunfire—and probably damaged 85 more.

We have mentioned more than once the S.S. *Penshurst* that was so excellently disguised. She had sunk the minelayer *UB-19*, taking 16 prisoners in November 1916, and on January 14, 1917, shelled *UB-37* till she sank her by shells when she let go with depth-charges. But now on February 20, 1917, the *Penshurst* drove a U-boat to refuge below the surface: yet despite this fact and the 'Wasser-boms' which again were rained upon her, the enemy on both occasions reached home. Now allow just time for the *Penshurst* to shift from the English Channel to off the south coast of Ireland. Unknown to each other, here were a couple of pretty tough rivals. Imagine *U-84* being sighted on the surface by the *Penshurst*. Quite a formidable submarine 230 feet long, having a surface speed of $16\frac{1}{2}$ knots, with two guns, a dozen torpedoes and enough fuel to drive her thrice across the Atlantic. Altogether as suitable a foe as either might desire.

The time was just short of noon when the *Penshurst* sighted her enemy steering west, but *U-84* on sighting the Q-ship supposed her to be an oil-tanker and tried stopping her by torpedo. The target was missed, though gunfire brought the 'tanker' up. Now further back in this picture was discernible H.M. Sloop *Alyssum* escorting the S.S. *Canadian*, also a rowing boat full of survivors. *Penshurst* escaped the intended torpedo by only 15 feet. The German opponent was Lieut.-Commander Rohr, an officer of high reputation, but he passed nearer to death just now than he quite realized. In fact Rohr was decidedly less clever than Grenfell. The captain of *U-84* demanded the ship's papers and the usual 'panic party' had abandoned their steamer to row off.

Now, however, supervened the *Penshurst's* action when the Q-ship's guns opened fire, hitting Rohr's *U-84* at the conning-tower five times; exploding inside, putting out the electric light over the magnetic compass, wounding an officer, and so holing *U-84* till her conning-tower became top-heavy with the water that was pouring in. After Rohr had dived for safety he decided to rise and fight it out on the surface, but the *Penshurst* hit her twice more and the German officer that had been wounded was now wounded a second time. Then came a further development when apparently a vessel twice her speed though painted navy grey intervened. Rohr in time woke up. This grey ship after all was no destroyer but as slow on the surface, and the two went on exchanging shot for shot until by twilight *U*-84 retreated further and further.

Thus the culprit managed to occupy her immediate environment, but she had been through a severe hammering. The *Penshurst* dropped over her a couple of depth-charges, so the for'ard hydroplane and main rudder were both injured. Shell holes were repaired with the tricolour of the captured French sailing ship *Bayonne*. But despite all these hard lines Rohr managed to extricate himself from a remote corner of the British Isles and get back to Germany. Admiral Scheer of all people was able then to inspect *U*-84, and this is what he wrote of the condition which she presented: "I realized that it was little short of a miracle that, in spite of such heavy damage, she reached home."

Rohr's luck did not always pursue *U*-84. In the following January Admiral Scheer was bound to add these words: "Lieutenant-Commander Rohr is, unfortunately, one of the many who have not returned from their voyage."

The truth is that she was sunk by H.M.S. P.C.-62, a low-lying craft with bows sharp as a razor for ramming. The German was caught on January 26, 1918, when our patrol craft was at work between the Smalls and Tuskar. Meanwhile the *Penshurst* continued to show wonderful gallantry, and on August 19 she was torpedoed by a submarine but help was sent out and they towed her safely into Devonport. Still it was quite remarkable how the ship and her commander held on. On Christmas Eve a U-boat torpedoed her at the southern end of the Irish Sea, and at last the *Penshurst* ended her eventful life. Nor must we forget that Commander Campbell in the *Farnborough* was torpedoed by *U*-83, for when the wily submarine appeared on the surface the *Farnborough* was hit with the initial shell from the German skipper. Presently a shower of British shells shattered the enemy utterly as *U*-83 descended into a sea mingled with oil and blood. It was February 17, 1917.

If *Farnborough* was beached at a corner of Berehaven, the old ship presently had to be repaired and returned to the Merchant Service. She had done exceedingly well to have survived so long. April 1917 was the peak month of the U-boats' successes, for during this month the submarines sank 516,394 tons of British mercantile shipping, which was the largest amount for any month during the whole war. In no other month did these figures exceed 391,004 of June 1917. During this period of maximum submarine intensity a considerable portion of activity occurred off the coast of Ireland and its Western Approaches even so far west as Long. 16 W. For the enemy was making a dead set against the incoming transatlantic trade. But now let us relate that unforgettable story of the *Prize*.

Well do I remember during the first days of war in the summer of 1914 a typically foreign-built, three-masted schooner arriving in port after she had just been captured outside Falmouth in the English Channel. And she was the first prize to be captured from the Germans, but had previously been named the *Else*, and now lay with a White Ensign flying over German colours. And she was there as something notable. No longer the *Else* but the *First Prize*. Eventually she was sold by auction and the managing director of the company owners decided to lend her to the Admiralty free of cost. Changing her name to the *Prize*, alias Q-21, this topsail schooner was fitted with a couple of concealed 12-pounders. The Admiralty appointed in command of this 'mystery' ship Lieut. W. A. Sanders, R.N.R., who was a native that had come from New Zealand.

On April 26, 1917, she left Milford to cruise off S.W. Ireland and at 8.35 p.m. of April 30 was in Lat. 49.44 N., Long. 11.42 W. The evening was clear, spring-like, with a light N.N.E. wind, calm sea, and excellent visibility. She was heading N.W. under all sail, doing about two knots. But distant about two miles off the port beam appeared a submarine 225 feet long with a couple of guns. That was U-93, which had come out of Emden only a fortnight ago (Friday, April 13). In command of the German was Lieut.-Commander Freiherr Spiegel von und zu Peckelsheim. The Hun Count was not dissatisfied with life, the new craft well pleased him. In all he had this cruise sunk eleven merchantmen. Why not complete the list of sinkings to a round dozen? Then a week's work having been satisfactorily accomplished, he proposed to leave this station in time for seeing two of his horses winning at the Potsdam races. The weather just now was very settled but why should any sailing vessel such as that schooner be allowed in these modern days to be alive encalmed, whilst sheets and canvas slatted about aimlessly?

Freiherr Spiegel was somewhat spoiled by good luck in the past and future. At three miles' range he opened fire with his 4-inch gun, invited on deck to witness this easy conquest so many men as could be spared. But it should be mentioned that when *Prize* immediately sounded her alarm gong, Sanders, together with Skipper Mead, R.N.R., was concealed inside the steel companion-cover amidship, six hands being visible on deck, the rest hiding under the bulwarks; whilst Lieut. W. D. Beaton, R.N.R., in charge of the guns, lay by the foremast with his ear to a voice-pipe leading from Sanders' observation post.

Prize having been luffed into the wind, the 'panic party' consisting of seven launched the boat and abandoned the schooner. But the submarine maintained a slow fire to make sure the schooner had been deliberately deserted, and from astern drew nearer. Through twenty minutes of suspense the U-boat got closer and closer, till she fouled the schooner's patent log-line. Spiegel now approached on the schooner's port quarter, and at last enabled the latter's guns to bear from the port quarter.

The orders came quickly.

"Down false screens! Up White Ensign! Range seventy yards. Open fire."

The hatchway slid back, deckhouses collapsed, a gun rose in position. Within two seconds the first British shells leaped forth. As the White Ensign was seen to be run up Spiegel realized all too late that his turning circle was too wide. He was past his reckoning, but he hit the schooner again. In mighty anger twice more he deliberately at full speed tried to ram this sailing vessel, but being inside his turning circle reversed the wheel. The *Prize* had an opportunity slender enough, but took it. That is to say the schooner fired her after gun which struck the submarine's conning-tower and destroyed it, whilst a Lewis gun raked the Germans on the after deck.

Another of the brave schooner's shells so damaged *U*-93's engine-room that after another 500 yards the German machinery, like the wind, stopped utterly.

Spiegel's plan for a pleasant time at Potsdam had been altered strangely. The submarine had slewed broadside to the schooner and was now without way. Shot after shot came from the *Prize*, the enemy seemed to be settling down slowly, a red glare could be noticed through rents in the hull. After the thirty-sixth shell and four minutes since the action began, *U*-93 vanished below surface entirely. Let it be mentioned that it was the last shot which knocked Spiegel into the sea, together with his navigating warrant officer, and let it be added an engine-room petty officer. Three survivors.

The action was about to conclude as night was throwing her cloak over the scene, but Sanders bade his own 'panic party' to row off and rescue this trio. They were brought on board the much battered schooner and Spiegel promised his parole not to attempt escape. Seeing how damaged was the Q-ship, the racehorse-owner promised also that he and his two colleagues would render their best help to save the *Prize*. So the navigating warrant officer began by dressing the wounds of those Britons who had been hurt, whilst the German engine-room petty officer went below and gave his British opposite number petty-officer a hand to start the much damaged motor. Yes, a strange alteration of fate that prisoners should be so situated by circumstance. A curious yarn? But wait till it all ends. I was myself on patrol off that coast at this time amid quite attractive environment.

Just before midnight a gentle breeze sprang up, so by filling her sails and with one motor working the *Prize* next day got hold of the land to the N.E. Lieut. Hannah in *M.L.*-161 towed her from five miles west of the Old Head of Kinsale right into Kinsale Harbour. And from there a steam drifter was assigned to tow *Prize* with the three prisoners to Milford Haven. Believe it or not, but some readers will agree that this is the most amazing story that ever came out of the sea. Just consider the 'might have been'. For in that short voyage to Wales how curiously fate hovered over their heads and the Author of all knowledge was withholding from them something vital. Call this an incredible yarn, yet it happens to be true. On the way across the Irish Sea *Prize* had the thrill of sighting a German minelayer who took such a thorough good look that for a whole hour the two vessels steered on a parallel course and the nerve-tried crew of the schooner had to wait at their action stations expectant of the uncertain. Finally the enemy became suspicious, drew ahead and thought it best not to be mixed up in an unusual contest; for Germany was aware that 'trap ships' had been achieving some surprising things off that coast. So had there been a fight to the finish and people from the *Prize* taken prisoners, what an amazing situation when the submarine discovered Spiegel and his two companions!

We can learn a few things by piecing together the strands of contemporary history even if the actors themselves knew less than the weaver could learn before the design was completed. The other two U-boats in that area were U-43 and U-67. How do we know that? Because U-43 had been attacking the British S.S: *Swanmore* when the engines of U-43 suddenly and temporarily broke down, so the latter bleated wirelessly to *U*-93 for help. And it was only very shortly after this submarine crisis that *U*-93 torpedoed the S.S. *Swanmore* 230 miles W.N.W. of the Fastnet. It may be added that *U*-93 was on no chance visit but Spiegel had originally come out to relieve *U*-43. So meanwhile Spiegel passed him unawares for a whole hour.

Is there any more to tell?

There certainly is, but at that date it was unknown. By his brilliant performance Sanders was awarded the V.C., Lieut. Beaton in charge of the guns a D.S.O., two Trawler Skippers a D.S.C. and all the other men a D.S.M. But while the three Germans were sent to an internment camp we have something else surprising to relate.

U-93 got back to Germany!

Yes; despite those shell holes and the conflagration! She had been hit in her starboard fuel tank, she was terribly knocked about and numbers of her crew annihilated, but the most junior officer, Sub-Lieut. Ziegler, saved the situation. That is to say he found this U-boat unable to dive properly; three wounded, one killed and three still missing, but he managed to put out all the fierce conflagration, plug the holes, bring *U*-93 to the surface under cover of darkness. Then dodging his way through mists, fogs, night and loneliness, Ziegler with the luck that only goes to the daring finally got back to Germany by May 9. His craft was duly repaired, Ziegler rightly won officially both admiration and promotion. Finally this *U*-93 on January 7, 1918, was accidentally sent to the bottom by the S.S. *Braeneil* in collision. But the curious fact is that Ziegler at that moment was ashore ill. Ultimately he perished in another boat.

Spiegel survived the war and before these second hostilities began I was surprised to receive a letter from him in which he described his submarine life as that of 'purgatory', which was possessing some analogy.

Even now it still remains for the final narrative of the *Prize*, alias the *Else*, to be narrated. We may realize that since such a memorable May there must have been passed by German submarine officers using the Irish coast a memorandum concerning the three-masted vessel named the *Else*. By reconstructing facts, any astute person could now understand that this *Q*-21 had been built of steel and iron at Westerbrock and registered in Germany at Leer. She measured 112 feet long and was of 100 net tons. Thus with these details, the name and date of her builder, it would be easy enough to produce such a design with all canvas up. Photographs could be multiplied easily enough to supply every U-boat that ever came down the Irish coast. So it happened that in the following August 1917 a certain ruthless captain of *UB*-48 (Lieut.-Commander Steinhauer) was coming down the west coast of Ireland, heading for Gibraltar and Cattaro up the Adriatic. Steinhauer was a typical Hun who delighted to do his damnedest; young, cold as steel, very sure of himself. For instance, off the Butt of Lewis (Scotland) he stopped the British S.S. *Roanoke* (4803 tons) and destroyed her by bombs but took as prisoner her Master (Captain W. H. Williams). The date of that incident was August 12. Now on August 15 *UB*-48 sighted unquestionably the *Prize* but disguised as a Swede. Then the Q-ship hoisted the White Ensign before returning the submarine's shell-fire. Just after midnight Steinhauer, with little more than hull visible, made two hits from torpedoes. At 1.30 a.m. the German submarine successfully planned to avenge

U-93, thus sending Sanders and his ship to the bottom. And with Captain Williams an involuntary visitor the submarine *UB*-48 passed through Gibraltar Straits, up the Adriatic and into Cattaro. Three exciting weeks (Captain Williams tells me) were spent aboard her.

But *Prize*, though having played her part in the submarine campaign, could not win through at the very end.

CHAPTER X

SLOOPS AND SUBMARINES

THE manner in which the United States slid into the war was unostentatious to a remarkable degree. Rear-Admiral W. S. Sims was to travel to London at once and there get in touch with the British Admiralty in Whitehall. He and another officer went aboard the American liner and left New York for Liverpool with great secrecy.

That is to say Admiral Sims appeared in the passenger list as 'Mr. S. W. Davidson'. The liner was the S.S. *New York* which I passed at sea. With him as his aide went Commander Babcock who travelled as 'Mr. J. V. Richardson'. I have reason to remember that Easter Monday for the enemy had been kept secretly well informed. Not knowing the exactly intended date of the Americans' arrival, but guessing that this would appear to be at one of several times, it is to be remembered that a bunch of German mines was found laid at the Mersey entrance on March 24, another batch four days later and yet another on April 7.

Although certain channels were swept clear at the Mersey entrance, the S.S. *New York* on Easter Monday, April 9, struck a German mine north of the Mersey Bar Lightship. The weather was far from good; a strong cold wind being accompanied by snowstorms. It seemed unfortunate that the *New York* should meet with an accident at the very end of the voyage that evening, but despite a lumpy sea the ship's lifeboats were lowered, Admiral Sims and Commander Babcock taken off to be landed on Liverpool landing-stage. That mine had made a hole large enough to take a full-sized horse and cart. A special train was waiting in Liverpool and Admiral Sims found himself met at the Admiralty by the First Sea Lord, Admiral Jellicoe. The disconcerting position of the submarine menace was discussed frankly; and the truth faced that owing to the peak of German sinkings being reached in April there were not going to be more than two months' food for the nation.

To cut details to a fine point, the first American six destroyers left Boston on April 24, 1917, and on May 4 I was ordered to meet them soon after noon outside Queenstown Harbour, but the enemy's secret intelligence must have been still further accurate. For up went a few suddenly discovered German mines which just missed hitting the first arrivals.

In April too the Germans commissioned at Wilhelmshaven the large submarine *U*-155, otherwise known as the *Deutschland*, and at the end of June she left Kiel for America with mail and valuable stores. She was unarmed and merely made a gesture of a merchantman getting safely to the United States and back. In order especially to foul the trans-Atlantic routes passing off the South Irish Coast, mines were laid in April off Cape Clear and Old Head of Kinsale. For this purpose Germany particularly used the minelayer U-78. Her size (displacing 750 tons on the surface and 830 tons when submerged) made a formidable vessel. For she could carry 36 of these missiles. Very few submarines were capable of bringing so many at a time, but she discharged also torpedoes from both bow- and stern-tube.

When in the early hours Ober-Leutnant H. Degetau allowed his UC-68 to be torpedoed and sunk by H.M. Subarmine C-7, there were several remarkable facts that need stressing.

The exact time was 3.32 a.m. of April 5, 1917, the position being Long. 3.17 E. and Lat. 51.42. The night certainly was very dark and misty, but the enemy was first sighted on the surface 400 yards away. The British submarine's torpedo struck UC-68 forward and the Hun disappeared in about 10 seconds. Already we have mentioned that such officers as Captain Gordon Campbell and Captain Grenfell were remarkable in their fights with submarines, but these tussles were far from slices of luck. For instance, on April 30, 1917, Q-12, which had formerly been H.M. Sloop *Tulip*, had not quite satisfied the submarine U-62. Admittedly the latter at first took this disguised 'mystery' vessel to be a cargo steamer of about 3000 tons gross. But what made the enemy suspicious was that (1) this alleged British trader seemed to have no guns, (2) she hoisted the Red Ensign more smartly than would be done by a merchant ship, and (3) she exaggerated her course to such an extent that her people must be naval. And here, then, proved that play-acting with these ingenious ships needed very particular attention to details.

I used to pass this converted sloop at sea, but frankly, though she looked an ingenious bit of re-design, it was indeed her false stern that failed to inspire confidence; so when U-62 sank her, the German took as prisoner the British naval officer (pretending to be a Mercantile Master) and all through indifferent acting. Yet strange occurrences might happen any day. On April 19 UC-30 went to her last end because she struck a mine in the North Sea. Within the same twenty-four hours, curiously, H.M. Submarine E-50 whilst cruising below the surface rammed another German submarine but the enemy succeeded in returning home.

And when that converted sloop (once known as H.M.S. *Heather*) encountered a submarine at 8.15 a.m. during the forenoon on April 21 her captain (Lieut.-Commander W. W. Hallwright, R.N.) was selected as the enemy's target whilst using shrapnel. Everything points to the fact that 'Bill' Hallwright was about to give as much as he received and he was observing the movements of the enemy through the starboard peep-hole of the bridge. Five shots had the German loosed off, but now the sixth killed Hallwright instantly because one piece of shell passed through his head with mortal effects. Whilst Lieut. W. McLeod, R.N.R., then took over command and fired on the German, which received a shell at the base of the conning-tower, this U-boat dived and was not seen again. Perhaps such a fight is never wholly convincing: it was impossible to claim we had sunk the submarine.

Still, however, the U-boats were doing their deadly work in the Mediterranean, and the hand of fate would any day bring about the chance meeting that ended in tragedy. Take for instance U-73 and Rear-Admiral Sir Sydney Fremantle. They were destined to meet, no matter from what

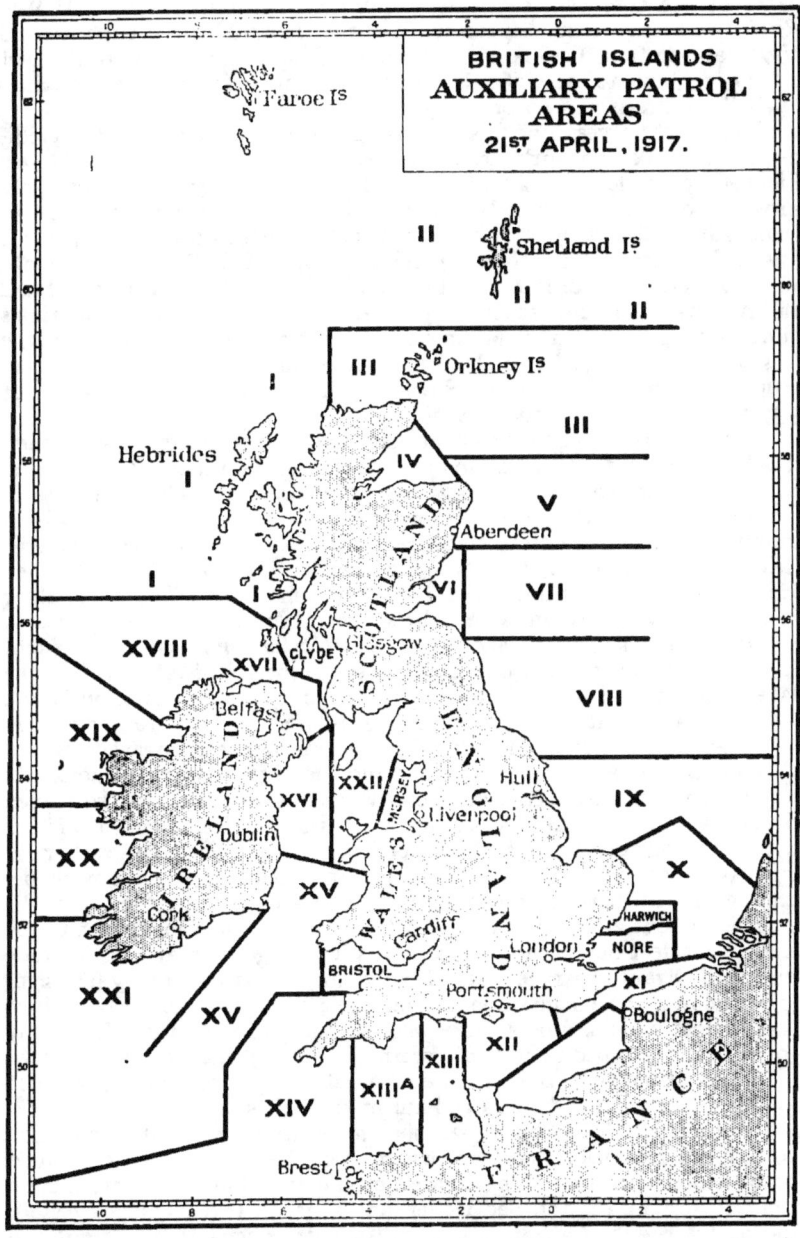

HOW THE PATROL AREAS WERE EVENTUALLY ASSIGNED
AS AMERICA WAS ENTERING THE WAR

parts of the compass they came, and the month was April. H.M.S. *Russell* was leaving the Aegean for Malta at the middle of the month and *U*-73 set out from Germany on April 1. The latter measured 185 feet by 21½ feet, able to carry 36 mines besides a couple of torpedoes and boxes of shells to fire from two bronze guns.

Russell was a vessel of 14,000 tons and *U*-73 was bound for the Mediterranean. We can fairly trace the German's route. Her captain was Lieut.-Commander Gustav Siehs. Siehs, by the way, had previously served aboard *U*-41 (sunk by the Q-ship *Baralong* in September 1915) when Lieut.-Commander Hansen had been the skipper. Today Siehs was on his way for Cattaro on the morning when H.M.S. *Russell* ran into an unexpected trap of mines laid by the Huns. Malta was close at hand and Admiral Fremantle reached his bridge at 5.30 a.m. The submarine's mines having been laid off Malta on the night of this April 26, it was the *Russell* which steamed straight into such perilous cargo—the enemy had dropped 22 mines off Grand Harbour four miles from Malta—and at 5.37 a.m. the first explosive was struck.

Despite this flagship's excellent discipline, 126 men were lost, though trawlers and other craft raced to help. Temporary-Surgeon P. D. Pickles, R.N.V.R., managed to get away from the *Russell* though badly gassed. He was on a raft with several wounded men, who were picked up by a trawler, and all the way into Malta Harbour he dressed the men's wounds. Having himself landed, he worked himself to the absolute finish, then brought himself to the hospital and died next morning. The whole affair was tragic enough when we recollect that H.M.S. *Wallflower* (a sloop) and two more sloops (the *Marguerite* and *Nasturtium*), also H.M. Yacht *Safa-el-Bahr*, had on this one day the same species of fatality, but the date could not end before H.M. Yacht *Aegusa* blew up. Even on May 4 —a very dark night with a strong S.E. wind—Skipper White was over in the water for more than an hour till picked up by another trawler.

Thus do we perceive how subtly could the U-boats operate thousands of miles from their base, creating secretly and unseen immense havoc, when dismay would come all of a sudden. British and Italian naval officers in the Mediterranean felt that our policy had been neglected rather for defensive than offensive purposes. For instance, the Italians were beginning to want nets to be laid across the Otranto Straits; the top of the net being about 24 feet below the surface and the mines made fast to the netting 200 feet below the surface. It was being felt that a fixed trade route and Otranto barrage marked by patrol vessels were really like signposts helping the enemy U-boats on their puzzled way. Net drifters were almost useless, unless there were so many of them that the enemy would get so trapped as not to discern the entanglements. They would require more netting, but bad weather added new difficulties, since it became necessary for drifters to haul in their nets.

On the night of April 20–21 six enemy destroyers left Zeebrugge, crossed the Dover barrage somewhere near 2A buoy then continued towards Dover without being sighted by our two flotilla leaders; though about 10.30 p.m. they shelled Dover, and engaged various patrol vessels. And as the result of a hot action with the destroyers H.M.S. *Swift* and *Broke*, the enemy began to understand that it was hardly worth while to attempt another attack on Dover barrage. That is to say, though the

Germans hated this entanglement they would be glad to make it less difficult for their U-boats in risking the bottle-neck. Those of us who so closely have compared the campaign of 1914-18 with so many features of the war begun in 1939 have frequently been reminded that in some respects there is common continuity.

Thus when the Dover defile had proved such a tough net, the Germans looked ahead and tried new efforts of air raiders. The series of our drifters watching the Goodwins-Snouw barrage began to be attacked by aircraft on May 25 and June 1, although on March 29, 1917, just two German aircraft had been crossing the barrage; but by the middle of June enemy seaplanes had sought to sink the buoys by machine-gun fire so as to make the U-boats' passage through this area less difficult. Other aerial instances accumulated. By the end of the summer in 1917 more buoys were laid down so as to support the nets higher, the buoys becoming only 250 yards apart. The intention was so that the enemy might otherwise more readily cross the spaces by expending their weight between these buoys. So in fact the Dover barrage was not much more of a hindrance to U-boats than was the Adriatic line of drifters cross the Otranto Straits, though of course the problem in the South was rendered less difficult by the absence of tides.

At home our minesweepers cleared the War Channel each day before the traffic was released after it had been at anchor during the night hours in such places as the Downs, the Black deep, Hollesley Bay and so on. But presently large protective minefields were placed off the Yorkshire coast to defend the War Channel. The paravane during 1917 already proved itself very valuable for this year saw the enemy doing treble the amount of minelaying than had been the trouble in 1916. To give you some idea, let me state that the enemy laid 536 groups of mines during the first four months of 1917, as against 195 groups in the year 1916. It was notable that during the former an average of one submarine cargo was laid off our coasts every 30 hours; and the shortage of minesweeping vessels now became acute because of submarines. Flotillas of Scotch motor drifters about 70 ft. long, 21 feet wide and $7\frac{1}{2}$ feet draught were fitted with light sweeps for working from such places as Liverpool, Oban and Aberdeen. But disasters occurred such as when H.M. Sloop *Carnation* struck in a snowstorm with considerable sea that was running off Auskerry Island in the Orkneys.

It was the following six destroyers which in 1917 were the first to reach Queenstown flying the Stars and Stripes—*Wadsworth, Wainwright, Conyngham, Davis, McDougal* and *Porter*; but by July 5 this number had risen to 35 and by November there were 52 destroyers sent over here to operate from Queenstown, Brest and Gibraltar. America had certainly entered the war on sea, and the anti-U-boat patrols had become considerably increased. Of course it needed a great deal of prejudice to be overcome in regard to the Convoys. As almost every shipmaster saw the problem, he pictured the escorted ships—perhaps numbering 30, 40, and even more than 100—becoming a danger to themselves and each other. Manœuvring in foggy or misty weather or by night, with inte ceptions of rainstorms, might seem unthinkable, but even before 1917 was out the use of convoys had become not merely tolerable but of prime importance. The American destroyers soon found themselves escorting convoys with consummate success and gradually these little throngs criss-crossed the ocean with much less prejudice when once it had been thoroughly established during that first Anglo-American summer. A German submarine was generally so clever and subtle that when a far more able British submariner had as good a chance as his enemy, you may be sure that the Hun would become badly beaten.

It was May Day of 1917 and the scene about 180 miles N.W. of the Fastnet. The reader will call to mind Captain Dunbar-Nasmith, that modest and retiring officer who had first won fame when he took his submarine under the minefield at the Dardanelles (for which he had been given the V.C.) was now in command of H.M.S. *Vulcan*, the submarine mother ship which looked after six of the E-class, two of the H-class and six of the D-class. The *Vulcan* and her children had recently come over to Ireland. At 3.40 p.m. that afternoon one of these submarines (E-54), commanded by Lieut.-Commander Robert H. T. Raikes, R.N., distinctly heard an underwater explosion and observed a steamer down by the bows but stopped. What happened in this story was a very neat affair: for E-54 proceeded to close the damaged steamer on the surface and she turned out to be the British S.S. *San Urbano*.

The condition of the latter was obvious, but E-54 remained on the surface till $3\frac{1}{2}$ miles off and then dived. An hour later Raikes sighted a U-boat apparently just come to the surface, and proceeding towards the *San Urbano*.

At 5 p.m., when 1500 yards distant, this enemy (being U-81) altered course to pass round the steamer's stern, whereupon E-54 altered course to pass round the steamer's bow and on reaching it saw U-81 quite clearly. It was just 5.11 p.m. and E-54 at 400 yards fired both bow tubes. Everything in such a case as this happened quickly. First, one of the British torpedoes hit the enemy between bow and conning-tower. The other torpedo struck U-81 between conning-tower and stern. The enemy immediately sank and about half a minute later a third explosion happened. What a scene! There were seven survivors, including the German commanding officer, but the latter was rescued because one of E-54's officers gallantly jumped overboard with a line. The rescue of the Hun captain was only just not too late, for this enemy officer, having been injured, would certainly have gone down to where he was sending the *San Urbano*. And only the survivors knew how nearly fate had brushed them and these seven were really most anxious to relate that another U-boat was cruising about the neighourhood submerged.

But Raikes, together with seven prisoners, hurried off to Queenstown. He climbed the hill to Admiralty House, and at 1 a.m. in the stillness of the night, through the blue clouds of tobacco smoke, gave Admiral Sir Lewis Bayly the above simple but dramatic account. The late captain of E-54 has long since become an Admiral.

Germany used, and continued to use, her submarines quite as generally for minelaying as for torpedoing merchantmen and men-of-war. For example on May 2 and 3 UC-26 dropped nine mines off Havre, four off Caen, and five off Cherbourg. Then on May 11, and 21, mines were again laid off Havre and Caen in the same position. In fact it was quite remarkable how regular was the minelaying by UC-boats in the English Channel and down the west coast of France.

Thus as regards the English coast the positions were within a couple of miles of the Royal Sovereign (off Eastbourne), off the Shambles, near to Portland, Start Point and Eddystone. As for the French coast the enemy laid his mines near Havre at the S.E. and N.W. extremities of Belle Ile and Ile de Ré. Another characteristic of the Huns' minelaying methods was that such traps were laid between 10 p.m. and 1 a.m. Approximately this depositing of the batch of missiles went on every seven to ten days. And if one takes the trouble to trace the connection between cause and effect, we shall not infrequently find that today the U-boat is successfully aggressive but tomorrow consigned below the water for the last time.

We might quote the affair of H.M. Sloop *Lavender*, which was torpedoed and sunk in the English Channel on May 5, 1917, by *UC-75*. It seemed on paper quite an accomplishment that another of these 'herbaceous border' sloops should become wiped out. We have only to wait till the spring of next year and witness one of our convoys being attacked by *UC-75* off that favourite rendezvous Flamborough Head; though this time not a modern sloop but the very old destroyer *Fairy* on May 31, 1918, made quite a fine job. She drove herself on to *UC-75*'s hull, then did the same thing a second time and shelled *UC-75* till 'all the stuffing' was knocked out. Down below, the decrepit submarine descended with 26 Germans. Certainly the *Fairy* after all this ramming was so ruined that she also sank, but the great thing was that *UC-75* would never again injure our warships or convoys.

Yes, the war on sea was rarely dull in those days. Although the first six destroyers had so recently reached Queenstown in 1917 from America and were soon on patrol, they instantly became very busy. For on May 9, 1917, the American destroyer *McDougal* whilst proceeding to her patrol was only just missed by a U-boat's torpedo, and three days later the United States destroyer *Wainwright* had a similar near shave. But how little was the distance which separated bad fortune from good luck. Consider *UC-42*, which was commanded by a German named Muller. She was another of those enemies which specialized in marauding off the N.E. coast of England, and on May 9 sank the steam fishing trawler *Kitty* some 25 miles E.N.E. of St. Abb's Head. She then cruised between Whitby and the Longstone Lighthouse, her tactics each day before dark being to motor forth seawards and then submerge for the night; but just before daybreak she would rise to the surface, steam towards the land and then resume sinking ships off the Yorkshire coast.

When on this same May 9 a British destroyer attacked *UC-42* about 3.45 in the afternoon, the submarine was compelled to nose-dive suddenly to about 190 feet and remain at this depth which started making her hull leak. But though she had been down to her limit—the safe diving mark being about 150 feet—she feigned damage by releasing some oil into the sea.

Fake? Pretence? Well, it was not always so, and more than once have we instanced the risk which a U-boat ran when about to negotiate the Dover Straits. Granted a well-handled destroyer was on patrol at night, and the enemy working his tide-time correctly, the scene was set for a submarine's disaster. The loss of *UC-26* on May 9, 1917, occurred in practically the same position as the loss of *UC-46* on February 8. Let us follow what happened on May 9.

H.M. Destroyer *Milne* was a very modern vessel and Commander V. L. A. Campbell, D.S.O., R.N., an exceedingly able seaman who had earned much merit when serving in an Antarctic expedition. He was on patrol this night (May 9, 1917) near No. 7A buoy when a German submarine about 11.50 p.m. G.M.T. was espied travelling on the surface heading to the eastward. At present the Hun was about three points off the *Milne's* port bow and the latter went full speed ahead to ram. *UC*-26 tried to dive, but the destroyer with her sharp bow was ideal for the job. Commander Campbell rammed *UC*-26 just as the submarine attempted to dive. A terrific rasping sound told that the submersible's deck was now more than awash, much oil was coming to the surface and this was *UC*-26 sinking whilst the *Milne* had performed the good work quickly. But into that region burst another of our destroyers, H.M.S. *Miranda*, who picked up a couple of survivors. One turned out to be her commanding officer, Graf von Schmettow, and the other was Sub-Lieut. of Reserve Heinrich Petersen. It was learned that when *UC*-26 sank straight to the bottom the two were blown back to the surface by air-pressure. Von Schmettow had been in the engine-room when *UC*-26 sank. At the time of being rammed this submarine was trying to get back through the Dover Narrows on her way to Zeebrugge, using her gas engines at the time.

She had left Ostende on April 30 and today was May 9, but the idea of using this UC boat was to wriggle herself in and out netting, narrow spaces and—for that matter—indefinable trouble. For she was a thoroughly unhappy ship with a skipper that was over-confident; and pessimistic junior officers that found too little enjoyment in life. Trouble seemed always to be meeting her; defects always were occurring in the ship, fire bursting forth whilst in harbour, something always not quite right with the engines. Sub-Lieut. Heinrich Petersen had come from the Hamburg-Amerika Line and his diary was found which shews well enough that he would much rather be back in peace-time and aboard a liner.

So he wrote:

"2nd May, 12.4 a.m. Steered for Havre and laid mines just outside the buoys. I slept during this, but it was a painful process. We nearly got caught in a net. . . .

"4th May. . . . 1–1.35 a.m. Dived to attack two steamers, each convoyed by a destroyer, but of course we never got a shot in. . . .

"6 May. . . . 8–12. My opposite number (the second watch-keeping officer) is fed up. . . .

"7th May. . . . 2 p.m. Came to surface and again headed for Barfleur. It is a miserable existence. . . . 9 p.m. Sighted a convoy, which of course we do not bag. Vessels turn away."

CHAPTER XI

TURN OF THE TIDE

STRANGE it is to trace so many links of the same submarine with several happenings. On October 23, 1916, whilst another of these 'Flower'-class sloops (H.M.S. *Genista*) was escorting the S.S. *Alexandrian* off the S.W. of Ireland, *U*-59 suddenly torpedoed *Genista* in two halves and most of the sloop's sailors were drowned as the gale came on. But three days later *U*-59 torpedoed and sank S.S. *Rowanmore* (10,320 tons) and casually informed Captain Phelan, whom the German had taken prisoner from the *Rowanmore* that *U*-59 had sunk a light cruiser '100 miles west of the Bull Rocks' at this date.

He was, of course, referring to H.M.S. *Genista*. But on the following May 14 *U*-59 came to a fatal ending when she struck a mine and was lost with all hands off Heligoland. *U*-59 was being escorted to sea when she, with the minesweeper *Fulda* and a German 'outpost boat' all struck British mines and then sank. The enemy was completely nonplussed by our minelaying. He also claimed that whilst *UC*-76 had been embarking some mines in Heligoland Harbour on May 10 (1917) the latter also blew up. The minefield on which *U*-59 received such tragic punishment for boasting of the *Genista's* fate had been laid on April 18, 1917, by the three destroyers *Royalist*, *Blanche* and *Abdiel* in a kind of whalebone pattern and that made it very difficult for the German minesweepers to locate. The position was about 15 miles S. by W. of Horn's Reef Light buoy. Our British minefields in the Bight were indeed causing the Germans grave inconvenience; for whilst the enemy was trying to find the spot where *U*-59 went down, the German minesweeper *M*-14 on May 16 was herself struck by a mine. Thereupon when the German Torpedoboat No. 78 attempted to save *M*-14, both vessels foundered.

There can be no doubt that by now the British minelaying of German waters was having a serious effect on the enemy since the U-boat could hardly move out on her voyage; and this kind of terror had a most cramping effect. Even so long afterwards as February 2, 1918, a group of German armed trawlers which had been sent to escort a U-boat to sea came to grief in so doing; four of these trawlers foundering on February 2 and three more the next day. We perceive, then, that whereas at one time the enemy's submarines had been a mighty terror to our merchantmen it was our Navy which imperilled the Germans' every move. The tide was beginning to turn from German submarine offence to defence. The decrease of German minelaying was decidedly noticeable in May 1917, yet our sweeping operations were even more determined, and we were destroying these dangers so far distant as Aberdeen, Peterhead, Lowestoft and the approaches to the Thames. The enemy had noted our Coastal Motor Boats as a reply to the Germans' fast travelling efforts that he used to send out along the Flemish coast. We found that these so-called Patrol Motor Boats (P.M.B.s) which commenced their rushes in May 1917, were stationed respectively at Zeebrugge, Blankenberghe, Bruges and Ostend. They worked only at night and were all named after German battleships. Whereas British P.M.B.s were of two kinds (40 feet long and 55 feet long), the German P.M.B.s were of three kinds: (1) 20 feet long, 1ft. 10in. draught, with speed 32 knots and made of steel; also armed with a machine-gun; (2) The second class were about 29 feet long, 2½ feet draught, speed 25 knots, armed with a machine-gun and one light field gun. Made of wood as were these craft yet (3) there was another German type 45 feet long with 3 feet 3 in. draught, speed 40 knots, but armed with one machine-gun and two torpedoes. These little wooden vessels also carried wireless. In the present war we saw the Germans revive this idea for further employment in the English Channel from about the date of May 1940 onwards.

Yet the last war kept introducing so many instances of the fighting that even in those early days they were but anticipating the present mode of Channel warfare. It is worth noting also that on May 1, 1917, off Southwold the British S.S. *Gena* was attacked even by two German seaplanes. The steamer was struck by an aerial torpedo (carried forward) and sunk. But it is also significant that *Gena* (which was of 2784 tons) brought one of the seaplanes down by gunfire, both the pilot and observer being made prisoners. They were presently brought into Lowestoft by M.L.-29. Certainly it seemed a novel warfare that in those days a steamer at sea should be thus sent to the bottom but all her crew could be saved. This example again emphasizes that the naval war which began in 1939 was largely the sequel and further development of the Anglo-German hostilities of the 1914-1918 period.

So also whilst the Convoy system began somewhat shyly to reintroduce itself now in the age of steam during February 1917, it owed its organization to the French coal trade. This traffic was already arranged in a group of sailings on definite routes such as Lizard to Brest, Portland to Cherbourg, Southampton to Havre, Dover to Dunkirk. Timorously it was at first conceded that protection should be only during daylight and moonlight hours. It was to ensure full use being made of night zones and because it was accompanied by practically no sinkings, that the Convoy system very gradually led to universal adoption.

For those were anxious times which during April 1917 witnessed the U-boats at their intensity. Especially off the S. and S.W. of Ireland and Western approaches to the English Channel the savage onslaughts of the U-boats during that peak month amounted to the torpedoing of 189 ships, though the amount soon descended during May to 121 British vessels being torpedoed and sunk. In regard to the Convoys, they were now running across the North Sea from the ports of Lerwick, Immingham and Stornoway. Then there were Coastal Convoys between the Tyne and Intermediate ports so far as Kinnaird Head. But Ocean Convoys from Gibraltar to the United Kingdom were escorted by two special service ships, and met outside the submarine danger zone by eight destroyers. The North Atlantic Convoy was instituted on May 24, 1917; a highly anxious and responsible collection under escort of H.M.S. *Roxburgh*.

Matters very definitely were being improved in systematization. The 'D.A.M.S.' as they were called ('Defensively Armed Merchant Ships') by the end of May 1917 were already protected with 2375 guns; and smoke apparatus for making screens was also being supplied for eluding the enemy. But the most devastating of our offensive features on the U-boat was—what? Certainly our Q-ships had done wonders, but they had pretty well run their extreme limit by now.

THE BITER BIT

UC-44 after being damaged by her own mines off Waterford is salved and brought ashore.

U-103 (RUCKER) PHOTOGRAPHED IN HELIGOLAND HARBOUR

Presently she went on a long cruise but in the English Channel was run down and sunk by the White Star Liner *Olympic*. Rucker and some German survivors were picked up.

For the convoys had now become our finest method. And this escort assuredly seemed excellent. Yet it was the innovation of the depth-charge—filled with T.N.T. and resembling a mine that explodes under water around the submarine—which was the most notable offensive device contrived in 1917 by the British Admiralty. I doubt if any other of our subtleties did so much for destroying German morale: but when these bombs were plentifully supplied to the fast destroyers from British and American yards, it was like so many mobile mines arrayed against U-boats. From our present anxieties we may take courage that the German submarine once considered as a problem well-nigh insuperable was at last giving hints of being doomed.

Thus we may regard the climax of the submarine campaign as having been attained by the summer of 1917 and no one realized this fact so sternly as the German U-boat captains. Thus *UC*-77 (Lieut.-Commander Ries) which left Germany in May 1917 reported to her headquarters that in at least the Aberdeen area the principle of effective anti-submarine methods had been so effectively grasped by the British as to 'hamper our operations in the same way as the centralization of ocean shipping has done'. He was especially struck by our numerous groups of trawlers, yachts and M.L.s. This *UC*-77 herself had reason to remember once when her oil-tanks were burst open to the loss of many fuel tons.

Moreover we may call to mind the report of *UC*-55 that the countermeasures of minelaying were promptly taken after she had laid these snares in threes between the Fastnet and Valentia. As I happen to recollect having sunk these little groups near the Fastnet and also those in line with the entrance to Valentia at that time, it is not uninteresting to find the enemy appreciating our active measures so spontaneously. *UC*-55 was surprised and sunk on a later occasion by another craft. So too Lieut.-Commander Ries in *UC*-77 may be set down as a thoughtless fool. His undoing arose because he imagined he was trying to get through Dover Straits in the evening of July 10. But when he left behind a leak of oil and bubbles, two of our drifters finished him off with their depth-charges.

Now it was by no means a rare practice for the Huns in special need of particular naval intelligence to send a submarine on a reconnoitring cruise whilst seeming to be carefully invisible. One day in April 1917, owing to suspicions of our having introduced the convoys, Germany despatched *U*-49 twice on scouting trips to hover off the English coast and make report by wireless. The enemy strictly forbade her to attack shipping during such expeditions. Observation was the chief objective. For instance, *U*-49 was once ordered to find out what the Scandinavian convoys were doing across the North Sea. Our decoys, determination, and a nervousness which our patrols inspired made it very difficult that summer to entice the enemy into a fair fight.

It is a rare episode that we should find a sailing ship once more fighting a submarine. The story of the *Prize* we have discussed already, but this time it is the auxiliary schooner *Glen*, under command of Lieut. R. J. Turnbull, R.N.R., which on May 17 distinguished herself in a duel with *U*-39. This schooner had begun service as a Q-ship on April 5, 1917. Now, armed with a 12-pounder and a 3-pounder, this very lightly defended vessel about six in the evening was steering N.E. about 35 miles off the back of the Isle of Wight. The wind was a little more southerly than East, force four, and she was close-hauled on the starboard tack. The *Glen* was slipping along under all sail over a moderate sea when suddenly a shot flashed; whereupon *Glen* backed her foreyard to ease her way Over there lay a submarine. But the latter, which had just shown herself was *UB*-39, who evidently could not quite understand her adversary's behaviour. Rather foolishly the submarine ceased firing, closed the schooner, and the latter proceeded to 'abandon ship' after the usual custom of decoys. The 'panic party' were just leaving the *Glen* when *UB*-39 rose fully to the surface and at a distance of only 80 yards from the schooner's beam surprised the sailing people that any enemy could be so simple and without guile.

Turnbull gave the order for action and within five seconds the schooner's 12-pounder boomed forth but the shell flopped over the submarine's conning-tower. The German Lieutenant, named Kustner, was either very simple or completely without imagination. Had he failed to realize that we were at war? Or did he think we were fundamentally foolish? Anyway, Kustner actually opened the hatch in the conning-tower whilst next followed the head and shoulders of a man who seemed dazed as the second 12-pounder shell burst on the hull under the conning-tower. This man fell back down the hatch and *UB*-39 began diving. Evidently that rather junior officer was all confusion and surprise, and in his panic he allowed the craft to raise her stern out of the water, which made her a still better target. Two more shots from this British gun perforated the after part of the hull; but now the hull was badly holed, and listing towards the schooner, she finally sank without any sort of doubt. Thus did *UB*-39 disappear for the last time, and not one survivor was picked up, though as she descended there rose to the surface much oil with bubbles.

It was an incredible performance: so extraordinary that a decoy sailor accustomed to sail and yards might call the incident a dream of Heaven. Neither German nor British authorities have ever disputed this story of a very simple Hun. But it has another side.

Barely had *UB*-39 disappeared than about 4000 yards away approached another *U*-boat on the starboard bow. The *Glen* opened fire and the enemy submerged, but reappeared 600 yards away. The schooner in fact, was ready for anything though the newcomer was now becoming distant. Was the German biding his time? Waiting only for the schooner to recall the 'panic party' and torpedo the *Glen* during this delay? Turnbull was mindful of such a possibility, hurried away northward under sail and auxiliary motor, yet nothing more happened till at 7.30 p.m. a very large submarine was sighted with whom there was now a gunnery duel for half an hour; and then there was quietness again.

The Germans were therefore under orders to lie in wait concentrated in mid-Channel, so placed as to trap any of our ships proceeding up or down the route to Cherbourg, or keeping well off the shore. But in this summer of 1917 the Germans were both guilty of not learning the Q-ship tricks; then of being exceedingly cautious. In other words they could now believe the worst, which proved that our decoys though waning were yet of consummate influence. For only a few days later—June 25—and in much the same locality (14 miles S. by W. of St. Catherine's Point) the *Glen* whilst under sail was shelled by another craft under sail. The culprit was a second submarine using the old trick of setting a mizzen aft. This U-boat though expectant of the *Glen* was evidently more cautious and feared for her own skin; since the Hun dared get no nearer than 4000 yards, finally hid below surface and made off.

The upper hand in this Submarine Campaign, despite occasional bad luck, was becoming ours and the enemy had lost much of that free aggressiveness which till recently had marked his technique. One begins to feel that the stage had been reached when the Huns were asking themselves: Is the Submarine warfare really worth while? Have we Germans any hope of winning at sea? Do not the English manage to defeat all our tricks and seem always just a little better?

For we have mentioned just now how German aeroplanes were both daring and able to fly across to the East Anglian coast and sink our craft. Yes, but the reverse of that action occurred on May 20 when a little lower down the same coast *UC*-36 was bombed off the West Hinder Lightship by one of our seaplanes and sunk. The war became so varied by curious incidents that one could never prophesy exactly what might happen.

It was in the spring of 1917 that Admiral Sir Lewis Bayly had taken up for Q-ship work three more little steamers of 1200 or 1300 tons, and they were fitted out to serve from Queenstown. One of these was *Q*-25 (alias *Lady Patricia*, alias the *Paxton*) being armed with one 4-inch and two 12-pounders. Lieut.-Commander Hewett, R.N., was appointed in command.

Now *U*-46 happened to have a very wide-awake captain, and on May 20, having torpedoed certain other ships in Lat. 51.43 N., Long. 13.57 W., sighted a little steamer which also might be given the same fate. This was the *Paxton*, which had disguised herself as a Norwegian merchantman, but somehow the Hun captain of *U*-46 (Hillebrand by name) was not to be put off by her apparent neutrality, so fired a torpedo which struck the small steamer aft. This was not exactly Hewett's lucky day although anything might be expected in the Atlantic. The impact of torpedo caused the *Paxton's* bulwarks to drop which surprised the Hun seamen to remark: "Look out! That's not a Norwegian. She's an English trapship."

"Is she?" asked the German captain. "Then give her another torpedo."

They did, so without having ever fired a shot the *Paxton* foundered. It was a curious fact that the commanding officer of *U*-46 at first greatly hesitated whether he was justified in wasting a torpedo on her, but down she had to go. Then happened something which gave the Huns an alarming shock. Up burst a terrific explosion. *U*-46 shook and trembled to such an alarming degree that every German in the submarine thought *U*-46 was gone. But no: the sinking *Paxton* had become so low in the water by now that her depth-charges were well below the sea and went off with a most scaring effect. In sight of *U*-46 was another U-boat, and recognition signals were exchanged by firing a pistol giving coloured balls of fire. Thus it was something like producing a rocket, and it was possible also to exchange letters by means of the heaving line. In another week *U*-46 managed to get back with her story to Emden. She took also to

Germany the British captain and engineer, yet it was a considerable time ere the captors got over that alarming shock from the depth-charge.

On the whole German officers serving in submarines were by no means to be envied. We called attention on an earlier page to the anti-submarine sort of reception which *UC*-55 was having and there were at least two known instances of German U-boats having to return home sooner than intended owing to the damage done by depth-charges. In *UC*-55 the First Lieutenant happened to be a Reserve officer who had come from being Chief Officer in the Hamburg-Amerika Line; whilst the submarine's First and Second Under-officers had previously been Second Officers in the North German Lloyd and Hansa Lines respectively.

About 9 a.m. on May 29, 1917, when *UC*-55 was travelling submerged off the south-west of Ireland she was surprised to receive a series of dull explosions around her and began to vibrate heavily. Furthermore the exploding depth-charges had carried away the propeller at her port side putting the machinery there out of action whilst the hull began to leak alarmingly. So the captain was compelled to take her home for repairs A few months later, this time again off Lerwick (on September 29, 1917) she was once more caught by the gunfire and depth-charges of our destroyers so that she finally sank. Altogether Lieut. Ruhle von Lilienstern, her skipper, spent a fairly anxious time aboard her till the finish

Then there was the submarine which on September 30, 1917, sank by torpedo our armed cruiser H.M.S. *Drake* that was escorting a convoy bound for the Clyde. Along came one of the United States destroyer which on October 4 gave the enemy—her number was unknown—such a hot rain of depth-charges that the German's electric machinery was quite thrown out of action and the submarine so generally shaken up that this U-boat (new though she was) had to get back home quickly Although she had come out from Germany on only her second trip via the North of Scotland, she was glad to return to German waters via the Dover Straits.

But anyone could perceive that in the Otranto Straits our drifter were making it so difficult to allow passage of the submarines to and from Cattaro that the enemy must do something about it. Just as German destroyers had raided Dover Straits more than once, so May 15, 1917 was selected by Austrian cruisers for rushing south and making a tragic gap from west to east in the line of vigilant drifters.

In order to fix this line, regard the drifter nets as lying from May 12 till the early morning of May 15 from Lat. 39.50 N. to Lat. 39.55 N. and from Long. 18.37 E. to Long. 19.12 E. At 3 a.m. on May 15 there were eight divisions of these drifters (seven to a division) in the above position Daylight (Central European Time) was at about 4 a.m., but an hour earlier two four-funnelled Austrian cruisers without any warning suddenly crossed the drifter line from North to South in order to locate it. One cruiser then attacked the drifters from the eastern end; a second attacked from the western; and a third cruiser (the three were respectively *Helgoland, Saida and Novara*) attacked in the centre of the line. After having shelled this line of drifters and taken a number of our hardy fishermen as prisoners, the enemy ceased fire about 4.45 a.m. and proceeded to Cattaro

Frankly the Austrians, whose heart was not in their work but behaved in a chivalrous manner, gave the drifter crews opportunities to abandon ship. Of course it was a hopeless contest for the fishermen in their tiny craft to imagine themselves evenly matched against fast light cruisers; but, despite all this, there were several drifters who gallantly stood up and fought the fight. Actually 14 were sunk, but with only little success. We lost one officer and 70 men killed but eight officers were carried off to Austria as prisoners. Presently the night-netting was protected by two Italian destroyers and a cruiser. But after the above raid H.M.S. *Dartmouth* and *Bristol* came out from Brindisi and were at the job from soon after 5 a.m. till about 2 p.m. Unfortunately the *Dartmouth* was torpedoed by a submarine though succeeded in reaching port. The enemy had apparently placed a line of submarines across the return track to Brindisi and had also mined the entrance to Brindisi very closely. The French destroyer *Boutefeu*, which was going out to help *Dartmouth* in, struck a mine just outside the boom and blew up.

So altogether this Austrian incursion amounted to very little whilst on May 24 *UC*-24 was sunk off Cattaro by the French submarine *Circe*.

CHAPTER XII

U-BOATS' HAZARDS

IN a previous volume* we alluded to the part which was played at the beginning of the last war, how that Germany's primitive Submarine Flotilla on July 31, 1914, was in charge of Commander H. Bauer destined to become Commodore of the Kaiser's High Sea Fleet submarines. Ships and men pass away. In April of 1942 Hermann Bauer had already reached his 50th year, already had brought up his son to reach an officer's rank in Hitler's Navy, but now had to confess that this only son who had entered Hitler's service in submarines had failed to return from his last trip.

Yet we look back to 1917 when Admiral Bauer (though still referred to as Korvetten Kapitan) was especially remembered for the memorandum which he issued to his officers in those days on the subject of 'Submarine Traps' (i.e. 'Q-Ships'); he warned these young captains that as regards vessels larger than 3000 tons his personnel should always be suspicious of the opposite ship not returning fire immediately, even after the attack had been going on for some time. In that case, Admiral Bauer warned, "you are most likely opposed by one of the 'traps'." She might be cargo vessel, tank steamer, or sailing vessel with motor, and doubtless he was thinking of such units as the *Prize* and the *Glen*.

We spoke, too, just now of the enemy building a large submarine which at first they used to call the *Deutschland*, but after the U.S.A. entered the war the Germans converted any mercantile submarines into fighting vessels and gave each a number. Thus by the end of April 1917 there were about six of them. The *Deutschland* became *U*-155. She left Germany for her second outward voyage on May 24, 1917, and returned about September 4 that year. Proceeding via the North of Scotland, thence to the southward of the Azores, she sank shipping on the surface, for this submarine was nothing else than a submersible cruiser of about 1700 tons

---
**Fighting the U-Boats*, pp. 13 and 17.

displacement armed with two powerful 5.9-inch guns. She carried a crew of 73 and her best speed was six knots. One has to think of such a craft normally travelling or fighting as a small, light cruiser on the surface and submerging only rarely; but she took some time to get below the waves When I went aboard the *Deutschland* at the Armistice, she appeared well if plainly built, but everywhere aboard her to the smallest cabin was a prevailing odour of stale coffee.

There had been built, too, a sister out-size trans-oceanic submarine named the *Bremen*, but to this day the Huns have never learned her fate, though she left Germany for Virginia. Probably whilst submerged she collided with two vessels of the 10th Cruiser Squadron, but anyway she failed to make port. To clew up this story of cruiser-submarines, *U*-154 was sunk in Lat. 36.45 N., Long. 12 W. by H.M. Submarine *E*-55 on May 11, 1918; *U*-156 was sunk by a mine on September 25, 1918, and *U*-157 was interned in Norway on November 11, 1918, after the signing of the Armistice. It was characteristic of German impudence that when *U*-155 (the converted *Deutschland*) during the summer of 1917 captured the neutral S.S. *Benguela*, the German ordered the latter to give the submarine a tow.

It was not unusual for these great submarines to make a cruise of even 100 days, but never were such slow and ungainly monstrosities a success. Although we have emphasized the nascent tendency to use German aircraft against our shipping, it was not until May 25 the first aeroplane raid over England caused about 290 casualties over Kent and Folkestone, though on June 1, 1917, at 8.20 in the forenoon our cross-Channel drifters which were protecting the Dover barrage were in action with three enemy seaplanes. There were in fact so many instances of these unusual hostile actions during the last war, that the enemy seems only reluctantly and after many years to have developed this new technique in the war which began in 1939.

When we wrote just now of Lieut.-Commander Ries who was captain of *UC*-77 we thought of one who frequently bungled his duties. It was on May 27, 1917, that having left Germany for Aberdeen with orders to bombard the port and entice us into a minefield, Ries had to clear for action when a British destroyer suddenly appeared on the scene and made the enemy dive in a hurry.

It became notable that during the latter part of June when fine summer weather might be expected that the U-boats journeyed an unprecedented distance, sinking shipping so far out in the Atlantic as 19 W., i.e. about 400 miles away from the nearest land. At the same time UC-boats were laying about 120 mines a week especially in the Atlantic approach routes. Actually du ing this month there were 127 encounters with submarines, but altogether there had arrived 28 of the United States destroyers which would come out of Queenstown to protect the Atlantic approach routes. Even after the first Atlantic Convoy, escorted by H.M.S. *Roxburgh*, left Hampton Roads it used to exercise daily in zig-zagging. The second Atlantic Convoy was already leaving America on June 4 and the third on June 13; so the custom of these ships quite speedily began to be adopted when once the prejudice of shipmasters had been overcome. And there would always be the welcoming by the American destroyers off western Ireland as further protection through the Danger Area.

For the German submarine, life round the British Isles was never enviable. He was harassed from the very beginning of his outward voyage. Even when once clear of British-laid mines, he had to look out for our submarines on watch in the centre of the North Sea. Further north the U-boat would encounter destroyers, steam yachts, trawlers and aircraft which were on to him with desperate delight. Off our East Coast we messed up his navigation by placing dummy lightships; but Dover Straits with the newly begun type of deep minefield, plus all sorts of patrol craft formed the most strenuous obstacle to be encountered.

"In recognition of his conspicuous gallantry, consummate coolness and skill", Commander Gordon Campbell, D.S.O., R.N., had been granted the Victoria Cross for commanding the *Farnborough* and other Q-ships, but now he proceeded to fit out the collier *Vittoria*, a steamer of 2817 gross tons. She began service as a Q-ship on March 28, 1917, and changed her name to *Pargust*. In June *Pargust*, armed with one 4-inch, four 12-pounders, two Maxim guns and a pair of 14-inch torpedo-tubes, but with only a 7¼ knots gait and wireless, sallied forth from Devonport into the Atlantic once more. Just for appearances' sake, to resemble a merchantman, she mounted a dummy gun aft with a man in uniform standing by. At 8 a.m., being in Lat. 51.50 N., Long. 11.50 W., the *Pargust* on June 7, 1917, espied out of the Irish mist a torpedo rushing towards her, At 100 yards away it leapt out of the water and tore a large hole in the hull near the waterline, filling the boiler-room, engine-room, No. 5 hold, and blowing the starboard lifeboat into the air.

Captain Campbell then sent away the customary panic party in three boats and now a periscope was sighted 400 yards off the port beam, afterwards coming on the starboard quarter and broke surface. One Hun in the conning-tower shouted directions but these were ignored, and at 8.36 a.m. one more German acted foolishly as the enemy was now only 50 yards off and all *Pargust's* guns were bearing so nicely that these opened fire. Another perfectly planned affair! The very first shot from the 4-inch struck the base of the conning-tower and carried away both periscopes. About 40 more shells followed, and then the submarine took a list to port heavily. Several Germans came out of the hatch abaft the conning-tower, oil squirting from her sides.

And we know from so many instances that the German whether in sport or war is not an honourable fighter but a 'win-at-any-cost'. Huns who came on deck waved that they would surrender, yet as soon as the *Pargust* ceased firing, the enemy began to try and escape. What a silly trick to attempt! Captain Campbell had therefore to resume firing after 10 minutes, and one shell exploded disastrously in the forward part of the submarine without any further bluff. Down she descended 300 yards away and that was how the unskilful crew of *UC*-29 went down with their 'tin ship'. Her German captain and crew had been so stupidly unlucky, and a sub-lieutenant of Reserve who originally came from one of the Hun liners had today been washed off the deck, but he and an engineer petty officer were picked up by the Q-ship.

Thus was *UC*-29 beaten with only two survivors remaining, and that withering fire had killed the German captain before condemning the rest (other than these two) to being drowned. She seems indeed to have worked quickly but without much sense. For she had left Brunsbüttel on May 25, calling at Heligoland, then to have laid all or most of her 18 mines, for I remember sinking three of these near Dingle Bay, Ireland She was armed with a 22-pounder gun and three torpedoes but these too can be accounted for: one torpedo holed the *Pargust*, another she had fired at an Italian barque, and a third had passed underneath a destroyer

So *UC*-29, including the time on passage, had spent less than a fort night away from home but she was now wiped out of existence. Captain Campbell lost only one Engineer Sub-Lieutenant wounded, and a Stoker Petty Officer killed. For this gallant episode Captain Campbell received a bar to his D.S.O., whilst Lieut. R. N. Stuart, D.S.O., R.N.R., and Seaman W. Williams, R.N.R., each won the V.C. This was the first occasion when under Clause XIII of the regulation the V.C. could be balloted for by one officer and one rating.

The reader will recollect our mentioning that Lieut.-Commander Moraht torpedoed the French warship *Danton* on March 18, 1917, in the Mediterranean; but experienced and astute though he was normally, this officer became too confident on June 17, 1918, and fairly invited death though he escaped it. He had come out of Cattaro and on the day mentioned sighted a convoy not far from Cape Bon and sank the S.S. *Kandy* by torpedo. But instead of then clearing out from such an area, Moraht in his eager curiosity remained at periscope depth on the spot. H.M Sloop *Lychnis* then dropped depth-charges, with the effect that *U*-64 had some of her electric lights put out, her after hydroplanes damaged, her steering rudder jammed and other injuries. She now became so out of control that *U*-64 tried to escape from this dilemma on the surface but was immediately set upon by one of our auxiliary ships named the *Partridge*. In fact *U*-64 had foolishly surfaced among the escort and found herself among live shells. Moraht and four others were lost overboard and these five out of 41 men had the most narrow escape; Moraht surviving, but utterly exhausted was about to go down for the third time. So if *U*-64 was finally lost, Moraht was remarkably lucky to find himself one of our prisoners.

One of the unfortunate Q-ships was the S.S. *Zylpha*, a steel-built vessel of 2917 tons that was torpedoed by a submarine off the S.W. coast of Ireland on June 11, 1917. This *Zylpha* was totally disabled, though the U-boat was a cautious fellow who never shewed himself again. The U.S.A destroyer *Warrington* came to the ship's assistance and stood by from 2 p.m. today until 2.30 p.m. of June 13 when the *Warrington* must return to port for fuel. Meanwhile another American destroyer and two Queenstown tugs were being sent to the *Zylpha*, but under a casual sail rig the *Zylpha* made off at 1½ knots though she failed to last out and sank at 11.20 p.m. on June 15 near the Great Skelligs.* Only one man had been killed, yet already the Atlantic swell was shaking the bulkheads badly.

I have already emphasized the amount of chance in fighting a submarine and this was well exemplified during June, but how direct and simple it seems when the armed ship was a steam trawler which Commander Godfrey Herbert, D.S.O, R.N.—who had served for years in submarines and also had been one of the pioneers of Q-ships—commanded H.M. Trawler *Sea King* based on Falmouth. With him also was Lieut.

---
*Off the West Coast of Ireland.

Buchanan, R.N., who also had come from destroyers and now served in H.M. Trawler *Sea Sweeper*.

Suddenly an alarm on June 11, 1917, summoned them to sea with two other trawlers for a submarine was said to be somewhere near the Lizard. Was this yarn true? It sounded rather too good. But between the Lizard and Kynance Cove it was known that U-boats were fond of going to rest here on the sea-bed. At dawn of June 12 Commander Herbert thought he would stir things up by dropping a depth-charge. It was dawn at 4.30 a.m. and at any rate some fresh fish for breakfast would be yielded out of the sea by this explosion. Evidently *UC*-66 had chosen her resting-place hereabouts for at 11.30 a.m. when two and a half miles to the south-east "I spotted about 400 yards away, two or three points on my port bow, the periscope, stanchion, and jumper-stay of a submarine travelling westward," related Commander Herbert, who happily saw the enemy dive. Now the *Sea King* fired 16 large depth-charges but ordered the rest of his flotilla to let go 64 smaller ones. A most satisfactory occasion. For *UC*-66 had been burst into destruction, her mines and torpedoes detonated. She exuded a quantity of oil, and the Hun was gone sure enough—though not a body was found. The depth was 40 fathoms and after searching the locality for several hours Commander Herbert and Lieut. Buchanan had only one conclusion to utter regarding *UC*-66. Months later an Admiralty letter arrived and confirmed the event. Commander Herbert was given a bar to a D.S.O. (for he already possessed one), whilst Lieut. Buchanan received the D.S.C. and two of the crew a D.S.M.

So the German pest had been roused and then put to sleep again with ludicrous ease. Yes: these incidents of decoys might develop in the most surprising manner. Listen to the extraordinary case of the Q-ship *Wonganella*. It was 8 p.m. on June 19 and she was on her way back across the Atlantic from Halifax when she sighted a submarine on the surface approaching from the north. The enemy opened fire at 8000 yards, and straggled *Wonganella* in three rounds.

Difficult situation!

For the Q-ship today had on board 30 survivors from a steamer which had gone down so it was not practicable to do the usual 'abandon ship'. Smoke apparatus was therefore used, the *Wonganella* ran down-wind at various speeds and on various courses, and suddenly another ship now appeared off the starboard beam, heading E. But presently the stranger shewed that she was making direct for the spot which *Wonganella* had selected. And, moreover, the stranger proved herself to be . . . no! not an ordinary merchant ship but that vessel mentioned in a much earlier chapter: the Q-ship *Aubrietia*. Nuisance! *Wonganella* had to signal her that "no assistance is required", though the submarine awkwardly continued to shell through the smoke till the engagement continued till 8.30 p.m., when the episode ended after 50 shells had been fired to no purpose.

You can see how awkwardly could fate sometimes guide these events for decoys.

Yet the Atlantic was really in an extraordinary mood, for only the very next day (June 20), about 4 a.m., the Cunard S.S. *Valeria* whilst homeward-bound from New York struck some submerged object and directly afterwards saw what appeared to be a broken periscope alongside the ship—close alongside. Furthermore a sound like that of motor engines was heard and then the jumping wires and top of a conning-tower were seen as the latter passed astern. The *Valeria* acted pretty smartly for she rapidly fired three rounds at the conning-tower; the first (at 100 yards) and the third (at 500 yards) being both claimed as hits. It was afterwards announced by the Admiralty that thus *U-99* was definitely destroyed, for air bubbles and oil now came to the surface. And we may note that on July 5 the United States Ship *Tucker* in passing this way observed a heavy film of oil about a mile long and 100 yards wide whilst large bubbles of oil were still seen rising to the surface.

The reader may now well ask himself whether there was any connection between this affair and the *Wonganella* incident of June 19. The answer is that both episodes occurred off the south-west of Ireland and most probably when *Valeria* sank the submarine at 4 a.m. of the 20th in a position Lat. 52.20 N., Long. 12.28 W., this pretty well agrees with that of *Wonganella* at 8 p.m. the day before; viz. Lat. 52.3 N., Long. 15.14 W. Allowing for a slight movement during those eight hours, I submit that it was *U-99* all the time.

And let us not make any mistake over the names of Q-ships.

For instance, we have already mentioned how the *Zylpha* met her fate off Ireland on June 11. But the Q-ship *Salvia* was another vessel—one of the sloops rebuilt with a false counter-stern to resemble a 1000-tons tramp. She was cleverely redesigned and I had known her new captain for several years before he took me one day over the ship; yet frankly she never quite 'fooled' me and always I felt at sea she would not exactly 'fool' an observant U-boat. So on June 20 at 9 a.m. when in that region it was so thick with U-boats (Lat. 52.17, Long. 16.13 W.) she was at last sunk by a submarine. Her captain was picked up from a raft and taken prisoner to Germany till the war ended, when he returned to New Zealand. Unfortunately, however, five of the *Salvia's* crew had been killed by the enemy's shell-fire.

CHAPTER XIII

SUBMARINE CAPTURED BY SOLDIERS

THE days for our decoys had not yet quite finished, but we may reckon June 20 as the very apex of our Q-ship operations, and the successes limited to a very few commanding officers and ships.

A Fleet collier named the *Dunraven* had been requisitioned as a Q-ship instead of the *Pargust*. She was fitted out for Captain Campbell at Devonport, and the crew of *Pargust* transferred to her *en bloc*. Everything was done with wonderful meticulousness: in fact we may say that all the concentrated experience was summed up in this one steamer, all the ingenuity of years and brave men. The limit had been reached. Whatever happened after, there could never be sent forth a mightier counterblast to this anti-submarine unit. So the *Dunraven* left Devonport on August 6, 1917, and on August 8 in the Bay of Biscay she was torpedoed by a submarine some 139 miles west of Ushant. It was a wonderful fight of endurance in which effort was well matched and neither party could be overcome. Finally on August 9 at 10.15 a.m. H.M. Destroyer *Christopher* from a position about 60 miles west of Ushant wirelessed that the *Dunraven* was making for Plymouth at four knots. The decoy with her crew had surpassed the heights of gallantry and endurance and excelled all the records of incidents that have ever been chronicled in the book of sea warfare.* The ship and men could scarcely have sustained much longer, but at 3.25 p.m. on August 10 the much battered *Dunraven* capsized whilst in tow of tugs to be sunk by the *Christopher's* gunfire. Captain Campbell was awarded a second bar to his D.S.O., and of the summit of Q-ship contest King George remarked that "greater bravery than was shown by all officers and men on this occasion can hardly be conceived". It was the last chapter in Captain Campbell's strenuous story against submarines, so he now resumed uniform and in command of H.M.S. *Active*.

But likewise the Falmouth 3-masted topsail schooner *Mitchell*, at a spot some three miles from a position Lat. 47.13 N., Long. 7.23 W., sighted the conning-tower of a submarine and engaged her with shells. A further engagement with her was continued also on this June 20. This nice-looking mystery ship, which used to change her name as required from time to time, won for her officers many decorations in her fights with U-boats; but actually one began to wonder if all this ingenuity, all this courageous endeavour, were still sure efficacy in the fight against German submarines. Even the Granton brigantine *Probus* on the next day (June 21) had a tussle with a U-boat but did not succeed in sinking the enemy. Incident followed incident quite promptly; that well-known sailing decoy ship *Glen* on June 25 was once more in action with a U-boat, but again it was indecisive; and on June 26 yet another sailing Q-ship—the *Gaelic*—based on Milford, exchanged shots with a submarine in the English Channel.

There is some uncertainty about the fate of *UB-36*, but she disappeared in the region of the English Channel. Neither Germany nor Britain has ever been able to settle details of the matter. Certainly towards the end of June occurred so many Q-ships incidents and on the night of June 24 a French destroyer in the English Channel claimed to have sunk this U-boat by shells and depth-charges but an equally likely theory is that victory fell to the United States Destroyer *Cummings*, who was one of those that originally had come over to Queenstown. Now during the week immediately preceding June 26 no fewer than 24 of these American destroyers were temporarily withdrawn from Queenstown to escort the first contingents of American troops who arrived in France on June 26. And it was whilst escorting this American force that the *Cummings* sighted a periscope in Lat. 47.10 N., Long. 6 W., when this destroyer turned towards the submarine and released a depth-charge. Whether, therefore, she sank *UB-36* will never be known though the attack on the convoy is claimed to have been frustrated.

One does not usually associate a fighting ship with the work of trader, but in many cases the Q-ship, though properly commissioned as a warship, was as much use as a cargo-carrier; so the two extremes of ship-use met, and in some cases at great profit. Let me give actual instances of

*Details will be found in my *Danger Zone*, pp. 284-5.

certain Q-sailing ships that were now based on the Firth of Forth yet would be engaged in carrying coal to France, or pit-props; or, say, a cargo of herrings for Farnborough, or leaving Newcastle with coal for Halifax. Really it was remarkable trading when we think of the two-masted brigantine decoy *Merops* this June reaching the French port of Morlaix from Granton with coal. Being efficiently disguised, these ships could call at any port without their camouflage being detected. I remember that between May 4 and December 6 in 1917 the *Probus* earned £5797, the *Merops* earned £4429 between August 30 and November 24; but four of these decoys (sail or steam) between November 14 and December 11 earned a total of £11,000 for the ships besides four D.S.O.s, 11 D.S.C.s and 21 D.S.M.s for the personnel of the vessels. There was another vessel—the three-masted schooner *Fresh Hope*—which was so smart as to do 12 knots in a fresh breeze.

The development of our various anti-submarine measures definitely did not please the Germans, and the *Frankfurter Zeitung* of July 8, 1917, complained somewhat naively of the use of smoke boxes as making the work of submarines more difficult. Not without interest may we compare the present submarine efforts with the past. The Allies in 1917 were losing about 500,000 tons of shipping a month and the building capacity of the available yards within the next year was not more than 130,000 tons a month. There was no denial that the shipping situation was very critical in those days.

However artful and clever might be the submarine, we had after all these months developed a variegated technique of such a sort that few U-boats could expect to succeed for long. Now in those days we used to see what were known as Grand Fleet Kite-Balloon destroyers patrolling the sea able to obtain an excellent view of the water's surface 15 miles apart, though this was only a preliminary development to the aeroplane age that would follow afterwards. But about 7 a.m. H.M.S. *Patriot* sighted a submarine one day, caused the enemy to dive, proceeded to the spot later and when in Lat. 60.25 N., Long. 1.32 E., about noon dropped a couple of depth-charges after the enemy had dived; whereupon the sea became covered with thick brown oil for 400 yards.

This was how we sank *U*-69 on July 12, but for a brief period we seemed to anticipate once more the tactics of the war that was to follow. One of the earliest submarines to have been put in service at the beginning of the war * was *UC*-1, who laid minefields off the East coast in 1915 and became attached to the Flanders Flotilla. Her job principally was minelaying off the E. and S.E. coasts. One day in July 1917 she was sighted in the Thames estuary by some of our seaplanes who flew over and dropped bombs. A few days later a remarkable and ludicrous event occurred at 4.20 a.m. Indeed to no one could this incident have happened with greater fun though anger than to a German of the usual type full of his own dignity. The submarine *UC*-61 surrendered in the English Channel off the French coast to some French cavalry!

The episode sounds so amusing, yet I have had the story fully confirmed in France, just after the last war, by French officials. *UC*-61 had come past Belgium under the cover of night, but we know that too often these minelayers were careless of their navigation, and today the weather was

---

*See *Fighting the U-Boats*, p. 94.

thick. She got picked up on the Wissant Shoal near Gris Nez on July 26, yet this was her fifth cruise and she had left Zeebrugge at 1 p.m. the previous day, passing the Goodwins-Snouw barrage during the dark hours, shaping her course along the shore between Gravelines and Blanc Nez, intending to lay mines off Boulogne and Havre. With a f lling tide the Germans fell into the hands of the French horsemen but, after abandonment, the Huns did manage to blow up their craft. Of course the Allies took every advantage of going through her equipment, so the German hydrophone was removed and sent to England for examination when it was found to be of a type inferior to ours.

On this day, too, another notable incident took place at the other end of the English Channel. Were German submarine officers becoming more careless as the months sped by, or must we attribute their quaint actions just to stupidity? Certainly these Hun submarines failed to keep up their early standard of efficiency. It was at 7.42 p.m. that H.M.S. *P-60* (a low-lying type of craft, swift and handy, designed for anti-submarine work) sighted a periscope three cables off the starboard bow when near the Lizard.

The patrol vessel worked up to full speed, tried to over-run the submarine, dropping first one depth-charge, then another, and presently some portions of a broken spar were sent up from the water. The conclusion was that this was another of the Flanders U-boats who must have got damaged in the fray. Evidently she hoped against hope and although three days later (July 29) it was ascertained that this was *UB*-23 which put into Corunna to lick her wounds, she had to admit her damage was far too serious to go out again; so the Spanish Government interned her.

There happened to be based on Lowestoft H.M.S. *Halcyon*, an old-fashioned torpedo-gunboat, not of great value or other attainment, but on July 29, 1917, she came outside and was steering to the northward at a speed of 14 knots when at 10.57 a.m. she saw a periscope 400 yards away and made straight for the stranger. *Halcyon* whacked up to 17 knots, steered direct for her, felt a collision, and dropped a depth-charge which was exploded off Smith's Knoll—by which there had been many an encounter with German submarines. Indeed this Spar Buoy was quite a favourite spot with the Germans, who sometimes made the land near by when her raiders came over on a minelaying-bombarding expedition. This time it was *UB*-27 which was the culprit, and she was definitely located by a sweep in 24 fathoms.

The blight which had now settled down over the German Submarine Service seemed to have been continued in one shape or another. *UB*-20 was yet another Flanders submarine bombed by our seaplanes in the North Sea by a surprise and fatal attack. On July 31 the British S.S. *Belgian Prince* was torpedoed by *U*-44 without warning 175 miles N.W. by W. of Tory Island. Her commanding officer was Lieut.-Commander Wagenführ who was so incredibly brutal that he deliberately dived with survivors from that ship lined up on his deck. At any rate, 39 persons were thus sent to their doom in the wild Atlantic. But Wagenführ was punished for this massacre more speedily than even the most callous German would suspect.

It so happened that Wagenführ had been assigned to operate in that North Channel (between Scotland and Ireland) where liners bound for

Liverpool or the Clyde might be expected. Now in a curious round-about fashion this *U-44* was destined to link herself with a certain Q-ship which was not a successful vessel, yet somehow fate decided that at least she would perform one important thing in life. The Admiralty had been employing a 2905 tons collier named *Bracondale* as a warship but decided that she would make a useful decoy, so at the beginning of April 1917 she was thus commissioned and her name changed to *Chagford*. She was fitted out with a 4-inch, two 12-pounders and a couple of torpedo-tubes. By the end of June she was ready for sea and sent to Buncrana (N. Ireland) whence she entered the Atlantic on August 2.

On August 5 at 4.10 a.m. she was about 120 miles N.W. of Tory Island looking for two enemy submarines which had been reported the previous day. But there appeared a U-boat (which was afterwards learned to be *U-44*) that torpedoed *Chagford* just below the bridge, disabling both the torpedo-tubes and the 4-inch gun besides doing other damage; though about this time *U-44* exhibited her hull and a couple of periscopes. Very shortly *U-44* came fully to the surface, when she was received with a hot fire from the *Chagford's* two 12-pounders, besides Lewis and machine-guns. In anger therefore *U-44* dived, but at 4.40 a.m. fired a second torpedo which struck *Chagford* abaft the bridge. However, the latter was settling down when one of H.M. Trawlers fortunately arrived and taking off the survivors finally landed them at Oban. Still the *Chagford* on August 7 could endure no longer, took a plunge and disappeared.

Now though *Chagford* was never a great Q-ship she had really done wonders, for those shells had crippled *U-44* to such an extent that the latter could only keep on the surface a short time at a stretch. It was going to be a slow business to reach Germany via the North of Ireland and Scotland and then down the North Sea, so Wagenführ might well wonder if it would be possible through all this distance and past so many headlands to evade every sort of patrol. And she could now dive only for short periods but made the effort to disguise herself as a trawler by setting a mizzen sail.

And now arrived August 12. *U-44* had got no further than the North of Scotland when H.M.S. *Oracle* (a destroyer) coming along sighted her obviously still unable to dive properly. So the unmerciful German was shelled and then rammed mercilessly. That, then, was how *U-44* came to her end, and Wagenführ's crime avenged, first by the *Chagford* and finally by the *Oracle*.

But the first indubitable hint of a great change was coming, for on August 3 and 4, 1917, there was a mutiny in the German Fleet at Wilhelmshaven. The initial outbreaks occurred in the battleship *Kaiserin* and other units of the 4th Battle Squadron. The immediate cause was insufficiency of food and the high-handed treatment of crews by their officers. And on August 4 a general outbreak occurred, so better food was promised. On August 5 some of the most disaffected battleships were ordered out of harbour as plans for a general demonstration ashore had been arranged for August 6. It was, however, indicative of the Fleet's feeling that when on July 25 Captain Thorbecke, commanding officer of the battleship *König Albert*, was stepping out of his motor-boat to the gangway of his ship, after having spent a convivial evening aboard another unit of the squadron, he had been fatally stabbed and his body not picked up for several days.

During this August other mutinous acts were happening. The downfall of Germany's sea power was now becoming nearer and with it the peril engendered by submarines towards us could be seen to have reached its limitations. Little more than another year would suffice to bring about the final crisis.

Of all created things using the sea none was more insidious than the minelaying submarine. Like some mysterious monster she moved beneath the waves depositing terrible death-traps that may remain hidden for hours and days till all of a sudden an unsuspecting surface ship comes steaming along and fouls those ugly horns protruding from a pear-shaped black-painted object.

Then follows a violent explosion, water rushes into the gaping hull, and one more vessel is doomed.

With her typical lust for frightfulness, Germany originally developed out of her U-boats a special type for minelaying known as UC-boats. They were originally only 111 feet long, with 10 feet beam and drew 9 feet on the surface. Small, handy, their best surface speed was $7\frac{1}{2}$ knots, and 5 knots when under water. As fighting units they possessed little value, having only a machine-gun and few torpedoes; yet these smaller boats were quite useful for going across from Zeebrugge or Ostend—doing most of the North Sea passage along the surface—then diving off the Lowestoft area, or the South Goodwins Lightship neighbourhood before releasing their dozen mines. That being done, the submarine scurried back home to fetch another deadly cargo.

It was the German occupation of Belgium which made this a comparatively easy project, the first of these minelayers to reach Flanders from Germany being *UC*-11 in the summer of 1915. Soon, however, actual experience evolved a bigger and more efficient class in the *UC*-16 to -79 boats. Measuring 165 feet long, 17 feet beam, and drawing 12 feet, they had a two knots superiority, a surface radius of 6000 miles, but besides carrying 18 mines and a machine-gun mounted at least one 22-pounder whilst able to discharge about half a dozen torpedoes.

In other words, here was a most formidable creature which might penetrate the Dover Straits even to western Ireland and the Bay of Bscay, besides serving a dual purpose. In actual performance such a crafti prudently avoided all shipping till every mine had been laid, when she could go about her job as an ordinary U-boat torpedoing victims or (if the silver missiles were becoming few) shelling the merchantmen from deck gun at long distance.

It was my experience to discover quite a number of these UC-mines. As a rule they were skilfully laid off prominent headlands past which steamers might be expected to pass on their lawful voyaging. If, suddenly, one mine became visible in the swell, we looked around expectantly for two more. Why? Because the German method was—more often than not—to deposit these 'eggs' in threes. I recollect one day locating a mine exactly in the right position for entrapping any vessel making for a certain western port. Sure enough, the other two were presently found right in the approach of the fairway from seawards.

For the German UC-boats were so constructed that about the first third of their length from the bows consisted of vertical tubes, extending from top to bottom. These tubes were six in number, each containing three mines apiece complete with sinkers. Thus one tubeful might be released off (say) the Old Head of Kinsale to destroy a homecoming Atlantic liner, whilst the next trio of mines would be dropped off Queenstown in the hope of catching patrol vessels bound out.

The captain of a minelaying submarine having arrived off the selected spot was wont to go about his work as follows. With the chart before him, he fixed his position accurately by taking bearings of lighthouse, church spire, or any suitable prominence. Then on referring to his chart, he knew exactly the depth of water beneath. Preferably he would wait till darkness, and either for top of High Water or dead Low Tide. The sinkers having been set to the required number of fathoms, all that he had now to do was to release his freight. Sinker would anchor itself to the sea-bed, but the mine (attached by a long wire hawser gradually unwinding itself) should then float at the assigned submergence.

It was often that, by some slight error, instead of the mine mooring itself 10 or 12 feet below High Water level, it revealed its presence sufficiently to afford valuable warning.

CHAPTER XIV

GERMAN MORALE

IN earlier chapters we have shown some of our North Sea fishermen bravely fighting under sail against German submarines.

Could anything be more glorious than the story of Skipper T. Crisp of Lowestoft who on August 15, 1917, was aboard his sailing smack *Nelson* fishing in the North Sea? About 2.45 that afternoon the trawl had been shot, the Skipper happened to be below packing fish, one hand on deck cleaning part of the catch for next morning's breakfast.

Then Crisp came on deck, glanced round the sea and sighted an object.

"That's a submarine. Clear for action!"

Almost immediately from the U-boat a shell dropped within a hundred yards, yet the Lowestoft men continued perfectly cool and collected. They slipped and buoyed their net, manned their little gun, but German 4-inch shells had quickly got the range and the seventh was the worst. It maimed the wooden smack, penetrated the skipper's body, came out through the deck and via the ship's side into the sea.

So now the skipper's son, Tom Crisp, took charge of the tiller whilst missiles still rained and the *Nelson* began to sink. One of the crew came to assist the unfortunate sufferer, but this grand old man, well knowing the proximity of death, made light of his terrible wounds.

"It's all right. Do your best," he cheered. Then turning to his son he ordered: "Send this message: '*Nelson* attacked by submarine. Skipper killed. Send help at once.'"

The bit of paper having been attached to a carrier pigeon, the bird flew in the direction of Lowestoft's naval office.

Commander Rucker, to the left without a hat, was one of the most notorious U-boat captains, and is here seen being landed as a prisoner at Milford Haven.

THE TORPEDOED Q-SHIP "ZYLPHA" IS ABOUT TO SINK

Meanwhile the *Nelson* sank lower and deeper, only five rounds of ammunition remained.

"Father——" the grieved son was comforting.

Captain of his vessel and of himself to the last, the grand old fellow interrupted:

"Abandon ship. .... Throw the books overboard"—he remembered those confidential documents which must never fall into enemy hands. "Tom, I'm done. Throw me overboard."

It was time to quit the ship if anyone were to be saved. Leaving their skipper almost breathing his final gasp, the crew went away in the smack's boat and a few minutes later *Nelson* disappeared below the waves, taking below the body of one whose death was as gallant as anything the North Sea ever witnessed. Through the dark hours a boatload of destitute, heartbroken men, hungry and thirsty, drifted hither and thither. Another day and one more night had to be endured till rescue came.

Posthumously Skipper T. Crisp was awarded the V.C., whilst Tom Crisp received the D.S.M. Tom came up to Buckingham Palace a few months later to obtain both decorations.

There is no finer breed of men than these fishermen, and today they have again left their nets to serve our country against an old enemy. Nature's gentlemen, reckless of their own lives, hardened by gales and misfortune, they never let you down when once there has been extended the fidelity of friendship. But German injustice, Nazi murders of innocent women and children travelling by sea, they will not tolerate. It will go badly with any U-boat daring to come within range of their guns or depth-charges, as happened one evening in April 1918.

It was about half-past five when the drifter *Pilot Me* on patrol off Torr Head, North Ireland, noticed some 50 yards distant an unmistakable periscope; whereupon Skipper A. Walker turned the *Pilot Me* round, made for the object and zigzagged across its path. Then a shower of depth-charges was unloaded.

The Skipper stopped engines to listen on his hydrophone, heard nothing. Fifteen minutes later a dark mass rose to the surface between *Pilot Me* and another drifter named *Young Fred*. Like a lot of terriers after a rat, other drifters joined in the chase. They were not going to be done out of the evening's sport.

Little guns banged away at the surfacing submarine now less than 300 yards off, and compelled the German to dive for safety. Not for long, however.

The *Young Fred* could not be cheated, steamed towards the spot where the sea had been disturbed, let go more depth-charges, and had not long to wait. Violent explosions sent up a column of water higher than drifters' masts, and next appeared bits of woodwork, painted gratings, and seamen's caps. Outside the latter were ribbons bearing the words 'Unterseeboots Flotilla', whilst inside the linings were the names of German sailors.

No survivors.

For *UB*-82 had gone below surface for the last time with all hands.

Yet another submarine was bombed by one of our seaplanes when *UB*-32 was caught in the English Channel. It was in August that *UC*-41 left Germany with orders to lay mines near Dundee and Aberdeen. Now on August 21 H.M. Trawlers *Jacinth* and *Thomas Young* were sweeping the Tay estuary heading towards the S.S.W. when just before 5 p.m. an explosion occurred on *Jacinth's* starboard beam about one mile S.E. of the Tay buoy. On altering course and sweeping towards this position something was about to happen. For the sweep had fouled some sort of obstruction and parted. After some difficulty *Jacinth's* portion did at last come clear, but the *Thomas Young's* remained foul till it was finally cleared with difficulty. A German mine rose to the surface, but while the *Thomas Young* destroyed it, then the *Jacinth* proceeded over the position and dropped one depth-charge after another.

When an explosion had occurred with great violence and a second one was heard a few seconds later, there rose to the surface large quantities of air and oil; so a third depth-charge was let go. The trawler *Chikara* now closed and dropped four more depth-charges which all exploded, and then four pieces of woodwork were picked up. *Jacinth* and *Chikara* next used their hydrophones, and the sounds of an electric engine could be heard. On the following day another mine was swept up, and three days later oil was still seen coming to the surface. But when a diver was sent down he reported that a submarine was lying against the sand on an even keel. Thus it was that the minelayer *UC*-41 was disturbed into activity from resting on the sea-bed. Or she may have been startled out of inactivity on hearing the minesweepers approach, and tried to clear out, fouling one of her own mines, and was blown up. By September 21 after many days of salvage work her 3.5-inch (22-pounder) gun was salved.

Curious things at sea were so frequent that their nature ceased to be surprising, but sometimes they were sufficiently odd to arouse suspicion. On the last day of August 1917 in the darkness that precedes dawn an old boat used for fishing was taken from Druridge Bay (Tyne Area) without being seen by anyone. About 9 a.m., however, the fishing trawler *Ranter* spoke a boat, answering more or less to her owner's description, but here she was 20 miles eastward of the Tyne. Well, of course since the boat contained several foreigners who insisted that they were Danish seamen who belonged to a torpedoed sailing ship and were now making for Holland, the story sounded somewhat fishy.

Moreover they declined the *Ranter's* help, since they professed that they had already been torpedoed twice and wished to sail home. That did not sound too convincing either. And when the trawlermen noticed that the foreigners' present course was not heading for Holland it looked still less convincing than ever. That same evening about 9.20 the *Ranter* fell in with H.M. Armed Trawler *Vedette* and reported the facts to the *Vedette* who in turn reported the affair by wireless to the Senior Naval Officer at the Tyne. Thereupon H.M. Destroyer *Bonetta* was sent out who eventually discovered the stolen boat with six escaped German prisoners, so the *Bonetta* took them on board and brought them back.

Nor was this the only occasion when this type of prisoner made for the coast and committed the same kind of theft. On the other hand, although things in the U-boat service were better than in the High Sea Fleet generally, there existed a real spirit of unrest in the German Navy. Apart from the dissatisfaction in regard to food, the men were angry at the small amount of leave granted and because of the heavy punishments for minor offences. As to submarines, it was noticeable that such crews were now less eager to serve, as the recent losses had lowered their morale and on many cases a man would miss his boat or feign sickness so as to avoid making a cruise.

The enemy preferred to work well out in the Atlantic in the hope of meeting the convoys before the latter were joined by their escort force. Whilst the utility of the Q-ship was still on the wane, her service was yet fruitful: in fact we could afford to put one decoy in the convoy, let her keep astern in the danger zone, as if unable to avoid being a 'straggler', and then suddenly surprise the submarine.

Now among the sea surprises I suppose that which was created on the forenoon of September 2, 1917, to a vessel named the S.S. *Olive Branch* whilst proceeding on the Archangel route was fairly unique. A certain German submarine opened fire on this cargo-carrier which was bringing to Russia ammunition and warlike goods. The submarine was U-28 and presently opened fire at 250 yards. Her second shot was directed into No. 4 hold and the *Olive Branch* blew up. That was not surprising, but the unusual affair was that in detonating the hold full of munitions the explosion sent a motor lorry into the air whose descent was upon U-28, sinking her utterly.

We have already conveyed some idea of those so-called cruiser-submarines and we gave U-151 (Commander Kophamel) as one number. We shall find between her and the long distance U-boats of the second (1939 and after) global Submarine War more than a little in common. This converted U-151, no longer mercantile but a cruiser, type left Germany about September 3, 1917, and proceeded to the Atlantic via the North of Scotland. Then going south she operated off Madeira and the Straits of Gibraltar, next along the African coast to Dakar, westward to the Cape Verde Islands, finally northward again, so reaching Germany about Xmas Eve, 1917, after a cruise of some 112 days during which she torpedoed two Brazilian steamers in St. Vincent Harbour (Cape Verdes); purloining copper and stores from a Norwegian vessel. In all this submersible cruiser sank 13 merchant ships of British, Italian, Japanese, Brazilian, Norwegian, French, Portuguese and American nationalities. Total 34,566 tons. For doing this Kophamel received the order 'Pour le Mérite', which corresponds to our Victoria Cross.

Among the other stratagems that were employed against the enemy's U-boats were our own submarines. The Germans always had a dread of so being surprised, as for instance towards the end of August when H.M. Submarine E-54 sank one of the UC-class in the North Sea near the Schouwen Lightship. Thus still one more of the Flanders units had made a journey across the North Sea guided by such fingerposts as lightships, lighthouses and buoys could direct.

But there was one German commanding officer whom no mysterious force could guide through peril, for already he was so steeped in inquity. I refer to Schwieger. Punishment still awaited him.

Who was Schwieger? Even now his name is still associated with the Atlantic as some soldiers on land will always be remembered for their brutality. Schwieger was in command of U-20 that sank the Cunard S.S. *Lusitania*, sending over a thousand men, women and children to death; but at a later date he became commander of U-88 and concerning some of his adventures in her the reader is already familiar.* But one day (September 7, 1917) Schwieger when outward bound in company with another submarine was aiming to get beyond the Horns Reef minefield, when in diving he and his craft crashed into floating explosives, that dealt fatal revenge for the *Lusitania* tragedy. Three days later *UC*-42 (like *UC*-44 of whose fate we gave details just now) was sunk $2\frac{1}{2}$ miles N.E. of Daunt's Rock Lightship (Queenstown)—sunk on her own mines. She had been sent from Germany with a desire to foul the entrance to this port that was kept busy all day and every day and night by all sorts of shipping. For instance, just to enumerate one section there were 38 U.S. destroyers based on Queenstown but any amount of British sloops, trawlers, drifters, destroyers, convoys and other craft. *UC*-42 had a terrible disaster. Divers were eventually sent down who discovered that only her foremost mine-tube was empty and that she still contained 15 mines. The damage to her stern was similar to that of *UC*-44 off Waterford. It was likewise ascertained that the hatches were open and her foundering on mines had been at night. When a diver brought up part of *UC*-42's starboard light it was reminiscent that these craft were now going out for a long time and a long distance. Hitherto the longest known cruise in Home Waters for a UB-boat was 24 days. But more than one of these fatal mistakes pointed to the inefficiency which had most firmly bitten into what was at one time a high grade.

In spite of the enemy's efforts in the Arctic, the German seemed too unfortunate for his choice. It was the eleventh of September when one of our merchant ships, the 4143-tons S.S. *British Transport*, whilst on passage from Brest to Archangel, passed through Lat. 46.51 N., Long. 14 W., and at four in the afternoon sighted a submarine which surfaced about 50 yards on the port quarter. She dived, and appeared again about that distance away. Then she dropped back to five miles' distant but kept following the steamer till dusk. Evidently the enemy meant business, and waiting only for a favourable opportunity. Just before eight o'clock that evening when the last flicker of light was departing, the steamer deemed it time to throw overboard a couple of smoke-boxes: for our mercantile mariners had been trained at such special anti-submarine marine courses as were being held at Devonport, Liverpool and other ports just then. And one instruction comprised the use of these gadgets for making an artificial cloud. Unfortunately, however, this September the two boxes burned with a flame; and an hour after dusk, having zigzagged away from the submarine, an unusual noise was heard on the port quarter when the tracks of two torpedoes were seen.

The ship's head was turned to starboard and the torpedoes passed along the port side without striking her; but a luminous patch of water was shortly seen and the form of a submarine made out. As the ship struck it, there was a heavy shock felt, and a grinding noise heard for perhaps three seconds. There was no question that the ship was checked by the collision, and the submarine's bow was clearly seen up in the air. The second officer observed a round hatch opened between the foremost gun and the conning-tower. The figures of some Germans were seen emerging, and considerable shouting was heard. The moment had now come for the *British Transport* to act.

---

*See my *Fighting the U-Boats*, p. 215.

At close range she fired a couple of rounds, the second being a hit with flames and sparks. Then the engagement petered out and having arrived at Archangel, the steamer's stern was examined to reveal some sharply defined scratches. Thus by having rammed the German, and dealt him two shots, the submarine was overcome and *U*-49 definitely sunk.

CHAPTER XV

THE U-BOAT'S TERROR

I HAVE to admit that though the Admiralty took up and commissioned for service numbers of steam yachts which had been originally built for summer pleasure cruising and, on the whole, were expensive units to keep in patrol, yet if their usefulness was distinctly limited there were some few occasions when these yachts justified their existence. We may mention such vessels as the *Sapphire*, the *Jeanette*, the *Lorna*, and *Narcissus*, as among those fine yachts which did such commendable work in Northern Europe and the Mediterranean. Now the *Narcissus* was commanded by that gallant Rear-Admiral John Philip Rolleston, D.S.O., who had come back out of retirement to serve again afloat. For this steam yacht on September 8, 1917, was in action with the submarine *UB*-49 (who occasionally but erroneously used to call herself *U*-293).

The latter received so much damage from the *Narcissus* that she put into Cadiz and had to be interned on September 11; but *UB*-49's skipper (Lieut.-Commander H. von Mellenthin) possessed such a curious sense of honour that on October 6 at 5.45 p.m. she escaped from this restriction and was last seen steering to the north but eventually got back to Cattaro. Curious how some ships keep on living! By the time war was resumed in 1939 most of these steam yachts had been sold abroad, or broken up, though the *Narcissus* had changed her name to *Grive* and was back in the war—this time under the command of another gallant and retired naval officer, Captain the Hon. Lionel Lambart, D.S.O., R.N. She was a vessel of 816 tons who at the historic withdrawal from Dunkirk distinguished herself for three terrific days and nights in which she rescued 2000 of the B.E.F. Then on her fourth trip to Dunkirk the Germans sank her and most of her crew of 43.

There have not been so many vessels of her age to fly the White Ensign in two great wars and to succumb with distinction after such a strenuous life. It was also in keeping with the standard of German morality that *UB*-49 when driven by homelessness from the Adriatic by the tide of German events at the end of war, left that sea on October 28, 1918, beaten and disgraced like her service generally.

But life for these Germans was full of surprises. Already we have reminded the reader that the Huns for some time had been paying attention to valuable ships that we were sending through the North Passage (north of Ireland). For this reason one of our submarines (H.M.S. *D*-7) was patrolling this area on September 12, 1917, and shortly after 10 a.m. sighted on the surface in Lat. 55.48 N., Long. 7.30 W., the German submarine *U*-45. With an impudent self-assurance, she had one day in January 1917 stopped and demanded oil of the American tanker

Westego and sunk next day the Dutch S.S. *Gamma* bound from New York for Amsterdam.

Now *U*-45 on September 12 was not immediately concerned with warlike matters. German, or Central European, Time is one hour ahead of ours, so that when the enemy was reckoning 11 a.m., the crew had just finished their mid-day meal and two of them had just come on deck to smoke a cigarette. Perhaps they yearned for the fresh keen air since it was not too pleasant with a big sea running and a certain amount of heat developed from the engines in the middle of September. *U*-45 had reported her arrival here by wireless to her station. These North Channel Hun submarines were becoming serious enough in this bottleneck, and *D*-7 manœuvred carefully to make this an excellent target. The British captain was Lieut. O. E. Hallifax, R.N., and he was assisted by two other officers.

He dived in this tideway and fired his stern tube, but when he came to the surface he sighted oil ahead and three Germans swimming in it. *U*-45 had been sunk. The British picked up two out of their new habitat though the third sank. This bottleneck was becoming exceedingly popular, for at 2.55 p.m. *D*-7 tried to torpedo another submarine. Probably she may have been *U*-54 who h. d been working with *U*-45. The nation has not always appreciated the pluckiness which was sometimes performed by vessels of the Auxiliary Patrol under most ordinary circumstances. However lightly we may consider the live mine, it is still a globe of explosives ready for dealing out death. One day in the middle of September 1917 some Holyhead trawlers were sweeping when they caught sight of a drifting mine.

It was blowing a fresh breeze with a choppy sea and a considerable swell. Unsuccessful attempts were made to sink it by gunfire. There was every possibility of this mine being lost in darkness, when Lieut. McNabb, the C.O. of *M.L.*201, lowered a boat, pulled to the mine, then jumping overboard passed a line through the lifting eyes, thus enabling the M.L. to tow this danger into smooth water where it was sunk by rifle fire. Having regard to the sea, this was considered a very fine piece of pluck.

The submarine *UB*-63 had left Germany for the British Isles on September 4 whilst on her maiden voyage, and her captain (named von Gebeschus) first sank the S.S. *Santaren* about 40 miles N.E. of Muckle Flugga. This steamer had left Lerwick at 5 p.m. on September 14 in convoy with six other ships, but at 6.30 a.m. the next day the destroyer escort had left this convoy and presently *UB*-63 isolated the *Santaren*, taking the Master and Chief Officer prisoners. The former was Captain Chapman and he soon found himself in conversation with his captor. It was during the second day on board that Chapman turning to von Gebeschus asked him bluntly:

"Well, and will you get back home safely?"

"Why not?" wondered his enemy in great surprise.

Chapman understood the German's nature and knew how to work on a Hun's fears. For there were too many things happening to leave the fellow ignorant.

"Well," repeated the British skipper, "for goodness' sake keep clear of our destroyers. They have terrific depth-charges."

". . . terrific depth-charges," Gebeschus, kept repeating to himself but not quite understanding; then called his second-in-command, Leutnant Drier, to interpret.

"Oh," came the next exclamation. "We don't care for your destroyers or depth-charges."

That was a barefaced lie, but Chapman well enough understood the deceit and pretended to sympathize. "No," he affirmed, "you are quite right. Depth-charges were no good up to last May. But now look out. They have a new explosive four times as powerful as the old ones."

"Who told you that?" asked Gebeschus and Drier, both speaking at once.

"Nobody: it's common talk."

But this idiom puzzled Gebeschus quite a lot until Drier explained. Then the former guffawed and gave a weak laugh, so that Chapman saw that the remark had hit home.

"Anyhow," ended the captive, "whatever you do, keep clear, because it does not matter whether they come over us or not: if it explodes a certain distance from us, the whole side of the submarine goes in."

A few days later when the submarine came up alongside a convoy, the Hun dived immediately, swearing the destroyers were on top of him. And the same thing happened on a subsequent night when he met a convoy bound the opposite way.

Pass over a while. *UB*-63 had duly gone back to Germany where he handed over his seafaring prisoners and on January 28, 1918, was again in Scottish waters. He could not forget Chapman's warning, ". . . terrific depth-charges. . . . Look out."

Two of the Granton Q-ship trawlers, *W. S. Bailey* and *Fort George*, were today about 14 miles East of May Island listening on their hydrophones when they heard a submarine some distance off. After fifteen minutes these sounds were heard in the direction of May Island much more plainly. That happened at 7.30 p.m. but at 9.10 p.m. the *W. S. Bailey* steamed in the ascertained direction, dropped a depth-charge and, still hearing the enemy, let go a second charge. The trawler next went full speed astern to take the way off, and then were sighted two periscopes 20 yards away. A third depth-charge was dropped over the spot where these periscopes had disappeared. Nothing further was heard on the hydrophone but a fourth depth-charge was released and the position buoyed.

For several days these trawlers remained in the vicinity, and it was finally established that it was the incredulous *UB*-63 had thus been destroyed. The *W. S. Bailey* had swept over the spot with a chain sweep, which kept bringing up in the same spot, and oil was seen also. So von Gebeschus had been wiped out of existence in the Firth of Forth despite his being warned.

Around the British Isles few localities, with their gales of wind and tumultuous seas, are so persistently merciless to shipping as that part of West Scotland between the Outer Hebrides and the Mull of Kintyre. Unimpeded for 2000 miles, the wild Atlantic comes rolling in with full force till it spends its fury against cape or island; making moderate-sized vessels dance to a lively measure and causing even great liners to perform strange capers.

It was on the twenty-fifth of September, 1917, that H.M. Tug *Flying Falcon* together with H.M. Tug *Milewater* raised steam and set out from Lough Swilly with sealed orders to be opened when abreast of Fanad Head, where they arrived at 9.30 a.m. The *Flying Falcon's* Master now learned that they were to proceed as far out into the ocean as Lat. 57 N., Long. 11.20 W., a position considerably west of the Outer Hebrides. His instructions told him to meet an eastbound convoy, which was coming along at eight knots escorted by H.M. Sloop *Primrose*. The rendezvous should be reached on the 26th by 7 a.m.

Now, almost from the first, these tugs—magnificent bad-weather craft as they certainly were—wallowed into an atrocious equinoctial which tested men, hulls and machinery to the limit. The south-west wind kicked up an ugly cross sea, *Flying Falcon* was being hurled about like a toy model, and the crew could hardly stand on their feet: night seemed to bring worse waves than ever. And when a man went to ascertain the distance run by log, this instrument was found to have carried away.

Still the little steamers plugged on bravely; they fell in with the convoy at 9 a.m. and were ordered to take station in the rear: *Milewater* to the north, and *Flying Falcon* to the south. So they proceeded until one of the convoy, the S.S. *Antillian*, about 5 p.m. broke down. Even she could not endure without injury this incessant battering, so, whilst the other units carried on, *Flying Falcon* stood by till *Antillian's* steering gear could be repaired, when they again got under way.

The gale showed no sign of easing during the dark hours: definitely the heavy waves were growing worse all the time. At midnight the tug gained the southern extremity of the Outer Hebrides, picked up the Barra Head Light and set a course for the Oversay Light on the island of Islay, this direction bringing wind and sea on her starboard beam, so that she now laboured very badly.

Tides round that island run strongly, and within the Sound attain to six knots. There exists at Port Ellen the one and only harbour, yet at all times it is an uncomfortable anchorage, but in a gale of wind no sort of place to rest without anxiety. *Flying Falcon* in any event would be safer at sea.

Just when she came abreast Oversay Lighthouse, Nature lost all restraint, sent a tremendous wave which broke aboard, turned the tug into a half-tide rock, swept away the top of the companion, poured tons of water down below, threw her on to her beam ends, and left her balancing between life and death. The end of things could not now be far off.

She sent out wireless calls for assistance, yet only the slenderest hope of survival remained. Should a ship come to her aid, what chance of being rescued from amid the storm? She bleated again, yet once more, and then it looked as if the untamed forces were laughing human sailors to scorn; for another towering sea broke over the tug and brought in its train much worse damage.

Everybody will have noticed in the stern of a tug a wide wooden grating whereon she coils her thick rope hawser, which is no light weight. This time the deluge smashed the strong grating, washed overboard the hawser as though it were a piece of string. The engines were still revolving, firemen and engineers hanging on like insects, but all of a sudden the machinery stopped. Stopped dead. Hawser had fouled propeller, jammed itself tight, and *Flying Falcon* possessed about one chance in two million.

There she lay in the Atlantic trough, utterly helpless, bullied to immobility. Men looked at each other with that silence which is more powerful than any words. Doomed! Nothing could extricate them from this crisis. The only thing which could happen now would be that she would roll right over, and this began to look more certain every time the ocean swell smote her side.

From bad to worse!

One terrible roll brought about the climax when the coal in her bunkers shot to leeward, and there she lay determined not to right herself. With two of her furnaces put out by the water, propeller not working, ship hove right down, how could the most heroic of mortals brought up to seafaring contend any longer? Convinced that the *Flying Falcon* was sinking, her Master ordered the port boat to be launched. The shore was not far away, so perhaps they might yet cheat death.

No easy matter in present conditions putting a boat over the side before it smashed itself to pieces against the steel hull; but they succeeded, and in jumped the six hands together with their Skipper. Instantly surged another of those lofty seas, filled the boat, washed it away, and swept the seven people into the angry Atlantic. Miraculously three of them and the Master managed to get back aboard their vessel, but three were carried away and drowned. A piteous tragedy for their shipmates to behold.

Meanwhile the tug was drifting before the gale like a child's balloon. The land began rushing towards them. One danger after another. Yet where life holds out, hope is never dead. Master of his ship, captain of his fate, *Flying Falcon's* Skipper did not yield to fear. Calling for volunteers, he asked his men to go below, trim the coal, and try getting her back on to an even keel.

Work? They toiled as supermen, stuck to it for a frantic hour, actually succeeded in reducing the heavy list and restored her if not to an upright condition, at least to a less serious inclination. Wonder of wonders, those gallant patient engineers persuaded their machinery to move. Altogether the tug's crowd deserved the highest awards, or at least complete success for their endeavours.

Alas! That was not to be. By the time they had achieved so much, the tug had drifted dangerously near the shore. What then? Let go both anchors, and with luck these might hold till the gale should blow itself out.

The holding-ground round Islay is notoriously indifferent, and here was a ship jerking at her gear with each scend of the sea, putting an unreasonable strain as she plunged and raised her dripping forefoot. Yet one hour of anxiety passed, and neither anchor dragged. Two hours, and still she was holding pluckily.

Then the final climax of all, and the drama ended quickly.

It was not the anchors which yielded, but the cables which snapped. Nothing more could now be done. All human efforts had failed. The

Flying Falcon sped off on her own, but—this was the most remarkable occurrence of all—in her flight shorewards she chose a sandy patch and there decided to remain. Captain and crew at last found safety by means of the rocket apparatus.

Pass over some months, and we come back to this Atlantic scene, though a little further south-westward and to the north of Ireland. On July 19, 1918, there was bound homeward the mammoth S.S. *Justicia*, 32,234 tons, which at the beginning of that war was being built for the Holland-Amerika Line as the *Statendam*. However, she never was employed on the Rotterdam-New York run, for the Anchor Line took her over and she became selected as a British troopship. Well conscious of her great monetary value, as of her immense utility for fetching soldiers from America, she was being attended by no less than a dozen escorts.

Germany, already extremely jealous of the way reinforcements from Canada and the United States were coming over, determined to make every effort to torpedo troop-carriers; wherefore she sent a number of submarines to lie in these North Atlantic approaches, especially just now between Tory Island and that lonely rock Skerryvore (south-east of Barra Head) where a lighthouse erected by Robert Louis Stevenson's kinsman makes a good navigational mark for liners to or from the Clyde or Mersey.

At 1.50 p.m. *Justicia* with her conspicuous top-hamper and three funnels was some 20 miles W. by N. of Skerryvore when *UB*-64 sighted her, sent in a torpedo which hit on the port side just abaft the bridge. Turning over the pages of his recognition book, Ober-Leutnant von Schrader could not find who she was; for, being a new ship, her name did not appear. He assumed her to be the ex-German *Vaterland*, which at the outbreak of hostilities had remained in New York till America took her over on joining the Allies and used her as troopship.

UB-64 was both lucky and determined. At 2.33 p.m. the escorts released so many depth-charges that von Schrader counted thirty-five, but less than an hour later, seeing the injured liner was stopped and blowing off much steam, made ready for another attack. That he accomplished by 4.15 p.m., sending two torpedoes from a distance of 2000 yards, but his presence was rewarded by 23 more explosives which shook him considerably. Unfortunately, he had kept outside the fatal zone. Biding his time, he crept within half the previous range and at 7.48 p.m., whilst tugs were trying to salve the steamer, *UB*-64 fired a fourth silver 'fish' which again holed her port side.

No mercantile steamer has ever been built which could endure that amount of punishment, and he must have marvelled that now low in the water and with a serious list the *Justicia* still remained afloat. Whilst tugs were doing their very utmost to save the costly ship, von Schrader hid himself below surface that night, rose to sea-level next day at 6.40 a.m., and then realized the price of victory. Looking astern, he became unpleasantly aware that all was not well with his submarine. *UB*-64 was leaving behind a broad and tell-tale track of oil. Those depth-charges had badly damaged his fuel tanks.

Still, he did not depart for some time but kept away from any more nerve-disturbing 'water-bombs'. At 9.10 a.m. of July 20, awaiting developments, he was startled to observe a couple of torpedoes making for the maimed liner. Then he counted another 35 detonations.

What had happened this time?

The explanation is a story in itself. A fortnight previously, at 1.30 p.m., Ober-Leutnant Wutsdorff in *UB*-124 had set out from Heligoland on her maiden voyage, escorted by one destroyer, six mine-sweeping trawlers, and one auxiliary cruiser. Wutsdorff had not got very far when the British-laid mines frightened him. Still less did he like the sight of British destroyers outside, so he decided to give that exit a miss, returned to Heligoland, next day came out again, put into the Elbe, entered the locks at Brunsbüttel and passed through the Kiel Canal.

Giving the Skaw a good berth, and crossing the North Sea, he made the land at Peterhead, whence via Muckle Flugga and St. Kilda he reached the north-west Irish coast in the forenoon of July 18. The next day was spent cruising about in search of victims, until at 4.30 a.m. of the 20th he sighted a large vessel some five miles away to the north. This officer likewise mistook her for the *Vaterland*, but on getting nearer descried the tugs which were towing her at four knots.

Wutsdorff perceived that as she slowly moved southward, *Justicia* had the protection of 17 destroyers. To attack the liner therefore seemed too difficult. Yet he waited nearly five hours to get in position, manœuvred beneath the destroyer cordon, and at 9.10 a.m., from a distance of 658 yards, torpedoed the troopship twice. Those were the missiles which the damaged *UB*-64 witnessed coming apparently from nowhere, but if you would understand how inefficient and stupid German submarine personnel could be, please read on.

Wutsdorff now gave orders to dive, though his second-in-command —Leutnant G. Seevers—and the crew generally were anything except a smart lot. One might even say that during peace-time they would be a danger to themselves. By sheer carelessness they forgot to compensate for the weight of two torpedoes just fired from for'ard; so that instead of doing a quick submergence, *UB*-124 lost trim, her bows broke surface and she advertised her presence in the most ridiculous manner.

To counteract this, the sailors were sent hurriedly into the bows, and regulator tanks ordered to be flooded, but such a combination caused the boat to take an excessively sharp angle and down she went into an involuntary dive. Actually she descended to 130 feet, and then above and around began the deluge of bursting depth-charges, which shook everybody both literally and metaphorically. Seevers was so agitated that he lost his head and clean forgot to stop flooding the regulator tanks. Not a very bright thing for a submarine officer!

And the consequence?

UB-124 continued to sink down and down like a stone—150 feet, 200, 250—there was no holding her . . . 275 . . . plop! At 282 feet her descent ended. She could go no further, because at that depth she hit the sea-bed five minutes after the torpedoing.

Then Wutsdorff found himself in a serious dilemma. He wanted to rise, his submarine was being jeopardized, the external pressure would soon prove intolerable; but above him he heard the thrashing of destroyers' propellers, then another bomb burst followed by plenty of others.

His men counted at least 50 between 9.30 and 11 a.m., so the German captain chose that of the two evils it were better to remain on the ground till things became quieter.

Meanwhile at 12.15 p.m. *Justicia*, unable to sustain her wounds any longer, finally sank. It was a considerable testimony to British shipbuilding that she could have kept afloat all these hours. Only one thing was lacking in this drama: her immense weight in its downward flight should have collided with *UB*-124 and crushed the enemy flat.

Shortly before 5 p.m. Wutsdorff decided it was time to rise. The atmosphere, after 34 human beings had been consuming air for most of eight hours, was already pretty foul. And doubtless those cursed English would have relinquished their hunting, gone home, left the sea now clear?

Commanding all tanks to be blown, his depth-gauge indicated she was coming up but he soon appreciated that something was very wrong. The boat lost trim, her bows broke surface but her stern was 50 degrees down. Either the depth-charges, the excessive pressure at 282 feet, or both influences, had caused her to leak, and now terrible fate took charge. Acid ran out of the batteries, bilge water entered the battery wells, so that chlorine gas now mingled with the canned air. It would be absolutely essential to get the craft to sea-level, open up conning-tower, and let the breeze enter.

Wutsdorff, like so many of his countrymen before and since, failed to understand our British character. The destroyers had not forsaken the area, though *Justicia* was no more. Altogether some 40 patrol vessels of one sort or another remained in the district. It was 4.55 p.m. when the three fast destroyers *Milbrook*, *Marne* and *Pigeon* caught a glimpse of *UB*-124 and ten minutes later Wutsdorff likewise espied these foes so unwillingly sought refuge below water, whereupon *Marne* let go two depth-charges and *Milbrook* dropped one. No results were observed and, the trio having now exhausted all their 'wasser-boms', resolved to quit the area for a time, but left behind H.M. Submarine *E*-38 to keep a good look-out. Of her the Germans were completely unaware.

Actually, however, this final unloading of the destroyers' explosives created such an effect that Wutsdorff no longer could remain submerged, even had the atmosphere within been less vitiated. At 5.23, using both Diesel engines, working up to 13 knots, he sought escape on the surface when the three vigilant destroyers again sighted him. They in the meantime had noticed a periscope (of either *UB*-64 or *U*-54) which they chased, but, having returned, now switched their concentration on the escaping *UB*-124. Opening fire, advancing like express trains, they quickly got the range and gave the enemy 'hell'.

It has never been established which projectile did the first damage, but either the second round from *Pigeon* or the third from *Milbrook* did the job, both shells being fired simultaneously, and with *Marne's* twelfth round the submarine's bows uprose vertically from the water and she sank stern first. Wutsdorff with his crew after the first hit took to the water, leaving the unfortunate Seevers and engineer to sink the ship. They went down with her to death.

Some survivors were picked up by H.M.S. *Marne* and landed at Rathmullen. Next day *U*-54, who had been operating the Skerryvore area, spoke *UB*-64 at 8.45 a.m., learned of *Justicia's* demise, and now it was time for von Schrader to take his leaking craft back to Germany. There would be some thrilling stories to relate concerning those dreaded British depth-charges.

CHAPTER XVI

WAYLAYING THE ENEMY

THE part that Q-ships took in this long story of defeating the submarines was virtually at an end. If it had been a comparatively short period, it was indeed a brilliant epoch, but one of most extraordinary yarns concerns the 1680-tons S.S. *Stonecrop*, alias *Glenfoyle*, which was under Commander M. B. R. Blackwood, R.N. A curious vessel, she was very slow, almost unmanageable in a head sea, and in September 1917 was sent to serve off S.W. Ireland. About this vessel there was for a period some error when it was thought that she espied on the surface *U*-88. That was quite wrong, as we have seen from an earlier chapter in which we learned that *U*-88 with Schwieger, the guilty assassin of the *Lusitania's* passengers, perished on mines off the Danish coast during September 7, 1917: yet no one has yet discovered with absolute certainty which was the enemy *Stonecrop* saw on September 17. They were engaged in a fierce duel, though the submarine is now thought to have been *U*-151 who carried on to the Azores.

These submarines round Ireland rarely worked alone: generally the one could summon a second by wireless, and even a third could be called up from further off still. So it was that on the next day a second *U*-boat arrived (probably *U*-43) and torpedoed this decoy beyond any pretence or make-belief. The British personnel took to rafts and boats. Whilst steering east when about 150 miles S.W. of the Fastnet she had been torpedoed at 12.30 p.m. on September 18, 1917, and at once began to settle by the head. I have before me a statement from one of her officers who remarks that all wireless was cut off at 2.30 p.m., and she was practically standing on her stem; owing to one boat having been smashed by the torpedo's explosion there was accommodation for only 44 men in the boats, whilst the rest (23 in all) had to do their best on rafts. At 6 p.m. the boat set out for Berehaven and at daylight next day the second boat rigged up an oar and a piece of canvas. At dark, however, a heavy sea swept these destitute mariners. It was not till most of a week passed with the deaths of 4 officers and 40 men that this sad story came to an end.

It was strange that these separate incidents of the U-boat campaign occasionally recurred in connection with aviation. For near the Sunk Lightship *UC*-72 was bombed and sunk by our seaplanes on September 22, 1917. Four days later Ober-Leutnant E. A. Arnold in *UC*-33, was destined to repeat some of the ill-luck which had brought both *UC*-44 and *UC*-42, to tragic ends off the south of Ireland. *UC*-33, which had been sent to lay mines from Brownstone within three nautical miles of the land and within a radius of $1\frac{1}{2}$ miles from Coninbeg Lighthouse, to bar the entrance to Waterford, came to a hurried finish when she was sunk by gunfire and the ramming by H.M.S. *PC*-61. Waterford approaches seem to have given the enemy something to remember whilst alive, but the incident was one of those short, sharp disasters.

It happened at 5.57 a.m. on September 26 in thick, misty weather that *PC*-61 sighted *UC*-33 on the starboard beam about half a mile away. There was a moderate sea and *PC*-61 at the time was escorting the S.S. *Zan Zeferino* which had been torpedoed. Now *PC*-61, with her low-lying hull, inconspicuous funnel and stern, but with bows resembling a razor's edge, was commanded by Lieut.-Commander F. H. Worsley, R.D., R.N.R., and with him as second-in-command was Lieut. J. R. Stenhouse, R.N.R. These two officers were born to adventure, and both had earned fame under Sir Ernest Shackleton in the Antarctic. Stenhouse was in command of the *Aurora* during the expedition of 1914–15 and later served in the Q-ship *Penshurst* under Commander Grenfell, of whose victories against U-boats we have already spoken. Worsley made a reputation for having endured with Shackleton the most terrible boat voyage in the world. To me he always seemed to have been born in the wrong century. Hearty, brave, blunt and resourceful to the utmost limits, perhaps somewhat unconventional yet a first-class sailor; Worsley had a genius for finding himself in tight corners and it was nothing extraordinary for him to find himself wrecked in some sailing ship and compelled to clamber ashore from the end of an overhanging jib-boom. I don't think he was everyman's friend, and the world could not contain his zeal indefinitely. He passed out of this world early in the year 1943. Stenhouse also went out of this life about the same time in 1943. For sinking *UC*-33 Worsley was given a D.S.O. and Stenhouse a D.S.C. One might say, concerning each, that these neo-Elizabethans were the saltiest sailors of our day.

Certainly it is surprising to note how incident succeeded episode. *UC*-21 was commanded by an officer with the Italian name of Zerboni de Sposetti, and on September 27 was no less rash than some of these young captains. When in Lat. 51.30 N., Long. 1.34 E., he was stupid enough to allow his boat to be trapped in the North Foreland mine-nets, and the body of her watch-keeping officer was afterwards washed up on the Dutch coast but minus a head. The second loss of a submarine due to our aerial activity occurred on September 28 when *UC*-6 permitted herself to become a victim near the Sunk Lightship to the bombs of a seaplane. It was exactly the same disaster as happened to *UC*-72 in the same locality.

However long the war continued around the British Islands and the submarine tried to do his tricks, you might be pretty sure that when there were destroyers around, armed with guns and depth-charges, and able to whack up to high speed, you could be sure that the submarine was severely handicapped, except perhaps at night or during thick weather. Let us see how co-operation of different craft could bring about success. At 7.30 on the morning of September 29, 1917, the minesweeping trawler *Moravia* reported that she had sighted a submarine about four miles east of Monsa (Scotland) running along the surface at full speed. Thereupon the two destroyers *Sylvia* and *Arab* were despatched to hunt the enemy. At noon the *Moravia* reported having swept up a moored mine three miles S.W. of the lighthouse. Two hours later the trawler again reported the submarine stationary, and the *Sylvia* also made the same report, but within 15 minutes she further announced having sunk the submarine six miles east of Bard Head.

Now it has been established that the enemy on this occasion was *UC*-55. She had left Germany with orders to mine the entrances to Kirkwall and Lerwick; these mines being laid in equal numbers and at irregular distances but not more than five miles from the shore. It was with great joy that the patrols learned that *UC*-55 had been wiped out, for during 1917 the Orkneys and Shetlands were believed to have been mined by this boat.

These mining operations had been largely directed against the Scandinavian Convoys. It was indeed significant that though these explosives had been here found in all the months from January to September inclusive, such activities suddenly stopped and were not begun afresh until November and December. The key to the whole affair is that when *UC*-55 was first seen by the *Moravia* she was caught in the very act of laying her 'eggs'. Germany then sent a successor to this submarine, since the attacks on neutral shipping meant assaults against our trade.

Perhaps the reader may be interested to have a few details of *UC*-55's sinking in the Shetlands. It was the second shot from H.M.S. *Sylvia's* 12-pounder that killed Ober-Leutnant zur See Ruhle von Lilienstern, the commanding officer, and disabled the submarine's steering-gear. Another hit was made, and she began to sink. Two depth-charges were dropped alongside *UC*-55, and blew her up. Another vessel also arrived, hitting with two shots and letting go another depth-charge. The *Moravia* claimed to have hit the enemy by gunfire. There was no question about the Hun having been finally destroyed, and some of her crew leapt into the water; but 17 officers and men were taken prisoners though 10 officers and men were killed.

But how was it that *Moravia* surprised the submarine into making a blunder? The answer is that *UC*-55 had lost trim whilst minelaying and began to sink nose first. She actually went down to 165 feet and the hull plating could not sustain pressure at this depth. The sea water rushed in forming chlorine gas, a battery caught fire, and she had to come again to the surface for recharging her air-bottles. It was then that the vessels chased heartily to her undoing.

The German submarines failed to obtain from their attacks on our convoys the considerable success which they had expected. Even some of real star-turn U-boat captains which had distinguished themselves in the Mediterranean were fetched back to Northern Europe but were quite terrified when they found themselves amidst a convoy threatened every moment by steamers' sharp stems. Indeed I can compare this situation only to that of a puppy dog who gets mixed up with traffic and horses' hoofs when Piccadilly Circus is at its busiest. By October 1917 the submarines were operating in the Atlantic, Bay of Biscay, off the south coast of Ireland, English Channel, N.W. coast of Africa; but laying mines off headlands, and especially in the North Channel, against our convoys.

So well did we acquire information about the routes of the submarines between Flanders and the English Channel that their movements could be watched most of the time, or at least comprehended. Therefore small minefields or nets came into existence for making these passages perilous. Thus by laying down traps backed by able patrols, it was almost certain that the enemy would be caught on more than one occasion. For a period from October 1 to October 11 we carried on combined operations that consisted of destroyers, submarines and net drifters which brought about the destruction of U-50, U-66, and U-106. Of this trio one evidently became destroyed in the mine-nets of the drifter *William Tennant*, which was anchored in Long. 2.31 E. and keeping constant hydrophone watch. At 10.27 a.m. on October 2 the drifter heard the high-pitched sound of a submarine running on electric motors, followed by a heavy underwater explosion close to the nets, shaking the drifter severely. The submarine was never heard again but destroyed.

U-46 had cruised in various waters. Once she attacked H.M.S. *Marlborough*, and there was a different occasion when at Christmas she lay quietly on the sea-bed of the Bay of Biscay and presented gifts to the crew, as well as to prisoners, from the Christmas tree. She left Germany on September 19, 1916, for a cruise in the Arctic, returned north on October 13, 1917, sinking several ships. U-46 perished this late summer (probably on Russian mines) and on October 5 UB-41 was sunk off Scarborough by an explosion. A fortnight later H.M. Submarine E-45 at about 6.20 a.m. in Lat. 52.16, Long. 2.46 E. observed a Dutch merchant vessel being attacked by a German submarine. The date was October 19, 1917, and the enemy partially below the water. The British submarine dived and approached: E-45 fired her stern torpedo but missed. At 7.11 a.m. E-45 fired her bow torpedo, and hit the enemy at 800 yards, sinking her. Some say that this culprit was UC-79 and others that she was numbered UC-62; but that we sank the enemy is beyond doubt.

Enemy submarine activity off the Yorkshire coast by the autumn of 1917 had been going on for some time. It has always been surprising that the Germans displayed so much interest off Scarborough and Flamborough. Surface ships, submarines and minelayers had all at various dates displayed their energy, but off Flamborough Head there was such an excellent landmark that even during the Second German War which began in 1939, both peaceful traffic and German warlike aeroplanes have used these conspicuous cliffs. During October 1917 it was decided to lay a mine-net barrage and the clear result was that UB-75 was lost on December 10, 1917, though on October 3 the minefield which we had laid off Zeebrugge blew up UC-14. Once again the destroyer proved herself the finest antidote for submarines when on October 23 H.M. Destroyer *Melampus* in about Lat. 50.24 N., Long. 0.30 W. by using her paravanes and depth-charges managed to sink UC-16 about two o'clock in the afternoon.

Besides the moral deterioration with which the commanding officers of submarines were undoubtedly being afflicted, there must have been something utterly disappointing at this time in Germany's Submarine Service; for the losses were so marked and so frequent that it looks as if these officers had lost all interest in life: the kind of outlook which says

U-BOAT VICTIMS
Disguised Officers of a Queenstown Q-ship.

A SUBMARINE'S TORPEDO DOES HER DAMNEDEST

"I really don't mind whether we live or whether we die". Gone was that moral ascendancy which in *Fighting the U-Boats* we found so pronounced. Otherwise how can we account for such stupid, really silly victims?

On October 19 *UC-62* was torpedoed and sent to the sandy sea-bed off Lowestoft by H.M. Submarine *E-45*; and *UC-51* off Harwich was similarly dealt with on November 13 by H.M. Destroyer *Firedrake*, but the carelessness in so many of these UC craft entering or leaving the vicinity of Zeebrugge may be explained partly by the wild, excessive orgies which used to mark the habits of the Flanders submarine commanding officers and unfitted them for the austere reception with which we were awaiting them not far from Dover. By sheer negligence *UC-63* omitted to observe H.M. Submarine *E-52* lying to the eastward of the Goodwins. The Flanders craft was homeward bound. Doubtless the German may have been wearied of the sea, longing again for the shore and hard drinking. But the British submarine was so quick on the trigger that she torpedoed *UC-63* on November 1 and *E-52* upset the welcome that was waiting at Bruges. I have also to mention *UC-65* who in February 1917 had sunk H.M. Cruiser *Ariadne* but on November 3 was coming up Channel in a hurry to get back to Flanders when H.M. Submarine *C-15* torpedoed the Hun.

We mentioned just now the strange fact that on November 13 off Harwich H.M. Destroyer *Firedrake* sank the submarine *UC-51*, but the story of *UC-63* deserves further elaborating.

One hears so much of U-boat activity that we forget how efficient was the British Submarine Service whilst 'playing the game' honourably as gentlemen warriors. H.M. Submarine *E-52* had come out of Dover for her patrol at 4.30 p.m. on October 31, and nothing happened until the next morning at 1.12 a.m., when in a dark patch clear of the moon she sighted *UC-63* off the port bow distant 1200 yards. Two minutes later *E-52* was 500 yards away when our submarine fired both torpedoes, which were followed by a big explosion, a great flame, and a column of water 100 feet high. *UC-63* was thus destroyed completely and indubitably, but so vehement was the concussion that it discharged the beam torpedo of *E-52*. Only one man was picked up from the German craft.

Now this survivor was Petty Officer Fritz Marsal who related how *UC-63* had laid mines inside the Isle of Wight, then proceeded to the Bay of Biscay, next operated in the English Channel and had been proceeding through Dover Straits on her way back towards Zeebrugge, passing the barrage submerged at night; but when about 16 miles E. of this barrage, *E-52* had sunk her. It was a clear moonlight night when Marsal as Petty Officer of the Watch was on the bridge with the Officer-of-the-Watch, and one able seaman as lookout. Marsal was detailed to keep a lookout on the starboard side, the officer on the port side, and the able seaman watching astern. The boat was controlled from the control room below and the conning-tower unoccupied. Just about then the engineer had come up on the bridge and in that silence of the night which brings mariners to share their thoughts was exchanging yarns with the officer who in consequence failed to keep a proper lookout just when it was most needed. On such occasions as when running the gauntlet at night and the enemy might congratulate himself

G

that now they were 'nearly through', it was the grossest folly to relax. Marsal chanced to look to port and was astounded as he saw E-52 on the surface. The rest of that story we know, but the affair happened like a flash as the reward for E-52's unceasing vigilance.

Conversely we may note what happened to H.M.S. *Drake*, that armoured cruiser which was being employed frequently in escorting our transatlantic convoys. On October 2 she had just dispersed her incoming convoy and was passing through the North Channel to the southward when an unseen submarine torpedoed her on the starboard side. The *Drake* then proceeded under her own steam, screened by 11 destroyers, and made for Church Bay, but about 3 p.m. capsized and lay on the bottom. The enemy was up to all the tricks, despite vessels of the Larne patrol being on the alert. When H.M. $M.L.$-476 one night at 9 p.m. sighted a fishing vessel, it was afterwards ascertained to be a submarine, three miles S.W. of Corsewall Light (Wigtonshire), disguised and proceeding at 12 knots on the surface, but before the M.L. could fire the enemy had disappeared in the mist and darkness.

So we can really understand how pertinaciously was this North Channel bottleneck being visited by German submarines who lay in wait to catch richly laden vessels approaching home after days of open sea. Further south we were about to lay some 40 feet below the surface those lines of mines in the Dover Straits that eventually were to neutralize the German submarines which had once more tried to rush this narrow defile. Of course it required several months before the narrow stretch of water was, so to speak, 'thick with the weeds of mines' but certainly it was going to be no healthy passage for U-boats. At the same time we employed M.L.s to lay mines athwart the channel between the Galloper and the Outer Gabbard, and this minelaying took place between October 29 and December 4. It is true that U-boats when outward bound had recently been giving up attempting the English Channel, but the detour round the North of Scotland was so seriously delaying a submarine's voyage (already protracted by the British-laid minefields in German waters) that the Dover Straits route became imperative, and this once more gained for the Huns an increased peril by the laying of our sub-surface minefields.

Discontent in the German Navy was not easing and by November 1917 volunteering for the Huns' Submarine Service had become largely abandoned. It had been found in practice that most of the men volunteering for such risky work were attracted by the higher rates of pay. So the general system was now to draft into the Submarine Service men under the age of 32, considered suitable irrespective of their own wishes. U-boats were sent out from their bases as soon as ready, very little leave being granted and the crews made to work hard. The result was that we find so many of these crews 'fed-up' with the life and (as at least well instanced by one submarine lurking in the Larne Area) only too willing to surrender without firing one shot against the patrols provided they could be taken prisoners and save their own lives.

Yes: changes indeed were most assuredly arriving. The Irish Sea, once such a happy hunting ground for U-boats, was now more frequently—though not exclusively—avoided by German submarines because they found themselves surrounded by hostile craft so readily that the Germans found that this way led to danger. U-boats were still fixing their positions by directional wireless stations, but we were keeping the enemy on the alert all the time.

The Flanders submarines never operated north of Flamborough Head and consisted of 35 of the U.B. and U.C. types which used to take refuge under the concrete shelters at Bruges. But was it this security at home that rendered such officers still negligent when towards Flanders directing their course? Could the German commanding officers never get over their conceit and self-satisfaction? Let me quote yet one more act of silly carelessness. Did they seem to imagine that our submarine captains were not out for war?

This time H.M. Submarine *C*-15 when in Lat. 50.28 N., Long 0.17 E. sighted *UC*-65 at 3.12 p.m., dived, and three minutes later fired a double shot at 400 yards. One torpedo hit, but the other passed under. Of course *UC*-65 was sunk. It was yet another instance of the enemy returning home having used up her 5 torpedoes and laid 18 mines. When the British submarine rose to the surface and rescued the captain (Lieut.-Commander Claus Lafrenz) the Englishman was to learn that this was one of the most successful officers of the Flanders Flotilla and the first one that had taken a photograph of a Q-ship. The torpedo of *C*-15 had blown Lafrenz high into the air and he had come down into the water on his chest with plenty of severe bruises, but he was lucky to have escaped death even if his arrival back in Zeebrugge were delayed.

We, too, had our misfortunes. For we lost H.M. Drifter *Deliverer*, probably on November 3, 1917, since on that date she disappeared from Dublin Bay. She had been detailed on November 1 to patrol outside the Bay and on the 3rd her small boat was picked up undamaged one mile from Bailey Light, with cork fender and a couple of oars inside. Inasmuch as a German submarine was sighted near Burford Buoy in Dublin Bay at 6.30 that evening, it was presumed that the submarine had sunk the *Deliverer* in order that the German's presence might not be made known. There was thick fog tonight, so the enemy's 'sink without a trace' had been fairly easy.

CHAPTER XVII

UB-81 GOES TO HER DOOM

ONE thing leads to another. The arrival of our transatlantic convoys via the North of Ireland was one big problem, especially through the North Channel, but the presence and help of American destroyers based on Queenstown rendered the exit from this port another dilemma; and Germany was evidently resolved to foul that exit from Queenstown —however twisty might be the winding approach past the buoys—with some certainty of success. Already we have instanced one U-boat meeting with disaster at this entrance. Now let us examine a second. The villain of the piece was *U*-58 and perhaps she hardly realized her danger.

But it was very real. Let us begin with November 16, 1917.

That afternoon when some two and a half miles S.S.E. of Daunt's Rock Lightship, near the spot where had been welcomed in May the first of the United States destroyers to arrive, H.M. Trawler *James Johnson* about 5.15 heard suspicious sounds on her hydrophone, and next morning (November 17) H.M. Drifter *Sunshine* also listened to these noises quite near, and likewise discerned a small patch of thick oil only just ahead. She dropped a depth-charge and at 10.15 a.m. H.M. Trawler *Sarba* heard unusual sounds on her hydrophone and another small patch of oil was seen. On dropping a further depth-charge, she descried four distinct explosions, and oil continued to rise for a long while.

On November 17 this *U*-58 thought it was about time to manifest herself for the U.S. destroyer *Fanning* was now forming up the convoy and sighted a periscope heading across the *Fanning's* bow distant 400 yards. Presently the periscope disappeared, and *Fanning* dropped a depth-charge slightly ahead of the estimated position of the enemy, the U.S. destroyer *Nicholson* heading for the same spot.

What now happened was that the conning-tower came to the surface, but *Nicholson* also dropped a depth-charge alongside, then turned to port and fired three shots from her stern gun whilst turning. Thereupon up rose the submarine's bow rapidly. She righted herself but was still somewhat down by the head. Three more shots from the *Nicholson's* bow gun, and the Hun crew came running along the submarine's deck, holding up their hands, and surrendered about 4.30 p.m. Less than 20 minutes had elapsed since the submarine had been first seen. It was as quick as that.

A line was got on to the enemy but a couple of the Hun crew disappeared below through the conning-tower and scuttled their craft. She sank at 4.38 p.m., the line was cast off and the German crew swam to the *Fanning*. It was learnt that this was *U*-58 and that *Fanning's* depth-charge had wrecked her motors, her oil-leads and diving gear. Having submerged to 278 feet, she became entirely unmanageable. Certainly she now tried blowing tanks and rising higher, but the *Nicholson* let go another depth-charge.

U-58 had come from Wilhelmshaven via the Dover Straits, sighting the Lizard on the night of the 15th-16th. This was the German captain's first trip in her and she arrived off Queenstown on the late afternoon of the 16th.

Now the 17th happened to be an eventful day. It chanced that between November 5 and 11 we had laid a British minefield off the Start well below the surface, and within a week of its completion *UB*-18 ran herself into its midst, with complete destruction to herself. Thus had we accounted for two Hun submarines in one day. Germany's anger at all these submarine losses and the ease by which England was able to carry on trade with Scandinavia in security by means of Protected Convoys of course considerably irritated our enemies; so on October 17 also she resolved by means of a sharp raid to deal us a nasty blow. The proper kind of weather had been awaited exactly, and the arrangements for this occasion were typically Teutonic. A cold grey North Sea autumnal day.

It was a west-bound convoy, consisting of British, Belgian, Norwegian, Swedish and Danish cargo ships, bound from Scandinavia to Lerwick escorted by H.M.S. *Mary Rose* and *Strongbow*, destroyers, one armed trawler and one armed whaler. Suddenly at 6 a.m. two fast German light cruisers—*Brummer* and *Bremse*—pounced on the scene and H.M.S. *Strongbow* was shelled out of action, then *Mary Rose* was sunk, and having received heavy losses the former also went down. By half past eight a total of nine ships from the convoy, plus both destroyers, had been vanquished on fire. Not a soul was saved from the *Mary Rose*, which in May had accompanied us out from Queenstown to welcome the first American destroyers.

This North Sea incident was just one more German effort to assist the U-boat campaign in compelling the British to take protection against the U-boats from elsewhere. And again on the night of December 11-12 the enemy attempted another North Sea surface raid. Of course it was a serious assault on our food supplies as also on the Scandinavians, who were wanting to fetch home British coal. It became now a competition between ourselves and the enemy as to which of us could afford the best protection. Yet still we went on sinking submarines with such regularity and persistence that one could guess Germany would not last out more than another year. At the western side of the North Sea *UC*-47 was lurking around Flamborough Head, but equally watchful on November 18 was H.M.S. *P*.57 who shortly after 6 a.m. whilst patrolling at 15 knots caught sight of a large submarine on the surface. Speeding up to 17 knots, the P.-boat rammed the rival with a heavy impact, tearing through the hull just forward of the conning-tower, and as the enemy passed astern of the P-boat a depth-charge was dropped and exploded; then two more also whilst large quantities of oil rose as well. After the sweepers had come on the spot, this wreck was duly located in 30 fathoms. It was thus that *UC*-47 passed out; and the confusing fact has to be remembered that somewhere between November 19 and 22 *UC*-57 was definitely destroyed in the Baltic, though exact details are unknown. We had gradually ascertained with certainty that the Zeebrugge submarines ventured across the North Sea by the route: Schouen Bank Buoy, North Hinder Lightship and thence to the South Falls. But for the enemy going down Channel it was a terrible undertaking which would shortly develop. For on November 21 began to be laid by our minelayers in the Folkestone-Gris Nez barrage most of 400 mines of a new type* being adopted today.

Perhaps one of the most pleasing (to us) incidents of the last war took place on November 24, 1917, but it really begins on November 21 when *U*-48 left Wilhelmshaven bound for the Irish coast via the Dover Straits. This story is one more illustration of the bad pilotage and seamanship that gradually deteriorated Germany's personnel. Had she already used up most of the better-grade material; or was carelessness becoming marked beyond all belief?

On the afternoon of the 23rd, 60 miles east of Dover, *U*-48 began her mournful adventures when she was concealing herself below water so as to sit on the bottom till nightfall. She would resume her passage through the Dover Straits, but one of our aeroplanes exploded a bomb too near for her pleasure; and about 7.30 that night *U*-48 was motoring along the surface heading for the Straits when apparently Buch (her commanding officer) lost his navigational way, and being too far west fouled the old net barrage near the North Goodwins. Portions

---
*See Admiral Bacon's *Dover Patrol*, pp. 70 and 401.

still were festooned along the propellers, her oil engines began to give trouble, and even on the surface she was compelled to use her electric motors. It was an anxious night. But at 3 a.m. *U*-48 gave a sudden bump and brought up all standing at the N.W. corner of the Goodwins. Had she then made no allowance for the hot tide which carried her on?

Not a delightful situation this dark November night, terribly near the Ramsgate base and *U*-48 making herself a bed in the sands which have swallowed so many vessels up in the past centuries. Although Buch tried lightening her by discharging 60 tons of oil-fuel, his drinking water, three of his torpedoes, and much of his ammunition, trying also to ease her off by working his engines, *U*-48 still would not—could not—rise from that bed which she had dug for herself. To make matters worse, tide was ebbing.

But when 6.30 a.m. came round again and the two drifters *Majesty* with *Paramount* were sweeping the War Channel at twilight just before daybreak about 1½ miles N.E. of the Gull Lightship, the submarine had become sighted. She was fired on by one of our trawlers, by the drifters, and H.M. Destroyer *Gipsy*. Like a pack of hounds these little ships leapt after *U*-48. Suddenly they concentrated their fire. H.M. Drifter *Feasible* got so near the sands that she kept a couple of hands working the lead. Blazing away with their 6-pounders, 3-pounders, and the rat-tap of the Maxims to which the German replied with her 4.1-inch shells, the fight was eagerly brightening up and the *Gipsy's* 12-pounder was helping matters.

German shells were falling all round the drifters. But the submarine received 13 hits, and after 15 minutes was seen to be on fire forward. The Hun crew leapt overboard, the submarine blew up and there were rescued merely one officer and 21 men of the 43. It was a fine little show in which these fishermen cared nothing except to fire their guns. Wind and sea were rising, but the engineers off watch were keenly handing up ammunition and with this united zeal the small craft won £1000 presented by the Admiralty but likewise robbed the proud Germany of that big *U*-48 213 feet long.

Who would have expected that a handful of wooden fishing craft could make the Huns' Navy so ridiculous? And did the Germans forget this incident after 22 years?

If you should chance to have by you a copy of the *Daily Telegraph* for October 27, 1939, and glance at the first page, you will find the headlines read as if they were applicable to the above incident:

U-BOAT LOST ON GOODWINS
Midnight Admiralty Announcement

> The shattered wreck of a German U-boat was found yesterday on the Goodwin Sands. Our Deal correspondent stated that boatmen . . . could see the greater part of the conning-tower sticking out of the water.

Thus in the second month of this second German war did the enemy once more 'display his foolishness'.

We had not to wait long for another German submarine disaster, for on November 29, 1917, *UB*-61 foundered on a British minefield which had been laid that year. And it was indicative of German submarines

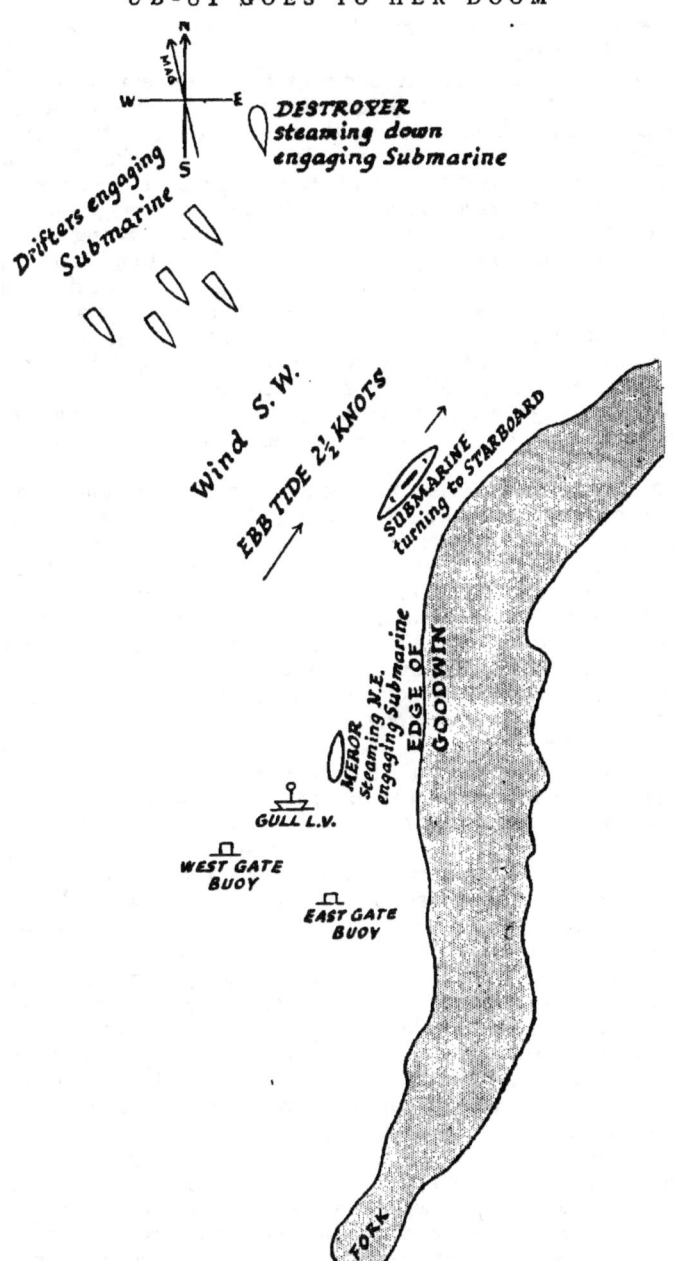

HOW WE SHELLED AND SANK U-48 ON NOVEMBER 24, 1917
An incident off the Goodwins that afterwards reminded us of the present war.

that in the period October 1–December 31, 1917, we had undertaken 200 encounters with them.

Notwithstanding the risks to our convoys, these revived formations were still proving themselves a decided success. In the last eight months of the year there had been no fewer than 98 North Atlantic Homeward Convoys, or a total of 1593 ships; whilst in the Scandinavian Convoy 6155 merchant ships had crossed with the loss of only 1·20 per cent.

It is interesting to trace the careers of some men through one adventure after another. Late in 1917, for instance, *UB*-53 set out from Kiel for the Adriatic and among her crew was one Erich Reich (boatswain's mate), who had served first in the raider *Emden* and afterwards got away in the sailing vessel *Ayesha*. *UB*-53 operated principally athwart the trade route converging on Port Said and Alexandria, but when *UB*-53 whilst submerged fouled the mine-nets of Otranto Fixed Barrage, two of these mines exploded violently on the starboard side aft and whilst she went down to 131 feet doing $3\frac{1}{4}$ knots, she was found to have been so badly damaged that she had to rise to the surface and be abandoned by her crew of 35.

The converted submarines of which we spoke just now (generally lumped together as representing the Cruiser class), numbered *U*-151–157, were not regarded by the Germans as successes. With a clean bottom these craft could do only 9 knots on the surface and little better than half that when submerged. It was a joke in Germany that any old 10-knots steamer could escape them, and the results of their cruises were held up to scorn. When Captain Gordon Campbell had his memorable duel in the Bay of Biscay against *UC*-71 on the occasion of his last tussle in a Q-ship, his opponent (Salzwedel) on that day—a clever submarine captain and very tough—was about to take command of *UB*-81. A memorable occasion, for on this, his first and only cruise in her after completing trials at Kiel, he proceeded down the coast to Zeebrugge and left there on November 28 via the Dover barrage, but on December 2 was operating on the surface between the Owers Lightship and Dunnose until 4.30 p.m., when he hit a small mine. Probably this accident was caused by her cable having fouled some mine moorings; for while weighing anchor at six o'clock that morning, the cable parted and 164 feet of it was lost or at least a certain amount of it was in tow; for the boat henceforth steered very badly.

Now when *UB*-81 was at 83 feet near Dunnose, a dull explosion was heard aft for she evidently fouled with this cable the small mine $10\frac{1}{2}$ miles S.E. of Dunnose. Trouble began quickly and two of the crew came running forward with the report that water was entering the stern compartment. Although watertight doors were then closed, the force of the explosion had started a number of rivets and water burst its way into the second compartment.

It was a cheerful outlook, yet land seemed not so far distant. Then a desperate effort was attempted. Even the duel with the *Dunraven* seemed mere child's play now. The stern was resting on the bottom in 15 fathoms, but from the upper starboard tube was extracted the torpedo, and the sea-cap was opened when it was found that the mouth of the tube was just a foot above the level of the water.

UB-81 was 180 feet long and with her stern on the sea-bed she lay at an angle of about 53 degrees. Three men were rammed through this tube, in fact altogether seven men were thus hauled out, a line having been taken up; but they also fired Very's lights to attract attention from passing vessels. The German crew were planning their suicides: so terrified of life and death were their thoughts. Those three men who with difficulty had been rammed outside now found the December cold so severe that they preferred to die in warmth rather than freeze to death outside. A well-known method of self-murder was to use the oxygen flasks, and as in a kind of *Theatre Guignol* Play the climax was terrible with suspense. Saltzwedel was having a fierce task to keep the men away from the flasks. Death seemed so difficult yet so easy. Discipline was almost gone, and one wonders indeed how many of these Huns were gazing into death, feeling its outstretched chilly fingers and remembered all the deaths of others at which they had assisted.

At the height of this terrific suspense, about an hour after the first man had emerged from the torpedo-tube, suddenly, as in a piece of fiction, the tenseness was relaxed. Rescuing vessels which had been attracted now began to arrive about 10 p.m. H.M.S. *P-32* was the first, but the Hun had become notorious with all his false cries for help that of course the P-boat suspected a trap and for some time circled continuously around.

"Some dirty work here?" she wondered. "You bet the Hun is up to some trick." Perhaps it was an ingenious 'wheeze' to entice a British warship on to mines? But when at last it was deemed advisable, *P-32* came close enough on the weather side to take the Germans on board. Of course it was a risk: the enemy could not be expected to behave decently. Yet still British sailors would save lives if allowed.

Chance forbade such willingness. Wind and wave suddenly combined to disallow such clemency. A little squall drove the P-boat to bump her weight against the submarine and the latter could no longer remain pivoted on her tail but immediately heeled right over. The sea-water torrented through the torpedo-tube, and she sank. The submarine had started out from Germany with a crew of 35, but only 7 were rescued, and the rest died probably very shortly owing to the water entering the tube and causing the emission of poisonous fumes from the batteries. But if Saltzwedel was among the lost, he did plan the method of life-saving and had refused to leave the ship till all his men had left.

Certainly towards the end of this long campaign the Germans were less lucky than hitherto. *UC*-69 operating off Cape Barfleur—a favourite region—was on December 6 accidentally rammed and sunk by *U*-96. It seemed as if so many murders were being avenged: so many incidents being atoned for long after the event. We mentioned that the white cliffs of Flamborough Head for long had attracted submarines into this area, till at last we laid again some of our very efficient minefields about a dozen miles from the Head on December 4, 13 and 16. Our patrols would endeavour to drive the enemy into these mines. Well, on December 10, 1917, the drive was successful and *UB*-75 was destroyed in this manner.

But those Scandinavian Convoys still gave anxiety.

It was on the night of December 11-12, 1917, that the Kaiser's Navy, jealous of the regular Scandinavian Convoys which were bringing over iron ore, sulphur, nitrates, paper pulp, timber, pit props and herrings, intended to 'clean up' these merchant ships; to stop such traffic once and for all by a deadly onslaught.

She therefore selected her 3rd and 4th Half-Flotillas, comprising the nine biggest and fastest destroyers which she owned. As rallying ship, on which they might fall back, she chose also the new light cruiser *Emden*.

On the morning of December 11 these ten units left port and set a course across the North Sea. By 2 p.m. they had reached the north-east end of the Dogger Bank, and here the *Emden* remained waiting whilst the two half-flotillas went about their business.

The 3rd, made up of four craft, sped off northward, but bad weather soon compelled them to ease to 12 knots. Night fell, their position became uncertain, so in the early hours of next day they closed the Norwegian coast at Udsire and obtained a 'fix'. It was intended then to await a convoy that was known through spies to be coming out from Drammen (Christiania).

But the weather seemed no worse, they again carried on north, until four hours later destroyer hulls could not endure the smashing seas. Speed must be reduced to nine knots, which for such fast craft meant a mere crawl. Turning round and heading south, they hoped for better conditions since the atmosphere was surprisingly clear, considering the month and locality. Half an hour later a streak of smoke sent German hearts beating with happiness and German crews to action stations. Dipping to the swell was an east-bound Scandinavian Convoy.

Six British, Danish, Norwegian and Swedish merchantmen, escorted by four armed trawlers—*Commander Fullerton, Livingstone, Tokio* and *Lord Alverstone*, together with the two destroyers *Pellew* and *Partridge*.

Mutual recognition occurred when seven miles off, and the fight began without delay when the foremost German opened fire and hit *Livingstone* in the vital engine-room. The two British destroyers steered at full speed towards the enemy in an endeavour to do battle whilst the slower trawlers and convoy might get away to the southward. But whilst *Pellew* and *Partridge* with no little gallantry were contending with three big destroyers, the fourth German proceeded to sink the whole convoy, the *Lord Alverstone, Commander Fullerton* and *Tokio*.

Meanwhile the *Partridge* had been disabled by a shell in her main steam-pipe but used her torpedoes in a vain attempt to conquer. One of these actually struck an enemy though unfortunately did not explode.

The nett result of this sad day was that *Partridge* also sank and nothing of convoy or escort kept afloat excepting the *Pellew*, which escaped in a squall of rain. The Germans took prisoners 4 officers and 48 men, besides 23 civilians of the convoy. A little later that day British ships picked up some more of the trawlers' survivors.

Now the 4th Half-Flotilla consisted of five destroyers which, after leaving *Emden*, headed for our north-east coast, expecting to trap another convoy. Their only success, however, before rejoining *Emden* was to wipe out one Danish steamer, one British trawler, and attack a Swede.

What followed?

By the employment of supporting cruisers and battleships, as everybody became aware, these raids ended at a sudden stop. German destroyer flotillas dared not risk themselves. So the winter passed, until finally in April (1918) a most ambitious scheme for wiping out the Scandinavian Convoy by using every sort and kind of surface vessel was launched.

Picture, then, a powerful expedition putting to sea on the 24th under Admiral von Hipper. There were battle cruisers, light cruisers, and destroyers who would do the raiding, but if pressed they were to fall back on Admiral Scheer having with him no fewer than three squadrons of battleships, a division of light cruisers, plus four flotillas of destroyers. In fact, practically the entire High Sea Fleet was out. Scheer had even posted his U-boats off the Scottish coast who were to wireless movements of all British shipping.

Looking back on this date, we see how untrue is the careless but oft-repeated statement that the German High Sea Fleet never again came forth after Jutland.

In truth, this April day only just failed to become one of the most historic occasions among naval records. The big 'Battle of the North Sea', that the world had been awaiting, seemed imminent.

Yet everything turned out exactly as unsuspected, and there resulted a fiasco as complete as it was ludicrous. Fiction could not invent such a strange chain of cause and effect.

Hipper's battle cruisers had reached a spot some 40 miles W.S.W. of Stavanger, when quite unexpectedly the 23,000-tons *Moltke* developed an extraordinary defect. Of her four propellers the inner starboard one dropped off, which in turn caused the turbines to race and created havoc. Engine-room and boiler-rooms became flooded, owing to the auxiliary condenser having been damaged, and the machinery ceased to work. She was taken in tow by the battleship *Oldenburg*, and the fleet turned round to make for the Heligoland Bight.

Now about this time Kapitanleutnant Spiess, one of Germany's ablest submarine commanders, chanced to be homecoming in *U*-19 when miles away off the Norwegian coast he sighted on the horizon the High Sea Fleet. These grey ships, however, he mistook for our Grand Fleet, so he wirelessed a warning that large British forces were coming along. This signal having been picked up by Hipper created further alarm, and guns' crews momentarily expected further trouble.

Suspense gradually lessened, the western German sandy shores revealed themselves at dawn. Home and harbour could not now be far away, all risk had passed. Thanks to her patient engineers, the *Moltke* could now steam at even 15 knots, so she cast off from *Oldenburg* and went ahead escorted by three destroyers besides a seaplane.

Then another surprising thing happened.

Barely had one hour passed than Lieutenant C. Allen in the British submarine *E*-42 sighted a smudge of smoke to the north-east. Time—6.30 a.m. He dived below surface, went full speed, got into position, watched through his periscope as the great *Moltke* with her destroyer screen approached.

At the long range of 2500 yards, Allen fired his starboard bow torpedo-tube, waited some seconds . . . then listened to the distant explosion. The missile had hit its target, making a gaping hole in *Moltke's* side through which poured the chilly sea.

Immediately *E-42* herself became in jeopardy, for those three destroyers had taken notice. Hither and thither they dashed, exploding five depth-charges and a score of hand-bombs, transforming the water into volcanoes.

Yet Allen managed to avoid all these attentions and brought his boat across to Harwich.

Still more remarkable was *Moltke's* fate. This 27-knotter, sister to the famous *Goeben* of Dardanelles fame, always flourished with adventures. Early that war she had assisted in the bombardment of Hartlepool, and then scurried home ere Jellicoe's ships could catch her.

Then in the following August she happened to be up the Baltic in Russian waters. The British submarine *E-1* was there also, and fired a torpedo which holed *Moltke* for'ard, killing eight men and admitting 450 tons of sea. Wonderful to relate, she kept afloat, made for Germany at 15 knots and then entered dry dock for repairs.

So, too, during this April of 1918, she simply refused to founder. Though Allen's torpedo had penetrated aft, and she drooped by the stern, yet slowly she limped into the River Jade's security for one more refit. Her numerous sub-divisional watertight compartments had saved *Moltke* once more.

But no more interference was contemplated by surface vessels against our convoys. When the High Sea Fleet again raised steam to come out, it was after Armistice when they steered for the Firth of Forth and surrendered to the Grand Fleet.

CHAPTER XVIII

OUT OF THE DEPTHS

WE have already related the story of how *UB-75* met her doom. But let us not mix up this yarn with the episode of that other submarine, *U-75*.

I would ask you to call to mind that on May 29, 1916, *U-75* had been ordered to lay mines against the exits thought to be used by the Grand Fleet. She did so off the Brough of Birsay.

Meanwhile the Battle of Jutland had just been fought and H.M. Cruiser *Hampshire* after Lord Kitchener had lunched with Admiral Jellicoe aboard his flagship at Scapa Flow received the distinguished soldier bound for Archangel. Instead of departing (as had been expected) east about, the gale of wind made it advisable for her to seek some lee via the west side. The result was that the *Hampshire* went straight on to these mines with the deaths of Kitchener and others. To the Navy, the Army, and the British nation generally, this activity left a heavy gloom. Just before the following year closed, H.M. Motor Launch 357 was—on December 12, 1917—in about Lat. 49.35 N., Long. 5.39 W. screening a convoy of the French coal trade whilst proceeding along the south Cornish coast. At 7.30 p.m. after passing through a small bank of fog, the M.L. sighted a submarine immediately ahead but submerging. This motor launch (which was commanded by Lieutenant

J. F. B. Kitson, R.N.V.R.) at once went full speed, attacking with gun and depth-charge, but only the conning-tower was visible. Travelling at 18 knots, the M.L. rammed the submarine violently, thus stopping the M.L.'s engines.

The submarine dived steeply, one shot was fired by the motor launch and then the enemy rose to the surface on her side and six more shots were fired at her, of which two burst against the hull amidships. The German disappeared rapidly this time and it was claimed that *U*-75 had been made to compensate for the loss of the *Hampshire*. But it was equally in the Eastern Mediterranean on December 14 that the deadliness of the depth-charge was to prove itself when the French destroyers *Mameluck* and *Lansquenet* were escorting the French cruiser *Château Renault* carrying about 900 troops. Fifty minutes later the cruiser was again torpedoed and this time sank.

Lasquenet then ran up the track of the torpedo and dropped five depth-charges, the second of which damaged the submarine causing a big leak. Presently the enemy on the surface was attacked by both destroyers' shells which compelled the Germans to leap into the sea and surrender. The effect of the destroyers' depth-charges was to stop all watches aboard the submarine, causing also a hatch to leak badly, water thus falling on the engines and fusing both. Finally this *UC*-38 had to be abandoned and thus she sank. The French destroyers had proved to the world their anti-submarine value.

How did the Huns take this attack?

Well, it was not exactly pleasant. When these survivors were taken on board the *Mameluck* the Germans all fell on their knees and pleaded for mercy. Wendlandt, the German captain, climbed up the destroyer's bridge and remarked that he supposed they would shoot him, whereupon the French commanding officer replied:

"Get off the bridge. And remember that in this ship we're not Boches."

The second Hun officer who had been very seriously wounded—he belonged to the regular Navy—asked permission to speak with his captain who was a Reserve Officer. The request was refused, and before reaching Itea in the Ionian Sea, this second-in-command together with three other Germans died. So perished *UC*-38, which had thought herself so successful.

Yet we need not go beyond British waters to perceive how well we were now in process of slowly if certainly wiping out the Submarine Menace. That secretly laid minefield below the surface in Dover Straits had now on December 19, 1917, begun a fresh chapter that was ultimately to settle this problem. Gradually, step by step, fate was leading the Germans to harsh destiny. It was at 11.42 p.m. that H.M.S. *Gipsy* (one of the old-fashioned destroyers) whilst patrolling the Straits heard a very big explosion, proceeded to search the locality, and half an hour later heard voices in the water calling. There were seen men struggling in the water, but before a boat could be launched they had all sunk. On switching the searchlight to starboard two more men were heard and then sighted, of whom one was picked up and the other sank also. The Hun picked up was undressed aboard the destroyer and everything done to revive him. He regained consciousness, but expired at 1.15 a.m. His clothes marked 'Bleeck' proved him to be an Engine-room Petty

Officer. *UB*-56 had thus shown that at last the Dover Straits were not healthy for German submarines.

The enemy still used to play his old trick of disguising himself by setting some sail. Five days before Christmas one U-boat in Lat. 49.56 N., Long. 7.29 W. did in fact set two sails: one forward and one abaft the conning-tower. It was stupid, unimaginative and certainly not convincing. So when the United States destroyer *Wadsworth* shortly came along escorting a convoy, the Hun took such a fright that she dived in a hurry with all sail still set. Of course the enemy had planned his attack on the convoy, for a second U-boat was close to her.

If around Christmastime the enemy was still doing his best to work havoc in the Dover Straits, firing torpedoes and then seeking to avoid vengeance, it was not because we had relaxed our vigilance but because our deep-laid minefield off Dover was not yet fully completed. Nor had the Germans yet realized how deadly was this elongated obstacle to become; even though *U*-87 was sunk off the Welsh coast on Christmas Day by one of our sloops and a PC-boat. Along the Dover Straits antisubmarine flares were constantly in use. Why? So that the enemy might be chased till he had to dive, and thus submerge on to mines that were ready to settle his fate.

The birth of another year in January 1918 came with a confidence that we had gained such a powerful grip over the U-boats and had hunted them so successfully that to beat them was no longer a possibility but a certainty. Only time would decide when, where, and how. In matters of detail we were strengthening the means of assault. Our submarines were stalking theirs, our destroyers and patrols beating theirs at their own game, our minefields making their lives a terror both in German waters and off such strategical parts of ours as headlands and restricted channels. At the same time it was one of their plans to mine certain exits from ports and then entice by bombardment the deep-draught units into the spheres of ambush. Thus the mining of the Harwich approaches was to coincide with the bombardment of Lowestoft.

The 6-pounder guns of our patrols were gradually being replaced by 12-pounders, and the 3-pounders by 6-pounders. As to Defensively Armed Merchant Ships, already nearly 4000 had mounted guns whilst in many cases depth-charges were given double the explosive strength, though submarines continued to lay their mines even outside the S.W. entrance to Scapa Flow.

Hundreds of these horned black 'eggs' they had previously deposited by surface ships, under cover of night, in such areas as off the Humber, Tyne, north of Ireland, and north of Scotland. When, almost immediately, we discovered these traps and swept clear passages through them, the enemy switched over to laying mines in small bunches by means of submarines. Headlands, harbour entrances, estuaries, the vicinities of lightships, thus became the selected spots; yet, having regard to the immensity of effort expended, the risks to themselves, the cost in time and mileage, Germany's submarine minelaying yielded comparatively puny returns.

Now Britain also knew something about mines, and the last war proved this to some purpose when we had once made our decision to enclose the enemy's activities. Months before hostilities finished, it was barely safe for the smallest tonnage to try getting out into the North Sea from the Elbe, Weser, or Heligoland. That is to say, our foes' naval exit was confined to the route via Kiel Canal, thence through the narrow waters separating Denmark from Sweden, and so round the Skaw. A long, indirect way with many navigational difficulties.

That was because our submarines, our destroyers, and other surface ships, with daring persistence were placing their cargoes more effectively than Germany had achieved in British waters. Let us see what this meant to the enemy's U-boats.

Take the case of *UB*-21. She was a modern craft; her commanding officer, Herr Hashagen, had trained his crew well before he transferred to *U*-62 and sank one of our Q-ships. The new captain of *UB*-21 set out from Heligoland at 5 a.m. of January 31, 1918, bound for the neighbourhood of Hartlepool, but found the utmost difficulty in working through the Bight's dangers, even though escorted. Next day she was still trying; the division of minesweepers still endeavouring to obtain a clear channel; and meanwhile the submarine had to let go anchor rather than suddenly be blown up.

Hours sped by, the barrage turned out to be so dense that all hope of a safe lane became out of the question. Those confounded Englishmen had hemmed-in the U-boats. Nothing for it, but *UB*-21 must return into Heligoland Harbour.

New instructions arrived; on February 3 she sallied forth again, ran into the Elbe, passed a long while negotiating Kiel Canal, thence into the Kattegat, so that by the date when she sighted Hartlepool it was already February 12. In that region she made two attacks on shipping, and both failed. Next day, having wasted so much oil-fuel, she began her return journey, spending six days on passage, reaching home with only one and a half tons of oil, and no sort of success to offer.

Sometimes this lengthy, roundabout route nearly proved disastrous. *U*-94, which had sunk the British S.S. *Rockpool* on March 2 of that year, found her resources running desperately low. From the North Sea on March 7 she passed into the Kattegat, keeping eight miles away from the Skaw's low-lying neck of sand, but at 6 p.m. there met her another U-boat. Luckily it was calm enough for them to lie alongside each other, and for enough oil to be pumped aboard. At the end of an hour they parted company; *U*-94 carried on to the south, reached Kiel the next day, thence via the Canal to Wilhelmshaven. But whilst some craft always seem to get what they deserve, others manage to dodge fate.

Less fortunate was *U*-104, and she certainly proved the efficiency of our anti-submarine measures right to the uttermost. As an engineering production, this 950-tons submarine, with her speed of $16\frac{1}{2}$ knots on the surface and half that when below water, was considered one of the finest things which ever came out of Germany. Kapitan-Leutnant J. K. Bernis had under him three other officers and 35 men.

On April 11, 1918, she set out from Wilhelmshaven, rounded the north of Scotland, passed outside the Hebrides and that lonely island St. Kilda, gave the west and south coasts of Ireland a good berth till she stole up the Irish Sea. She now lay in wait for the Holyhead-Dublin mail steamers. It was a brutal, barbarous intention, since these were always packed with passengers every night. Soldiers and sailors going on leave after months of duty, others returning from England, used to crowd these steamers' decks. The chief hope of safety lay in the speed and zigzagging.

Those two factors defeated Bernis for, though he made a couple of attempts to torpedo, he failed on both occasions; wherefore he shifted his billet further south to St. George's Channel.

It was between 1 and 2 a.m. of April 25, 1918, that *U*-104 motored along the surface, using both engines, and charging her batteries simultaneously. Smooth sea, a bright moon illumining the water, visibility moderate, speed about 10 knots. But, admittedly, a poor lookout was being kept. The old story—a well-built vessel with an indifferent crew. For by that date Germany's naval discipline had rapidly begun to get worse, no longer were volunteers easily persuaded into her U-boat service. Mass production at the shipyards did not synchronize with the supply of well-trained sailors.

Now in the neighbourhood patrolling, but keeping an eager vigil, steamed H.M.S. *Jessamine*, technically designated a sloop. Actually these single-screw ships—all named after flowers—were small light cruisers, built originally for minesweeping, though employed for a dozen purposes. Her captain, Commander S. A. Geary-Hill, R.N., had always maintained his crew on the 'top line' and a sort of affectionate awe existed between the Commander-in-Chief at Queenstown (Admiral Sir Lewis Bayly) and his ships. Officers and men would rather have perished than be found wanting in an emergency.

Suddenly about half a mile off the port bow *Jessamine's* Officer-of-the-Watch, Lieutenant Marshall Reay, R.N.R., spotted the submarine's shape, wasted no moment, rang down the engine-room telegraph to 'Full Ahead', pressed the bell for action stations, altered course to ram the enemy with a knock-out blow.

Obviously Bernis' craft ought to have been on the alert and seen what was coming, but not till only 500 yards separated the rivals did the Germans realize their peril and next sound the alarm inside. Then everybody woke up with a start. Altering direction eight points (90 degrees) to starboard, she began diving to 98 feet before this could be accomplished; whilst her periscope was just submerging, the sloop gained the U-boat's starboard side, and dropped four depth-charges in quick succession.

The first exploded near the enemy's stern, forcing her up aft. The second detonation drove the stern down and down, so that the gauge indicated 164 feet, and things looked ugly. Into the motor room the sea poured, short-circuiting motors, putting them out of action, forcing the air forward as if by an hydraulic ram, terribly accentuating the pressure till the Germans could scarce breathe.

That second depth-charge had closed the watertight door at the after end of the bow torpedo-room, but the air pressure continued to rise, being forced through voice-pipes and leads in the bulkhead. When the third explosion burst, an attempt was made to blow all ballast tanks. But because the after tanks had become damaged, only the forward ones could be emptied and thus the stern was depressed further.

So the bows rose to a depth of 32 feet, and the steep inclination made life on board one slippery slope. Discipline vanished, men crowded round the torpedo hatch, it was everyone-for-himself, and get away if he possibly could.

Now, after dropping her last depth-charge, *Jessamine* swung to port and by this time the submarine had created in the water a large disturbance some 200 yards away. To make additionally sure, the sloop therefore fired her foremost gun at this eddying; then began circling around at high speed in readiness for the U-boat's return to surface, but cries for help rose instead, followed by large quantities of oil welling up. After a while the Englishmen sighted a German, rescued him still alive, and found him to be Engine-room Petty Officer Karl Eschenberg, aged 22, and he had a thrilling story to relate.

Whilst his shipmates were crowding round the torpedo-hatch, Eschenberg succeeded in opening it, then came the inrush of water which swept the former aside whilst the power of escaping air forced him up and up through the hatch on to the sea's surface. At first the *Jessamine* could not descry him, but he had the sense to remove his clothing before commencing to swim. Dazed, but still conscious, he was at last picked up and hauled aboard the sloop where every attention of food, warmth and medical skill restored him to full health.

Until daylight the *Jessamine* cruised about searching the region for any more survivors, but Eschenberg alone had come up out of the 39 who left Wilhelmshaven. To Commander Geary-Hill the King gave a D.S.O., and to Lieutenant Marshall Reay a D.S.C. Such was the rewarding of constant vigilance. Lack of this sent Kapitan-Leutnant Bernis with his officers to their doom.

Two days after this incident *UB-72* left Heligoland after being delayed by our minefields, and even then she had to be escorted through these danger areas by five minesweeping trawlers. The commanding officer of this submarine was Kapitan-Leutnant F. Trager, who had under him two other officers and 31 men. Among the latter were Petty Officer W. Laabs, Able Seaman A. Diers, Stoker B. Gabriel, all of whom were making their first cruise in any submarine on active service. Moreover this was Trager's first command, and he suffered (as his crew believed) from over-confidence.

U-boat crews had long since begun to respect British sea-power with a deep feeling, and every voyage now had something in common with a suicide-trip. When Hans and Fritz and Herman used to come home to Wilhelmshaven or Kiel, with spine-freezing yarns of our anti-submarine measures, nervous temperaments were no more encouraged than their countrymen ashore by our Blockade's throttling grip. And from the moment submarines got outside Heligoland near the minefields they were never allowed to forget who still ruled the Narrow Seas.

All of which had a cumulative effect on morale.

Proceeding across the North Sea *UB-72* passed round Scotland via the Fair Isle Channel, through the Minch, then by the North Channel and Irish Sea so that on May 9 she was patrolling between the Scillies and mainland. Almost from the hour when she arrived in British waters she was continually harassed by our forces. Armed trawlers with their keen fishermen crews longed for no more welcome sight than a submarine: in fact I have often been told by British submarine officers that when approaching the English shores it was always unhealthy within gun-range of these hardy mariners.

But Trager realized that both our destroyers and aircraft were like terriers after a rat. His three raw hands were soon made wise that this was no yachting excursion. On the night when she was working through St. George's Channel (where *Jessamine* won her victory) *UB-72* experienced everything but annihilation. During two fierce hours a destroyer pursued her relentlessly, just missing her, yet dropping 23 depth-charges. *Twenty-three!* Laabs, Diers and Gabriel thought it was the end of all things! But so did everybody else with them.

And we have just seen what four explosives can do.

This *UB-72* had a remarkable escape, for a leak was started in the port ballast tank, which filled with oil fuel and thus a tell-tale slimy trail was left astern. On another occasion 20 depth-charges were heard to explode, which started the forward starboard oil tank leaking, and extinguished five electric light bulbs. Just to complete this nerve-testing of initiates, later that day five more powerful bombs were heard bursting.

Now from the Scillies area Trager went across to hang about off the approaches to Brest, then carried on up the English Channel, being by the early morn of May 12 roughly midway between Guernsey and Portland Bill.

So also was His Majesty's Submarine *D-4*.

UB-72 was today motoring along the surface at six knots, Petty Officer Herock (who had been borrowed from the German Merchant Service in which he held a Mate's Certificate) being Officer-of-the-Watch. He was standing on the bridge, Laabs and Diers acting as lookouts. Their friend Stoker Gabriel had just come on deck to throw some potato peelings over the side, and then remained to smoke a matutinal cigarette.

Suddenly tobacco ceased to afford the smallest pleasure, his face blanched, and he dived overboard—barely in time. The precise moment was 4 hours 50 minutes 8 seconds. Two seconds later nothing remained of the German submarine but a large patch of oil.

It had been at 4.30 a.m. that *D-4* sighted Trager's hull to starboard, moving southward, some two and a half miles distant. One of those calm peaceful May mornings with the sea like polished steel; clear atmosphere, but the light not too good. Five minutes later the German altered course. Coming in the direction of *D-4*, it seemed. The British submarine accordingly lowered periscope. She had not been noticed after all.

Several suspenseful minutes ticked by until 4.43. *D-4* ordered: 'Up Periscope!' A quick glance showed that Herock was steering on an easterly course, yet a little later had altered again till on the Englishman's port hand.

The captain of *D-4* now waited for the big chance—till his sights would come on. At 4.50 the target was excellently placed, and he released a torpedo, dipped periscope, fired a second torpedo . . . waited ten seconds . . . felt a terrible concussion, rose to the surface, perceived no German U-boat but a large patch of oil right ahead. Thither *D-4* hurried, and discovered three men swimming in the sticky mess. Now it is not too easy hauling exhausted men up the sloping hull of a submarine, but British sailors used their best endeavours and rescued the trio. The latter's names were Laabs, Diers, and Gabriel. An amazing coincidence that these war-initiates should have lost their ship on their first cruise to British waters, and that none other of their shipmates survived.

Gabriel had been more alert than the two lookouts, for no sooner did he sight the approaching British torpedo than overboard he sprang: two seconds before it struck the German's engine-room. Such mental and physical activity sufficiently indicates the nervous awareness which at that period characterized the enemy's submarine crews.

Immediately after the explosion *UB*-72 began sinking like a stone, stern first, with bows high in the air. It all happened so quickly that Herock and the two lookouts just slid below surface till 16 feet down, when a rush of air blew them up again. Still wearing seaboots, and those heavy leather clothes so popular in the German Navy, the men had an opportunity of learning the sort of anguish that British distressed mariners had too often suffered from torpedoes.

Herock cried out with pain and sank finally in a few minutes. Laabs and Diers and Gabriel swallowed a lot of oil, which made them vomit, and they had already forfeited all hope when out of the sea rose *D*-4 and British bluejackets with heaving-lines arrived as from nowhere. A few hours later the prisoners were transferred to H.M.S. *Loyal* and landed at Plymouth.

Somehow, apart from any question of age, I cannot imagine that either Laabs, Diers, or Gabriel volunteered for U-boat service in the 1939 war.

CHAPTER XIX

THE "CLOVER BANK II"

THE characteristic indifferent navigation of German submarines was indicated by *U*-93 on the night of January 7, 1918, when she was accidentally but foolishly allowed to be run down off the Lizard by the S.S. *Braeneil* in fine clear weather. It was a collision such as any Mercantile Master would have felt ashamed of, but for which so many German Submarine Naval officers seem to have been readily guilty.

The *Braeneil* was steaming at nine knots and her side lights had been unmasked as some craft had crossed her course a short time previously. At about 4.15 a.m. the Master, who was on the bridge, sighted the hull of *U*-93 about 200 feet away right ahead. The enemy was making north with her port side towards the *Braeneil* whose Master was now determined to ram the German and within two minutes the steamer struck the German amidships. After backing clear, the steamer heard above the leaden waters the cries of distress rising in a foreign language and smelt a very powerful odour of petroleum. Such was the rapid end to *U*-93. This, you will recollect, was that amazing U-boat which once fought the decoy schooner *Prize** but managed to reach Germany where she underwent serious repairs. But now she was sunk finally. After *Braeneil* got into Falmouth she was carefully examined, and her stem found to be twisted about two feet off the water line, with two plates on each bow dented.

Next day in the Western Mediterranean H.M. Sloop *Cyclamen* was

*See earlier chapter.

escorting a convoy off Bizerta when *UB*-69 passed near. Twice the sloop exploded her paravane, and on each occasion a depth-charge was dropped. The submarine was on passage from Germany, but by sinking her for the last time we realized that the German's intentions had now been altered. The skilful persistence with which we continued to lay mines in German waters was so regular that their submarines were still undergoing the greatest risks when setting out from home; whilst another sloop, H.M.S. *Campanula*, on January 18 dropped depth-charges over *UB*-66 and destroyed the enemy. It was also *UB*-22 which on January 19 foundered in the Heligoland Bight on one of our mines some 60 miles N.W. of Heligoland.

Yet the fishermen were the backbone of our coastal patrols. We had already lost one drifter named the *Clover Bank* by the enemy on April 24, 1916, off the Belgian coast. Then a new *Clover Bank II* was built to replace her namesake—slightly bigger this time—with a fishermen crew as before, and Lieutenant D. T. Webster, R.N.R., in command.

Just before eleven o'clock of a cold wintry morning on January 23, 1918, this *Clover Bank II*, as her predecessor used to do, was examining off the Belgian coast the barrage nets when suddenly a shell flopped into the sea. Only a thousand yards away Lieutenant Webster glanced astern, and noticed more shots. The visibility was from two to three miles. Suddenly he perceived the alarming sight of five German destroyers steaming at right angles towards him.

He summoned his fisher crew to action stations, the gun was swung round, but what sort of chance would a 6-pounder have against the enemy? How many minutes before *Clover Bank II* joined her namesake beneath the same waters?

Still, she would do her best.

Opening fire at 6000 yards, her first shot was seen to fall short of the leading destroyer. "Down 2000!" At 4000 yards a 6-pounder shell struck the second destroyer right on the bridge.

This infuriated the Germans, who concentrated a hot and very rapid fire so that a perfect shower of projectiles dropped all round the drifter, yet miraculously not one was a hit. But anyone who has ever been shipmates with drifter-men knows what fine gunners these clean-eyed fellows became. Quickly the *Clover Bank II* loosed off a third shell, and that too hit the target.

Obviously such contest could not be delayed indefinitely. Death and destruction must follow soon. One tiny gun against 10! And each of the enemy's weapons at least a 24-pounder! But nobody had a thought of giving in.

"Smoke screen!"

The British crew ran along the deck, ignited the smoke-box, threw it from the stern, and a black cloud shut out everything. *Clover Bank II*, with about one-quarter of the German's speed, essayed to get away, the enginemen below had never coaxed so many 'revs' out of the machinery —not even when the drifter was due back to Dover for 10 days' leave!

But it was of no avail. When the smoke cleared away, German destroyers had not sheered off. They had merely separated in commanding positions: two on one side, one on the other, two astern. "We've got you," they seemed to threaten. "Got you—like the first *Clover Bank*."

Bang! Bang!

The drifter pointed her gun and fired twice more, but now the enemy was about to punish thoroughly this impudence from a British drifter. Tearing aside the last vestige of artificial fog, sharp bows churning up the sea into feathery white, the destroyers astern were fast overhauling, whilst those units at each side were altering course.

"Going to cut us off!"

Webster saw through the intention, realized that within the next few minutes his *Clover Bank II* would be boarded and captured. All right!

"Stand by to open seacocks!" he called down to the engineer. He was determined to sink the ship rather than let her become a prize. Then he remembered the private signal book, and other confidential documents. So overboard they went, weighted with lead to sink. Now he was ready for the worst. He had, as a good commanding officer, done his very utmost.

Five destroyers. Nearer and nearer they rushed, firing every gun that would bear, even using their machine-guns. . . . Only a few moments now, and . . .

Clover Bank II all this time was steering to the westward, away from the Belgian sand-dunes, and at this crisis something right ahead caught his gaze. Something grey and long and lean, hurrying from the west towards him. Three miles off.

Then the crew looked in the same direction. During 45 tense minutes this unequal tussle had been prolonged, and it does not appear too creditable for the Germans that no casualties had been suffered aboard the drifter; not once had she been hit, and only a few fragments of shells arrived.

But next the distant objects shaped themselves into a pair of British destroyers steaming at full speed. The five Germans saw them also, quickly altered course with helm hard over, gave up the chase and then went back inside the defences of Zeebrugge Mole. It was all over now. Yes: it had been a thrilling episode for *Clover Bank II*, though by no means her last. To Lieutenant Webster and crew came finally an official letter of appreciation from the Lords of the Admiralty.

It could not be expected that this distant Belgian barrage would be a complete hindrance to U-boat movements, but across Dover Straits in those days stretched the secret minefield from Folkestone to Cape Gris Nez, and at night this was illumined by flares whilst drifters, trawlers, motor launches, paddle minesweepers, and other craft patrolled. The idea was that should a U-boat be observed on the surface, in the light he would at once be chased. Naturally the submarine would then dive out of visibility, but also on to the mines. A simple and most highly successful anti-German method of which our enemies long remained ignorant; though, when so many U-boats failed to reach Zeebrugge again, it was realized in occupied Belgium that something in Dover Straits had become formidable.

Let it be added that further east of the Folkestone–Gris Nez minefield extended a net barrage, supported by buoys, from the Goodwins to the Outer Ruytingen Shoal. U-boat captains often, when bound down Channel, would reach the Sandettie Lightship, descend to the sea-bed until night, wait till the tide began going west, then choose a spot where the nets sagged, and there work through.

Three days after the *Clover Bank II* incident, another drifter—*Beryl III*—had a sudden experience. With some of her sisters she had been patrolling over the Dover minefield but, during the night, a Channel fog had settled down. What with that and the strong tide, *Beryl III* had lost sight of her division.

At 8 a.m. the fog was less dense, but patchy. To verify her position, she was steaming over towards the French side of the Folkestone minefield and the fog signal on Cape Gris Nez sounded so much louder that she could not now be far from the steep grey cliffs.

O-o-o-o-h! It shrieked a warning from the lighthouse. O-o-o-o-h! It wailed again. Keen eyes were looking out to avoid being set ashore, when . . .

"What's that—right ahead of us?"

One glance sufficed. Lying low on the surface with conspicuous conning-tower, and a 4-inch gun for'ard, a 22-pounder aft, a net-cutter rising above the bows, was a great submarine some 225 feet long. Apart from her dozen torpedoes, she could have blown the *Beryl* out of existence and would then likely have peppered swimming fishermen with her machine-gun.

But the drifter reckoned nothing of the German's strength. After all, surprise is the very essence of victory, and the enemy had been caught napping. Skipper J. H. Bullock, however, was very wide awake, brought his little gun to bear, opened fire and—believe it or not—the second shot was a bull's-eye: it struck the base of the U-boat's conning-tower at the fore side. Evidently 'Fritz' had also been lost in the fog, but her crew were not keeping an efficient lookout.

And now, as if stung to activity, the submarine made a quick movement, more British shells came pouring forth. They failed to have any result. For the U-boat made an astounding dive into invisibility: so hurriedly that up went stern in the air, disclosing her propellers. Excellent! Let her grope about among the hidden mines.

Two hours passed, fishermen waited ready for any development. Then the inevitable followed. The stranger had not moved very far away when a terrible explosion was heard by H.M. Trawler *Elysian*. . . . A slight pause. . . . One more detonation, and oil-fuel rose to the surface. That was the end of *U*-109, one of the latest and largest of German submarines, which in her flight from a drifter was made to destroy herself with all hands on a row of mines. Quite properly was Skipper Bullock given the D.S.C., and the crew very justly were awarded £1000 to be divided among themselves. But why this sum never reached them we shall presently see.

Meanwhile, on this self-same January 26 another enemy submarine (*UB*-35) was fumbling about the Dover Straits, bound back to Zeebrugge. She still had four miles to go before gaining the Goodwins barrage and was just in the act of rising to the surface, seeking the line of net-buoys, when H.M.S. *Leven* (a destroyer) caught sight of her periscope and promptly rained a nice selection of depth-charges. Well, that concluded the career of *UB*-35, and only one of her crew could be picked up. He was aged about 21, and had a week's growth of unshorn hair on his chin. But before he could be landed life forsook him.

Now the German authorities in Flanders had become both anxious and angry. Several of their submarines on returning to Zeebrugge reported narrow escapes in the Dover area. Moreover, between December 18, 1917, and February 9, 1918, no fewer than five had been destroyed down there: *UB*-56, *UB*-35, *U*-109, *UC*-50 and *UB*-38. How did the Flanders Naval Corps know so much?

Because, firstly, their boats were ordered daily to wireless their present positions; and, secondly, when these craft did not reach home, it needed no more than a shrewd guess to discover the reason.

Wherefore, since Dover Straits had become (to quote the Germans) 'almost impassable', it was decided to raid this defile with a powerful force of fast destroyers under Captain Heinecke, an officer known for his ruthless daring.

On February 13 this flotilla left Heligoland Bight, hugged the Frisian Islands to avoid British mines, felt their way till abreast Haaks Lightship (near the Texel), but thick fog made them return as far as Norderney. On the 14th all fog changed to very clear weather, so anchors were lifted and the destroyers, giving the Dutch coast a wide berth during daylight, at length reached the previously mentioned Sandettie Bank at 11.30 p.m.

Here the flotilla separated to do their damnedest. Half were to attack our patrols from the north-west, and half from the south-west. Led by Heinecke himself, the former approached the illuminated section, sighted the moving silhouettes of trawlers, drifters, motor-launches, and then began. Time now 12.30 p.m.

The first half made for a vessel in the middle of the barrier, lighting up the sea with a specially bright revolving searchlight. This was the ex-pleasure paddle-steamer *Newbury*, whom the Germans claimed to sink. Then they fell upon Motor Launch 12, covered her with their searchlight beams, poured shell after shell at only 400 yards, claimed to sink her too.

Meanwhile the second half-flotilla made towards the Gris Nez end of the patrol barrier, fell upon the trawler *James Pond*, set her on fire, and did considerable damage to other units.

After one hour the raid ended as suddenly as it had begun, but it was far from the complete success which such a murderous force should have achieved against lightly armed craft, of whom so many were wooden-built. Just as they do today, the Germans made the most exaggerated statements. Far from sinking *M.L.*-12, the only thing they injured was a wire stay.

The *Newbury* went through hell, being simultaneously attacked on both sides so that her depth-charges went off, bridge was wrecked, four officers and five men killed. Yet, with real British pluck her captain and engineers managed to steam her till almost up to Dover breakwater whence she was towed safely inside. Of the other six damaged patrols all were drifters. One trawler, the *James Pond*, was sunk but her end forms one of the finest epics of the sea. Yet again did our fishermen show their heroic imperturbability. Listen to this plain tale of one who knew no fear.

Her commanding officer was Skipper A. E. Berry. Already at the Dardanelles he had won the D.S.C. for his gallantry in minesweeping when in charge of the Grimsby trawler *Frascati*. Despite Turco-German shells from the shore, he stuck to the job, but how he survived seemed a miracle. He remained out there till the evacuation, came back to England, was promoted to Chief Skipper, did excellent work, and tonight was on the Flare Patrol when three German destroyers in line ahead simultaneously opened fire.

Result: *James Pond's* fo'c'sle was pierced in many places, one shell exploded in the wireless room killing two operators in their bunks, and mortally wounding the third. Alfred Berry was in his wheelhouse cabin when another shell exploded, setting it on fire, wounding him in the legs. Ignoring his pain, he remained cool and collected, ordered all hands to lie down till firing ceased, then tried to put out the conflagration.

Impossible task. The flares which she carried would not yield to water.

"Abandon ship!" he commanded.

The falls had been ruined by shell-fire, but he encouraged his men to lift the heavy boat over the gunwale. They placed a dying wireless operator in it, survivors clambered in also, and off they rowed towards the French coast.

A few minutes later the *James Pond* blew up, but at Wissant they beached the dinghy where British, French and American officers dressed the wounds and showed every kindness to distressed mariners. "I cannot too strongly commend Chief Skipper A. E. Berry," wrote the head of the Dover Trawler Patrol to Vice-Admiral Roger Keyes, referring to the "cool, courageous and gallant conduct on this occasion. They all behaved with the well-known fearlessness of the Mercantile Marine and its Fishing Fleets".

But if seven drifters had been damaged, seven others tonight had been sunk. And one of them was *Clover Bank II*. Once more had she distinguished herself.

That was why the men in *Beryl III* refused to accept all the £1000. They asked that £500 of it should be given to the Mayor of Dover's Fund earmarked for the widows and children of those drifters whose lives had been robbed by the German destroyers.

And did this raid make things easier for U-boats negotiating the Dover Straits? It certainly did not. Out came the drifters and trawlers as before. They fired their little guns against the silhouettes, down fled submarine after submarine and up went the explosions. Many a German submarine lies on the sea-bed of Dover Straits today like so many steel coffins for men who had cruelly sunk our merchant steamers.

The Straits had become *quite* 'impassable'.

CHAPTER XX

GERMANY CRACKS

At four o'clock of that bleak dark morning on January 26 three German submarines were all destroyed. First H.M.S. *P-62* whilst patrolling across the Irish Sea between the Tuskar and the Smalls sighted *U-84* and before the latter had time to dive was rammed as a hot knife cuts through butter. In the darkness of night *U-84* was thus sent to the sea-bed without any further argument.

We have just mentioned how, four hours later, H.M. Drifter *Beryl III* and H.M.S. *Leven* sank today respectively *U*-109 and *UB*-35. The latter had been in the act of rising to the surface looking for the Dover barrage which was four miles to the N.E. Notwithstanding the dullness of the weather, these January sinkings of the enemy were quite numerous: the latter was approaching the end of his tether when on January 28, 1918, two well-known Granton Q-ship trawlers—the *W. S. Bailey* and the *Fort George*—heard a submarine on their hydrophones 14 miles E. by S. of May Island, hunted her for one and a half hours, dropped depth-charges over her and so destroyed *UB*-63. So also during this January—though neither the exact date nor precise position has ever been ascertained—*U*-95 just disappeared. Her adversary might have been aircraft, decoy, or patrol vessel, or perhaps another of our mines: but at any rate she was the ninth German submarine we had destroyed in January 1918.

From many a sign and portent the Huns realized that their submarine efforts were doomed. German naval historians of the pre-Hitler days confirmed that by the Spring of 1918 the Boches knew quite well that their U-boat campaign must fizzle out ingloriously. But like a dog which has gone mad and tries to bite everyone within reach, they threw aside meanwhile all rules, sank hospital ships when they could, concentrated against liners, ambushing ships passing between that lonely island of Inishtrahull and the Mull of Galloway.

In other words that vital area which includes the North Channel between Ireland and Scotland, embracing the approaches to Glasgow, Belfast and Liverpool, was to be made one long trap for Atlantic steamers at the very time when they were arriving continuously heavily laden with necessary cargoes or with thousands of American soldiers. Thus began the last and toughest phase of submarine warfare.

On February 4 the Cunard *Aurania* (13,936 tons) was 15 miles to the north of Inishtrahull when a U-boat sent her to the Atlantic bed with the loss of eight lives. That was the beginning, and next day the 14,348-tons Anchor liner *Tuscania* approached, bound from Halifax for Liverpool with 2000 troops and valuable cargo. For her protection everything was being done. Steaming in convoy, she had the escort of cruiser and destroyers, whilst more destroyers and other patrol vessels locally covered the North Channel.

But the Germans' concentration was fierce. Sometimes no fewer than five or six boats were working together, and replaced as others arrived on the station. I know that on a certain date *U*-43, *U*-54, *UB*-83, *UB*-90, and *UB*-126 were all co-operating in the North Channel district and that *U*-92 had just gone home after being rammed.

Not far from Inishtrahull a convoy in charge of H.M.S. *Roxburgh* (an armed cruiser) was ending its Atlantic voyage on February 12 under Captain G. W. Vivian, R.N. Time 11.20 p.m. A dark night with low visibility, and until a few minutes previously there had been a fog. Curiously at 11.10 this thickness lifted, and suddenly Lieut.-Commander A. R. Smithwick, R.N., Officer-of-the-Watch, peering out beyond *Roxburgh's* bridge, espied something on the surface. Barely 150 yards off the port bow.

The Navigating Officer too had a look. Both came to the same conclusion.

"Gosh! She's a submarine!"

Helm was starboarded, cruiser steadied on her course, less than half a minute elapsed, and there followed first a flash then a terrible explosion accompanied by violent shock. For when one steel ship of nearly 11,000 tons, travelling at the equivalent of more than 20 land miles an hour, rams another steel vessel of 1000 tons, something has to happen. From the leaden Atlantic swell Teutonic voices called loudly, but too late. Already the *Roxburgh* had sawn her opponent in two: one half immediately sinking, whilst the other portion before disappearing was observed to pass aft along the cruiser's port side. It was about as neat an action as ever happened in sea warfare, and not a German escaped that death which had been intended for one of the convoy.

So every unit got safely into port, and pieces of *U*-89 were still impaled on the *Roxburgh's* bows. Ordinarily when a British man-of-war has been in collision there would be a court-martial. But tonight's incident called forth the Admiralty's congratulations and to Lieut.-Commander Smithwick was awarded the D.S.O.

This happened as a most satisfying occasion for quite another reason. Months previously, on June 20, 1915, H.M.S. *Roxburgh* had been attacked in the North Sea by *U*-38. The latter fired a torpedo, which hit and did a certain amount of damage. But who could have foreseen that revenge, so thorough and complete, might come at the end of an anxious ocean voyage?

So this North Irish maritime struggle proceeded with a cunning and ferocity rarely equalled elsewhere in the Narrow Seas. Submarine onslaughts against our convoys in 1939 or 1940 bear no comparison with those perils of 1918. It was as if a nest of snakes had been concealed in the centre of a pedestrian's path. And the next incident was to happen on March 1.

That fine 17,515-tons Canadian Pacific Steamship *Calgarian* having been transformed into an Armed Merchant Cruiser had just escorted 30 merchantmen towards the North Channel at about 10 knots, when destroyers arrived and took over. It seemed rather asking for trouble if so valuable a unit were to go through those straits at slow speed in that fine weather. Permission was therefore granted for her to speed up and steam independently.

Now whilst approaching Rathlin Island at 20 knots, zigzagging, *U*-19 hit *Calgarian* with a torpedo, killing 29 men in the stoke-hold. The German officer was Kapitan-Leutnant Spiess (one of Germany's most experienced specialists) who, seeing that the ex-liner did not immediately founder though struck at only 550 yards range, determined to have another go. By this time the *Calgarian* was surrounded by 7 destroyers, 3 sloops, and 11 trawlers! Yet despite these 21 vessels, Spiess dived underneath and fired two more torpedoes, which of course finished her.

I mention those details to show the great difficulties in some waters with which our destroyers had to contend. Spiess certainly was both daring and extraordinarily lucky. He took *U*-19 home to Germany, returned to the North Channel area, and this time barely escaped with his life. Then, whilst again voyaging home, he did something which had never been done before and did not happen after. He brought *U*-19 close to that precipitous island of St. Kilda which lies 40 miles out from the Hebrides in lonely Atlantic detachment, sent some of his crew ashore by small boat to the one and only landing-place, waited till they shot some sheep, and then resumed his cruise. Throughout that war no other U-boat Germans ever landed alive on British territory except as prisoners.

Having regard to the numerous cavalcades of shipping which every week passed by the north of Ireland it was inevitable that occasionally some persistent submarine still found a victim. But our destroyers soon sought the culprit's track, and the following yarn shows something of the grand drama which was being acted away from public knowledge.

On February 25 there set out from Wilhelmshaven *U-110* on her third voyage. She was the newest thing in submarines which Germany owned: a big, powerful creature displacing 1000 tons below water. Her length was 225 feet, she mounted two guns, carried four torpedo-tubes, and could travel at $16\frac{1}{2}$ knots on the surface. Her commanding officer, Korvetten-Kapitan K. Kroll, both by seniority and experience, had quite a reputation. Three more officers and 35 men completed his ship's company.

Now *U-110* cruised some time between Ireland and Scotland and on the morning of March 15, being then some 30 miles west of Malin Head off the Ulster coast, torpedoed the Royal Mail liner *Amazon* (10,037 tons). Not far off were H.M.S. *Moresby* and *Michael*, two splendid destroyers, patrolling. At 9.50 a.m. they picked up *Amazon's* wireless SOS, hurried at full speed, and 15 minutes later found her already low in the water.

Moresby just had time to pick up survivors before *Amazon* went down, then joined *Michael* in making for the approximate position where *U-110* had been sighted by the liner. All this had to be done with great promptness lest the lurking enemy with other torpedoes should sink both destroyers. *Moresby* now dropped four depth-charges, *Michael* let go a couple, but then it was time for *Moresby* to leave the scene. She must hurry into port and land the shipwrecked people who crowded her decks, whilst *Michael* combed the Atlantic single-handed. She waited about but the time sped by and nothing like a submarine rose in the ocean swell.

Meanwhile aboard the invisible *U-110* things were not faring too well. After having torpedoed the *Amazon*, Kroll observed one of those two destroyers on the horizon and did not like the look of her, so he decided to hide, took his submarine down to 150 feet and presently it seemed as if Vesuvius, Mount Etna, and four other volcanoes were suddenly erupting. For those six depth-charges could scarce have been better aimed.

They shook her violently with their explosions, put the after hydroplane motor out of gear so that the boat lost trim, took a steep dive at an angle of 45 degrees and then more vicious than a wilful mule she went bow first to the incredible depth of 334 feet.

Certainly in October 1917, when *U-58* off Queenstown surrendered to American destroyers, she had already sunk to the preposterous depth of 278 feet and withstood the pressure. But 334 feet . . . ? Kroll was horrified. Especially when she now developed serious leaks and a stream of water some half-inch in diameter was being forced into the control-room.

Thoroughly scared, Kroll now had but one desire: to bring his submarine up to lesser depths as quickly as possible. Ordering his men aft to trim the boat, he blew tanks, and she rushed to the surface. What now? If she remained there, surely from the lofty bridge of a destroyer she would be visible. Try escaping back to Germany on the surface all the way, giving headlands and patrols a wide berth?

Well, that had been accomplished early in the war by one or two exceptionally resourceful commanders. But today there would be too many hours before nightfall. No chance of getting clear away under cover of dark. Besides . . . the English now were relentless with their patrols. Those destroyers any moment . . .

Bang! Boom! Bang!

Shells falling around. A fresh danger had developed.

It was 11 a.m., *Michael* was scouring the sea at high speed and suddenly, when five miles distant, sighted this blot on the waves. She opened fire. *Moresby* now returned and did the same with such accuracy that Kroll, against his will, dived again. But not for long. He was between the destroyers and the deep sea: whichever he chose would seal his fate. Punishment for wrong-doing was stalking him with deadly certainty.

In every record that has been made known where British submarine crews have found themselves finally up against fate, there is always some story of heroism and self-denial, of resignation to the inevitable; a firm determination to pass out exhibiting neither impatience nor panic.

Too often in the last war German submarine crews under such circumstances lost all sense of discipline. I know of cases when shipmates struggled against shipmates for escape; when others tried various methods of suicide rather than die nobly. That was during the Kaiser's regime.

Is the present generation of Germany's seafarers any better than the last? Can we really believe that Nazi youth with no great tradition to inspire them will surpass their fathers when clever gadgets cease to work and their craft are doomed?

British sportsmen who have competed with the Nazis tell me the latter are bad losers. It seems more than probable. Fancy being prisoner today in a U-boat when the depth-charges begin to explode!

CHAPTER XXI

THE VICTORIOUS "ZUBIAN"

Wasser bom!

Breathe those two words in the presence of a German prisoner-of-war who has served aboard a U-boat. Then note how the blood suddenly drains from his face, and a look of horror comes into his eyes.

Nothing on sea ever conjures up such terrible moments as those when a submarine beneath the surface, trying to escape, finds herself at the mercy of a British destroyer. For even should the German craft, with her crew of about 30, be so lucky as to survive, not one of her personnel forgets the experience to the end of his days.

These *wasser boms*, as our Nazi enemies designate them, are nothing wonderful to behold: just cylindrical iron drums, officially known as depth-charges but often spoken of in sailor language as 'ash-cans'. Measuring about a yard long, and half that in diameter, they are filled with several hundred pounds of explosive possessing the most devastating power; and I have personal recollection of a significant incident during the last war when at sea patrolling in the danger zone where U-boats busily operated.

We had exchanged signals with one of our Mystery (or Q-) Ships who warned me that presently she intended practising the release of a depth-charge. By the time we had proceeded over a mile distant, she let go the first 'ash-can', but such was the effect even at 2000 yards that one of my engineers came rushing on deck in alarm.

"We've hit something, sir."

Down below, such vibrations are always magnified, just as you can always hear more distinctly the sound of an approaching vessel if you place your ear close to bulkhead or hull. But on the bridge, despite all the intervening expanse of sea, that Q-ship's depth-charge felt as if a heavy log had struck us.

Imagine, therefore, what must happen when a succession of *wasser boms* are detonated within a few feet of the enemy: immediately above his submerging conning-tower, on either side of his hull, perhaps an odd one detonating under the stern as he desperately tries diving to obscurity! The pressure set up by the explosion against the steel boat is so devastating that within quite a moderate area every electric light globe in the submarine will be smashed, rivets of the hull-plating will be started and ominous leaks make their appearance. Gradually sea-water enters the electric batteries and generates that deadly chlorine gas which asphyxiates the crew.

Quite apart from the shock to nerves, and the groping about in total darkness, the moral effect on crews conscious of having murdered innocent men and women travelling aboard some victimized steamer needs no further stressing. The second depth-charge may be the beginning of the end. Why? Generally it jams those fin-like hydroplanes by means of which a U-boat is controlled in a vertical direction, as her rudder steers her horizontally.

At the best of times a submarine is a highly temperamental 'box o' tricks', an intricate mass of clever gadgets all mutually dependent. Let the hydroplanes refuse to operate, or become stiff, and what happens? First, the boat will behave like a wild mad monster, careering deeper and deeper till the water pressure threatens to crush her like a paper bag. That will never do, so her captain endeavours to persuade the hydroplanes in the opposite angle. Up she rises, impetuously, alarmingly, at so steep an angle that he can no longer prevent her breaking surface.

Then it is all over. The watchful destroyers rushing about sight first a thin periscope, then the conning-tower, finally the upper hull like some strange whale.

Flash!

Guns concentrate, shells burst around the conning-tower, others penetrate the oil-tanks, red-yellow flames and black smoke gush forth from the doomed U-boat. The nearest destroyer tearing along at 30 knots steadies a course straight for the enemy and a mighty impact ensues of steel forefoot ploughing through the German.

It is all over now, except to search for any prisoners fortunate enough to survive. Down to the sea-bed, gurgling on its way and emitting a heavy streak of oil, the Nazi submarine has gone whither she sent today's passenger ship or yesterday's cargo-carrier that was bringing us Argentine meat.

Occasionally a submarine by a miracle does escape. That happened once to U-84. Two depth-charges made her tremble from bow to stern, put out every light, damaged both for'ard hydroplane and main rudder, injured also her trimming pump. Then, under cover of night she retreated along the surface, plugged the shell holes, gave all headlands a wide berth and actually got back to Germany. Yet her commanding officer and crew never recovered from this experience, and a few months later when in combat again with one of His Majesty's ships U-84 was finally sunk.

Once during the last war a British submarine was able to confirm all that was claimed for our depth-charges. It was the end of February 1918, and three United States destroyers were on patrol off the Irish coast when they mistook H.M.S. L-2 for a U-boat. So they first attacked with gunfire, which caused the British submarine to dive without further protestation. First she went down to 90 feet, and finally even to 200 feet. Then followed the first depth-charge, whose explosion put L-2's after hydroplanes out of commission and sent her down to the perilous limit of 300 feet, where she hit the ocean bed. Four more detonations made things worse.

Eventually the submarine's commanding officer did manage to bring his craft up to the surface, but there—only a thousand yards off—were the three American destroyers ready for him.

Bang! Bang! Bang!

It was fierce. Shells came crashing across the wintry sea, and one actually hit just abaft the conning-tower. Just when tragedy seemed certain, L-2 managed to make the recognition signals and wave her White Ensign. Only then did the firing cease. Bitter disappointment for the Americans, but most valuable knowledge obtained by the submarine.

I remember another incident when a German U-boat, which had fallen into British hands, was presently employed for experimental purposes. After being taken out to sea, she was depth-charged and then salvage operations began. It was found that a hole was blown large enough in her side to make any patching-up an impossibility. But today, when destroyers are supplied with more numerous and more powerful ash-cans, the enemy has about one chance in a million if his presence be located. That is why the British Navy is gradually exterminating the Nazi menace till ultimately our mercantile vessels can proceed on their lawful occasions with little fear of being harassed.

Hunting-destroyers in threes, steaming line-abreast, using their listening gear and taking bearings of the direction whence suspicious sounds are heard of a U-boat's machinery, are daily making the lives of Nazi aggressors anything but one grand sweet song. By keeping the enemy always in a state of defence, causing the latter to use up all his electricity till he simply must rise and show himself on the surface, our fast light patrols render further security to the convoys passing along the sea-routes.

The strain on picked German personnel, chased and bombed day after day began to tell heavily. Once depth-charged, twice shy! And on the next voyage, after a refit at home, the German U-boat will not relish assaulting merchantmen unless that vessel be an odd homeward-bound unit which omitted to wait for protection.

At one time patrol units let go their depth-charges over the stern by the simple method of dropping them into the sea from a chute. Nowadays, these can be released indirectly by means of a mechanism on the bridge. So, also, small howitzers on either side of the deck can hurl these bombs in such a manner that the entire vicinity of a submarine is made alive with explosives. No matter what may be the U-boat's direction, she cannot steer out of the peril which surrounds her. I know of one case where no less than 40 bombs turned the sea into a series of marine volcanoes, making it impossible for any submerged crew to survive.

Strange things happen at sea.

Once upon a time His Majesty's Navy contained among her 'Tribal' class of destroyers two whose names suggested African darkness. The first was called *Zulu*: the second was *Nubian*. Then the Great War in 1914 broke out in which both ships played their good part until checked by hard luck.

For H.M.S. *Zulu* in the English Channel struck a mine which blew off her bows, so she was salved and taken into dockyard for repairs.

Now on the night of October 26–27, 1916, when it was black as any nigger, the Germans made their famous raid on Dover Straits, and forth to meet them rushed six of our 'Tribal' destroyers, including H.M.S. *Nubian*. At short range the enemy poured into her a heavy fire, so that later she had to be taken in tow. Before morning dawned the blackness turned into a full south-west gale—one of the worst that winter—and the tow-line parted. Buffeted about by wind, wave and strong tide, the *Nubian* drifted ashore near the Kentish cliffs. Everyone thought that was the end of her career. For her stern no longer existed.

Subsequently, however, they managed to salve her, tow her round to the dockyard for repairs likewise. Then a man with imagination and sense of humour said:

"Here is one destroyer with fore part missing, and the other ship which has no stern. Why not join the *Zulu* to *Nubian* and thus make a perfectly good unit?"

Since they were both of the same class and design, this union was effected with no great difficulty, and they even married the names so that the completed halves became H.M.S. *Zubian* and early in 1917 she steamed back to serve in the Dover area again. Of course lots of 'dismal Jimmies' thought this was tempting fate just a little too far. A monument to two disasters, she would certainly find a third!

'Adventures are to the adventurous', and she had not long to wait. One bitter day on February 4, 1918, whilst yet it was dark, H.M.S. *Zubian* chanced to be patrolling in the neighbourhood of Dungeness when a first-class surprise awaited her. Although the hour was 5.30 a.m. and long before sunrise, the lookout sighted on the surface heading north-eastward a submarine with both masts up and German White Ensign defiantly flying. Possibly the enemy, homeward-bound for Zeebrugge, was about to wireless his position before attempting the Dover danger zone? Probably the ensign (which so closely resembled ours) might have been hoisted to make the submarine in the distance and blackness seem to be British?

Very near she loomed up: in fact only 400 yards off the port bow. Her captain, Seuffer by name, certainly did not exercise that caution which many U-boat skippers showed when about to negotiate this death area with its patrols and hidden minefield. His boat was in no proper diving trim, and most likely she had been all night cruising on the surface charging her batteries.

Zubian altered course towards her, speed being accelerated, and something was about to happen. Call it slackness, sleepiness, or over-confidence, Seuffer failed to realize his folly till too late. Only when the onrushing destroyer was observed 40 yards away did the Zeebrugge foe make a crash dive: it had to be either that or be ripped in twain by collision.

Barely did the German escape the latter, for her normal period of submerging was 33 seconds, and it would have taken *Zubian* only 18 seconds to reach the enemy. The destroyer's engines were being worked up to 25 knots without delay, yet full speed cannot be attained instantaneously. All the same *Zubian* arrived at the right time exactly over the spot below which the 500-tons craft had disappeared; a depth-charge was dropped precisely in the centre of this disturbed water, and the reply came with remarkable celerity.

Large quantities of oil rose to the surface. Not one of those jets which some cunning commanders used to release, accompanied by bits of wood, to try and fool pursuers into believing they had conquered. This time a veritable oil deluge fell over the *Zubian* as far as the after funnel, staining white decks and heavily sprinkling sailors from head to foot. A second explosive created another large patch.

Lieut. H. J. Hartnoll, R.N., commanding officer of the destroyer, did not believe in half-measures. Releasing another couple of depth-charges, he marked the spot with a buoy; then an hour later arrived H.M.S. *P-12* (a specially built kind of torpedo-boat) which loosed off six more, while at 7.30 a.m. a mighty collection of destroyers, P-boats, and other craft repeated this intensity. Then, finally, the trawlers arrived with their wire-sweeps, located the wreck, sent up another big bubble of oil, and by that afternoon it was decided to call it a day. UC-50 with Seuffer and all hands had gone to their doom. Thus, some $4\frac{1}{2}$ miles south of Dungeness lighthouse lies a steel coffin with three German officers and 23 men who thought they could lay mines, sink British shipping, and then escape away home.

Lieut. Hartnoll was awarded the D.S.O. in proof that the enemy had got hold of the wrong idea. His destroyer avenged all that had happened to *Zulu* and *Nubian*.

CHAPTER XXII

YACHTS VERSUS SUBMARINES

It was so extraordinary and incredible that Germany's submarines should keep on attempting to get through Dover Straits at a date when the enemy so determinedly lost craft and crews, that even now one cannot grasp those undertakings with any comprehension.

Were the Huns so unimaginative that they suspected nothing?

H.M. YACHT "LORNA"

This armed vessel of 484 tons sank UB-74 west of Portland Bill. She was rammed with severe effect on May 26.

SALVING THE GERMAN UC-44. Notice the gun on deck and the wrecked conning-tower. After great difficulty she is brought ashore by lighters.

About 9.30 on the night of February 8, 1918, H.M. Drifter *Gowan II* was patrolling off Dover and half a mile from No. 15 Buoy when in the beam of a trawler's flare an object resembling a submarine was seen. The *Gowan* then steamed at full speed and lit a flare, but after 15 minutes could see nothing. It was *UB*-38, who evidently deemed it well to dive. Such folly brought her on to sub-surface mines and at 9.45 p.m. a triple submerged explosion shook the *Gowan*, likewise H.M. Destroyer *Greyhound* and other vessels. Not a German was seen, but a large patch of oil was found on the surface. The loss of *UB*-38 had been accomplished without the slightest difficulty. The sum of £1000 was awarded by the Admiralty among the Dover trawlers and drifters; but at the suggestion of the officers and men in the Auxiliary Patrol this sum was allocated to the Mayor of Dover's Fund, since this submarine had been vanquished by no particular trawler or drifter but rather by general co-operation.

And in spite of German submarines so frequently ending their days on minefields in British waters, what a hopeless setting forth it was from the first! Take, for example, the difficulties that awaited *UB*-21 which left Heligoland at 5 a.m. on January 31, 1918, and was met the next day by a minesweeping escort that was to guide her through some of the minefields we had laid in German waters. After half an hour the sea was so thickly strewn that *UB*-21 had to anchor and then return to Heligoland. On February 3 she tried another route: i.e. via the Elbe, Kiel Canal, and Kattegat, so it was February 12 ere the submarine could reach her destination (off Hartlepool) where she made two unsuccessful attacks against shipping, and on February 13 had so exhausted her fuel that she must start back home, which could not be reached till February 19.

So this submarine had been made to waste three weeks and done nothing. Our mines had upset that confidence which at one time inspired the German U-boat service. No wonder that they were growing desperate. Recently since December 19, 1917, in the Dover area alone the Germans had lost no fewer than six of their submarines up to February 13, 1918. No wonder, then, that on the night of February 14–15 another Destroyer Raid was made on the Dover Straits, but if this was intended as a terrorizing visitation it merely wasted the lives of a few ships and men.

Did the Dover defile, then, become a clear passage in the future for submarines? Perhaps the enemy thought that was so: but they were quite mistaken.

Let us pass on to February 25. At 5 p.m. H.M. Destroyer *Onslow* was escorting a convoy at the western end of the English Channel when a torpedo was fired at her but it passed underneath. After steaming at 20 knots for just over 20 seconds up the torpedo's track, five depth-charges were dropped. Up came the submarine's bows very slowly and vertically. She then listed over to port and sank. Other depth-charges were likewise dropped by four more craft and it was finally reckoned that UB-17 had gone to join the majority.

UB-58 was yet another of these submarines which simply asked for trouble in the Dover Straits and got it. At four o'clock in the morning of March 10 there was a thick fog and H.M.S. *P*-24 whilst on minefield patrol happened to be about 800 yards from the Varne Lightship when three underwater heavy explosions were heard in rapid succession; but despite the searchlight nothing was found until daylight at 6.18 a.m. when

I

pieces of wreckage consisting of bits of wood, loaves of bread, and a document in German (concerning the trials of this *UB*-58 at Bremen in the previous August) mingled with a lot of oil-fuel picked up. They were Auxiliary Patrol vessels whose firing had driven *UB*-58 to dive into the minefield and quick destruction. This was the first submarine wiped out in the Dover Area since the useless German Destroyer Raid of February 14–15. It is probable from the large quantity of bread found that this submarine was outward-bound. Another £1000 was divided between one trawler and five drifters who had compelled the enemy to dive to her death. These awards greatly encouraged the fishermen in their alertness.

Next day in the North Sea off the east coast of England the 5th Light Cruiser Squadron was being screened by destroyers when at 9.25 a.m. the destroyer *Sturgeon* sighted the conning-tower of a submarine a mile off. The German dived, but the *Sturgeon* steamed at full speed for the position and dropped a couple of depth-charges on either side of the track; after which the submarine broke surface showing her bows, her hydroplanes, and net cutters just ahead of another destroyer (H.M.S. *Retriever*) who ran clean over her, dropping some more depth-charges and marking the spot with a buoy. So yet again it was the old story of destroyers plus depth-charges finishing off a submarine. For *UB*-54, under the command of Lieut. Freiherr von Teichmann und Logischen, went straight to death.

Most probably when H.M. Destroyer *Loyal* attacked a submarine in the English Channel on March 20 with depth-charges this was *UC*-48, for the latter arrived at Ferrol only three days later and had been so badly damaged in the fight that she had to be interned. It really amounted to this. Provided your ship happened to be a destroyer and first sighted the enemy, then the rest was just simple. Keep the German submerged, calculate by watch when it was time to let go depth-charges after following the direction along which the torpedo had been fired—and the submarine would be 'done in'. If lucky, she would escape to a Spanish port all 'tattered and torn' with the German crew utterly tired of the game.

But May 8, 1918, was one of those occasions when vengeance, complete and devastating, seemed to descend exactly as it should, far beyond all human reckoning. A convoy was coming along and at 5.32 p.m. was 80 miles north of Algiers, being escorted by the U.S. Armed Yacht *Lydonia* and H.M.S. *Basilisk*. If ever any vessel for her hard and dangerous work deserved luck it was this British destroyer. She had served throughout the Dardanelles campaign, played a conspicuous part in the landing at Gallipoli as well as Suvla, and almost daily toiled in peril. Now her narrow escapes came with escorting.

Kapitan-Leutnant J. Remy in *UB*-70 had left Germany only three weeks previously and thought himself fortunate on his way towards Cattaro that this convoy should loom in sight. He sent a torpedo into the British S.S. *Ingleside* (3736 tons), and down she went with the loss of 11 men. *Basilisk*, steaming on her port quarter, spotted the missile's track crossing from left to right, followed it up, dropped at intervals three depth-charges, and *Lydonia* did the same. Result: loss of *UB*-70, Remy, and all hands. For, though the submarine bumped along *Basilisk's* hull, and a large brown patch of oil spread over the sea, those were the Germans' final activities.

That same memorable day Kapitan-Leutnant K. Albrecht in *U*-32 was hovering between Sicily and Malta when the aforementioned sloop *Wallflower* was seen escorting a convoy on her way from Gibraltar to Alexandria. Still a smart ship, always on the alert, she showed herself too quick for Albrecht whom she sent on his final journey below and in death his companions joined him.

Pass over a while, and we come to May 21. The scene was further up the Bay, on the west of the French coast. Out of the lock-gates from La Pallice harbour a northbound convoy was steaming, escorted by seaplanes and *Christabel*. The latter happened to be an American steam yacht. All of a sudden she noticed the wake of a submarine that was just about to discharge a torpedo, but the yacht again proved that a pleasure vessel could be the quicker in attack.

Depth-charges were showered over the spot, and if they dropped not quite near enough to cause complete destruction, they did enough damage to prevent this *UC*-56 from taking further part in the war. The German captain was another of those heartless submarine officers who had not hesitated to sink a hospital ship; for early one cold morning in the previous February, whilst yet it was dark, Kapitan-Leutnant Kiesewetter torpedoed the S.S. *Glenart Castle* with the loss of 153 nurses, officers, crew and R.A.M.C. people. Thus when this submarine limped painfully southwards and managed to enter the north Spanish port of Santander, where internment overtook her on May 24, she cheated justice. Evidently she thought this a suitable time for repeating the von Mellenthin trick for, on the very next day, she tried to leave Ferrol; but the Spaniards were not going to be fooled again. Still, she was a tricky creature, for after the Armistice rather than surrender to the Allies she scuttled herself.

The month of May 1918 really turned out for the Germans' submarines a most disastrous month. On the night of the 26th, H.M. Yacht *Lorna* (426 tons), hired from Lord Hollenden, had a most interesting experience. She was patrolling West Bay (beyond Portland Bill) just before ten o'clock, when about 50 yards away on the port bow appeared a periscope. Whether the submarine had been on the surface charging her batteries and ventilating her interior, but then been taken by surprise —and thus compelled to dive hurriedly—is not certain.

But Lieut. C. L. Tottenham, R.N.R., acted without wasting a moment. These steam yachts were not very handy, their turning circles too big, but this commanding officer starboarded his helm, went straight for the periscope and rammed the invisible conning-tower. Then he dropped a depth-charge, starboarded his helm a little more and, some 50 feet from the first attack, let go another explosive.

Not content with that, he was swinging round to pass over the spot once more when out of the sea disturbance four objects rose. He looked, listened, could not quite make it out; and while the rush of air was escaping upwards, he let go yet another depth-charge, dropped a buoy to mark the spot.

"*Kamerad!* Help! *Kamerad!*" he heard and stopped engines.

Three of the objects turned out to be dead Germans, the fourth was picked up thick with fuel-oil now spreading over a wide area. A German bluejacket's cap marked '*Unterseeboots Abteilung*' was also recovered. Although everything possible was done for the sole survivor aboard the

Lorna, he died three hours later. Thus did *UB*-74—a very powerful submarine 181 feet long, armed with three guns and 13 torpedoes—go to her destiny at last.

Lieut. Tottenham, who received a D.S.O., and Engineer-Lieut. E. Jones, R.N.R., who was awarded the D.S.C., more than deserved these acknowledgments after so many trying months of profitless routine.

CHAPTER XXIII

THE SUBMARINES WEAKEN

U-61 was definitely sunk in the Irish Channel on March 26, 1918, by H.M.S. *P*-51. This development of P-boats, that we have noted so frequently, was excellent, though, unless quite close to, many of our own people took them for submarines. It was whilst *P*-51 tonight was in the Irish Channel waiting for the arrival of her convoy that the enemy was sighted 250 yards off, steering to the westward at 13 knots. At first it was intended to ram the submarine at full speed, but unfortunately just then the helm jammed; and shortly afterwards the submarine was lost sight of. When, however, the German was sighted once again a quarter of a mile distant, the P-boat once more essayed to ram, but the Hun submerged and the P-boat dropped a depth-charge, followed by two others. They exploded with great vehemence, blowing much wreckage into the air and considerable oil. Thus quite simply *U*-61 was destroyed.

Finding herself fairly well frustrated as the sum of her efforts, Germany now planned that old scheme of laying a huge barrage in the North Sea, blockading the Grand Fleet in Scottish waters by means of submarine minefields from the latitude of Stonehaven Bay to about the latitude of St. Abb's Head. It took from April to August 18, 1918, to deposit this minefield, which was roughly in the shape of a quadrant of which the centre was about Fife Ness. Certainly it was a highly ambitious scheme laid by submarines fifty miles from the land. And all that the Germans desired was to lure the Grand Fleet into this barrier. But after much careful preparation the enemy realized that his series of minefields was being quietly swept up by us, so the ambitious plan completely fizzled out.

Somehow, whilst British mines so often answered their purpose, German-laid mines frequently failed of their intention. One of those big so-called cruiser-submarines—*U*-157—laid her mines within the vicinity of Sierra Leone. It was designed to be fired at the expense of torpedoes from a torpedo-tube; but although one merchant ship was lost, another of these missiles was recovered off Sierra Leone and the secret danger made known to shipping. Once more a Hun submarine foundered on April 11, 1918, in the Dover barrage. It was the ancient story where *UB*-33 was startled by the watchful drifters so that she dived, as previously we have narrated, to her death. Some weeks afterwards—on May 29—there was an interesting sequel when diving operations recovered from the wreck of *UB*-33 a steel box of confidential documents such as the German signal books, codes, and so on.

The submarine had probably plucked and uprooted the mine from the sea-bed and dragged it a mile and a half, shaking heavily both one of the patrols and the Varne Lightship. There were half a dozen drifters and one trawler engaged in the submarine's decease, and once more the Admiralty divided £1000 between them.

And now, though we shift to another part of the world we can still perceive the same technique so ending the submarine's activities that we are surprised how little does the enemy seem to operate against our well-tried methods. The area is that adjacent to Larne (N.E. Ireland) and the time was about 5.30 on the spring afternoon of April 17 when H.M. Drifter *Pilot Me* sighted a periscope off Tor Head, turned round, dropped four depth-charges in succession whilst zig-zagging over the mean northerly course that the enemy was steering. About 15 minutes later the submarine rose to the surface bows first. Thereupon various drifters shelled and hit the enemy until she was compelled to go back under the water stern first. More depth-charges followed from the drifter *Young Fred*, causing such a high explosion that *Pilot Me* thought *Young Fred* had gone. Oil and pieces of wreckage covered the sea, such as woodwork fittings, a shot-hole plug, some black-painted gratings probably of the gun platform, two seamen's caps and cap ribbons marked respectively '*IV Unterseeboots Flotilla IV*' (owner's name Rommel'), '*Unterseeboots Flotilla V*' (owner's name Schamewski'). It is thus that *UB-82* was destroyed.

Some of these submarine stories concerning the lives and deaths of apparently normal Germans seem but the records of simple fools, that I would again impress on the reader the plain truthfulness which requires no garnishing. The details and numbers are there for any confirmation: yet in cold print the accounts may seem to us an exaggeration. At least it became well clear that the skilful use of depth-charges was wiping out so many U-boats from wherever on the sea employed—North Sea, English Channel, Atlantic, Mediterranean—that the war's conclusion was foreseen as occurring within a very few months. There could be no uncertainty as to whether the Battle of the U-boats was still hanging in the balance: no longer any mystery as to whether we might be hunting the U-boats, but beating the U-boats within this next year.

We address ourselves to *UB-72* and the background is near the Straits of Gibraltar just before 4 a.m. of April 21, 1918. The *M.L.*-413 was keeping hydrophone-watch when she heard sounds of an engine proceeding at high speed and now she observed in the early light a large bow wave approaching from the west. Telegraphs were rung to full speed, and the bow lights switched on so as to avoid a collision, but two minutes later the new arrival was recognized as a submarine which had just altered course and passed across the M.L.'s bows only 30 feet away.

The M.L. followed in the enemy's wake and dropped several depth-charges, but nothing further was heard for some minutes when the hunter stopped. When daybreak followed, there was enough evidence to fill the eye—large quantities of oil welling to the surface and four pieces of wood. Two of these were fairly heavy pieces of white pine, creosoted and recessed apparently for ammunition, one piece of deal painted white on one side but black on the other; and two pieces of varnished mahogany fitted with steel hinges. Evidently the latter were part of a door. That was the last act of *UB-71*'s destruction and Lieut. Joseph S. Bell, R.N.R.V., commanding officer of the M.L., was given a D.S.C. for his victory.

And if you would realize all the agonies to which Germany subjected her submarine crews in running that terrible risk in the Dover Straits, please consider the following plain but overwhelming story which belongs to April 22, 1918. It is the most awful record of all these German adventures. No one can reckon these events without a shudder of horror that sailormen should take part in committing murder among themselves.

It was the drifter *Shipmates* who discovered whilst on patrol between No. 12 Buoy and the Vane Shoal that something quite abnormal was happening, for she felt a double explosion, and a very heavy one at that. She began to search the locality—it was a few minutes past 4 a.m. and already a large quantity of oil was visible on the water. Bubbles were still rising so the spot was buoyed and a search for wreckage made. Daylight came at 5.15 a.m. when the *Shipmates* picked up three live Germans, three more were found by another drifter, the *Seaflower*, and one dead body by the *Ivy*. At 8.30 a.m. the *Shipmates* heard another heavy explosion, buoyed the spot, and oil was noticed coming to the surface more thickly than before.

The submarine was commanded by a Hun named Wenninger, and the story reads more like that of a morbid scientific invention. She had left Bruges the previous night at 8 p.m. bound down Channel with the usual confidence and ignorance. Her crew numbered 28, but she was also carrying seven others as supernumeraries for training. Proceeding on the surface, she had not dived till Lieut.-Commander Ralph Wenninger at 4 a.m. gave the order to submerge to 39 feet. In fact she was just taking this depth, when a strange sound made Wenninger suspicious that all was not well: for his ears convinced him that a grating noise indicated they had fouled either a net or a mine. But this rasping sound was similar to that which Dunbar-Nasmith had once encountered when navigating submerged among the German minefield at the Dardanelles. No one would listen to such an interval without a feeling of suspense, but Wenninger's submarine—*UB*-55—had only to wait a few seconds when the first terrific explosion occurred on the starboard side aft.

The Germans at once understood the situation: even the supernumeraries needed no telling that a powerful mine had gone off: for considerable damage had resulted, the sound of water penetrating into the stern torpedo-compartment and engine-room was alarming and the boat began to settle aft. It needs no excessive imagination to picture the environment of desperate men with white faces groping in the dark and the stream of a leak growing worse. To restore the boat's trim, Wenninger sent his crew forward but without success. And even the dullest mind could foresee that their craft was doomed.

Matters were growing worse, the after ballast-tanks had been badly damaged, the engine-room was now filling with water. Engineer Sub-Lieut. F. Dietrich, seeing that he could not save the craft even with all her clever gadgets, managed to keep her on an even keel, and she finally touched sea-bed at 83 feet.

The sea-water now began to deluge into the control-room through voice-pipes and ventilating trunks. The batteries began to gas. But worse still the admission of all this water was exercising pressure of the air in the hull and gradually increasing this so that to the terror of environment was added the painful difficulty of breathing. Then German discipline quickly began to break down, there was no such thing as resignation to the inevitable. The German mind was not attuned to the spirit of self-sacrifice. Several unsuccessful attempts were made to open the torpedo-hatch forward so as to escape to the surface. But try as they might, these men who so often had sunk hospital ships, nurses, our sick and suffering; who had submerged with our shipwrecked men clinging on submarine decks; were now feeling the penalty which other jeering crews had imposed on our people.

Finally, as the Huns watched the water rising in the torpedo-room and listened to the swishing sound, they gave up every hope of seeing sunlight again and sniffing the sea air again. Stark reality with all its destiny faced them, all hope for escape gave way: a slow death by suffocation must come in that steel boat. Some tried to commit suicide by putting wadding in the nose and mouth and then throwing themselves into the imprisoned water already in the boat. Others tried to shoot themselves, but the pistols had become wet and would not fire.

An awful contemplation when the water within rose to a height of three feet, but then only was it found that the pressure fairly well eased the boat's external pressure, so they now discovered it possible to open the forward and conning-tower hatches. Of course there was a notorious custom in German submarines, which to most sailors of the sea is always regarded as discreditable, for the U-boat captain to escape first and all the rest to get away as best they might. Wenninger and Dietrich did manage to escape through the conning-tower hatch and about 20 of the crew through the foremost hatch.

Freedom at last?

Yes! for some, but not many.

The pressure in the men's lungs was so great that they were unable to keep their mouths closed whilst rising to the surface, and of the 20 who gained the surface only Wenninger, Dietrich, two petty officers and two men were picked up. Several unhappy creatures, because of the sudden change of pressure, burst their lungs and sank again screaming with agony. Nearly all the rescued six had lost consciousness; and even for some days after their capture were still expectorating blood and complaining of deafness.

It was between seven of our drifters and one trawler that the Admiralty apportioned £1000 for having vanquished this *UB*-55. And meanwhile on the night of April 22-23, 1918, we undertook that historic expedition against Zeebrugge in which the adventure was endeavoured to block the entrances to Zeebrugge and Ostende. Brilliant and brave as was this endeavour against the enemy, it may be remembered that the undertaking was not a complete success, but that almost immediately submarines could still get out of Zeebrugge, whilst the last of the ships which still partially blocked the entrance to Zeebrugge was finally removed in January 11, 1921.

Changes were happening in the German Submarine Service more thoroughly than the average person could appreciate; and I do not remember any separate incident which so completely indicated the change of morale which had already begun to alter. We have in this volume witnessed step by step the descent from aggressive independence to careless negligence. Now shall we see a kind of tired weariness that needs very slight persuasion to give up the whole effort. Yes: the enemy had changed for the worse considerably.

Indeed, had we prophesied aforehand that the following would be a true incident, we should scarcely have believed it.

During the early morning of April 30, 1918, H.M. Drifter *Coreopsis* (Lieut. P. S. Peat, R.N.R.), which had come out from Larne, caught sight of a submarine's conning-tower at 2.45 a.m. whilst on patrol. The stranger was distant about a quarter of a mile steering E. from the N.E. of Larne at 12 knots. The drifter now went full speed and altered course straight for the submarine, who came across the drifter's bows, but at point-blank range *Coreopsis* opened fire. The first shot exploded, the second was a miss, but the third exploded. *Coreopsis* was still proceeding East when the submarine actually fired two rocket distress signals, but the drifter began sending out wireless calls to inform all vessels what was happening.

Peat continued to fire on the enemy but owing to the heavy swell and being between the moon and enemy, accurate shooting was very difficult and the submarine went rapidly away but at 3.5 a.m. altered course, then stopped and fired a Very's light. It seemed all very curious and puzzling. What could the enemy be intending? Why all these rockets and what exactly was the German meaning to do?

The *Coreopsis* approached and then all the German crew in unison shouted:

"We will surrender. We are your prisoners."

What was that? Did Lieut. Peat hear correctly? Perhaps this was some German trick tonight? Surely the Huns would fight first, even if they did surrender?

But Lieut. Peat, seeing that the Huns made no attempt to escape or to attack, decided to try and capture them. Porting his helm and passing close astern of the submarine, Peat still heard these voices repeating the refrain:

"We surrender."

A red Very's light followed by a green occurred, and after four minutes' interval up burst another white light. So the *Coreopsis* brought the enemy direct into the moon's rays and once more opened fire as the German's gun was plainly visible, and it had best be put out of action. Indeed five more shells from the drifter were seen to explode, yet still the Huns made no sort of attack. Keeping directly for the submarine, the drifter steered bows-on with the gun duly trained and now reduced speed. It was still most mysterious, yet now the drifter stopped and approaching within hailing distance shouted:

"If you attempt to move, I shall fire again."

The enemy was watched carefully, he did not man the gun.

About 4 a.m. the other patrol boats began to arrive, so now Lieut. Peat despatched his boat with his Second Hand and two other men.

"Go near to the submarine, but don't close her," was the order.

Then hailing the Germans, Peat called:

"Jump into the sea and the boat will pick you up."

At this hour H.M. Drifter *Valorous* was arriving and bidden to launch her boat also. The latter made two trips and picked up nine prisoners. The submarine's captain and four Huns contrary to custom remained in their craft and at 4.33 a.m. this *UB*-85 sank. There were picked up by the *Coreopsis* boat members of the German crew to the number of three officers and 24 men, plus those nine who had been taken off by the *Valorous*.

And as they came on board, Peat searched them carefully for arms, taking all documents from them and then signalled Larne requesting permission to return to the base with prisoners. What an incredible signal! The patrol's dream of bliss!

Even now the whole thing seemed unreal. But if the Germans were just planning to capture Peat's drifter, that effort would be too late. Several more drifters, plus trawlers, had arrived on the spot and there would be a bloody fight with guns and rifles and sturdy fishermen's fists. But as they steamed back towards Larne and *UB*-85 gurgled beneath the waves, Lieut. Peat spoke plainly and bluntly to Lieut.-Commander G. Krech. As one sailor to another he must ask for a straight answer, whilst never easing up the suspicion that was felt concerning every Hun. But the dawn was fast approaching, they would reach Larne by 7.15 and any tricks would make the Germans sorry.

"Now then," Peat asked of Krech. "Tell me honestly. Why was it you people did not attack me?"

Krech replied in broken English as if grieved with life.

"I had been down two days. My crew were all ill with gas, and I could not submerge as my conning-tower was damaged. As I still saw you firing and watched the other ships arriving, what was the use of holding out?"

The Germans had set out from Heligoland on April 16, passed north-about, and been operating between Inishtrahull and the Mull of Galloway since April 23. These Hun officers complained that they had been obliged to keep submerged continually during the last two or three days, and were having a lot of trouble with their batteries. Moreover on trying to close the conning-tower door so as to dive, they had been reminded that the drifter's gunfire was very real. When first they sighted the *Coreopsis* and did a crash-dive, they went down to 40 feet with the water pouring through the hatch. Inside the control-room there was as much as 4 feet of sea. Krech had given orders to blow the tanks and rise to the surface, but something else went wrong. By error only the forward tanks were blown, and the boat took a sharp angle by the stern. As much as 15 tons of water had poured in and only her conning-tower emerged whilst even men standing on the super-structure were up to their knees in water.

Here, then, was a submarine that had been sent to do such wonderful things in the North Channel, yet had become full of forlorn hopes, 'fed up' with war, convinced of their ultimate defeat and seeing only death awaiting them When to all this fatigue and anxiety the batteries began to gas the craft, laying out the engine-room ratings, and Krech saw the *Coreopsis* drawing nigh across the dark waves, the Navigating Warrant Officer was ordered to flash S O S with his electric pocket-lamp. The submarine was at the limit of her ability, the men bereft of all desire to fight, resistance out of the question: for only nine rounds ready-use ammunition remained on deck and, owing to water, it was impossible to reach the rest in the magazine.

But Krech was an indifferent commanding officer. One of those obstinate and indecisive temperaments, he surrendered his ship too soon though most of his crew were very inexperienced. In short *UB*-85 till the conclusion of that war remained a memory that impressed us all of Germany's impending collapse. Krech during that cruise had indeed fired six torpedoes but he had never hit anything. And this general failure was characteristic of the dull rot which permeated the Hun personnel.

Something plus hard luck was the enemy's continuous bane. Take that odd incident which happened on the night of April 27, 1918. At first the S.S. *Ramsay* (Captain J. A. McLean) thought she saw tonight at 11.15 p.m. in Lat. 20.35 N., Long. 22.6 W. a fore-and-aft schooner carrying mainsail, foresail and small headsail, but it seemed strange that the *Ramsay* who was making nine knots was being rapidly overhauled. Presently down came the enemy's sails to reveal her as a submarine—one of those so-called cruiser-submarines of the converted mercantile *Deutschland* type. At 100 yards the submarine fired a torpedo but it missed by 50 feet. A second torpedo missed by much less, and the steamer began to reply with her defensive gun, claiming 9 hits out of 19 rounds whilst the enemy fired only one shot and then she had to disappear whilst covering her retreat by a smoke-screen.

Well, the truth is that this submarine had received some unpleasant damage from the steamer's 12-pounder and on May 1 did an extraordinary and impudent thing. She stopped on the high seas a Spanish steamer that was coming along, transferred to her two men who had become seriously injured when the *Ramsay* was defending herself; but having thus relieved herself of this responsibility, the German resumed her attacks against shipping.

CHAPTER XXIV

WEEKLY SINKINGS

IF the German submarines were now in their final phase, they were making determined attempts occasionally to maintain their sinkings. The approaches to the English Channel between 4.30 W. and 8 degrees W. were the concentrated area for intercepting convoys, fast liners, troopships and stores coming from America, but all that they could hope in regard to our Scandinavian convoys was to entrap them by mines such as laid in the Humber and off Berwick-on-Tweed. Nearly 6000 defensive guns were protecting our ships, and the German submarine commanders were still less liking our convoys which cramped the U-boats' freedom. Another source of anxiety to the Huns' submarines was the risk of being wiped out by British submarines.

During April and May 1918 the weekly rate of U-boat destruction averaged about two, which was serious indeed: the Germans could not supply boats and crews to keep up such losses. Let us examine the figures of German submarines sunk by ours in May 1918 alone. On the 19th *E*-34 sank *UB*-16; *E*-34 (again) sank *U*-154 on the 11th; while on the 12th *D*-4 sank *UB*-72; and on May 23 *H*-4 sank *UB*-52. Whatever the area might be, there could be no super-confidence for the enemy and at last the Germans began vaguely to suspect that we had done something to make the Dover Straits perilous, though at present these risks had to be endured.

May 2 opened the month for us with a double success when *UB*-31 was foolish enough to dive into the Dover mines and then be depth-charged by the drifter *Ocean Roamer*. It was notorious that Lieut. Braun, the commanding officer of *UB*-31, was a very unsuccessful officer, but he was lost definitely on this occasion never to return. And in very close position on the same day *UC*-78 destroyed herself by the mines with terrific effect and the additional depth-charges.

So also May 8 was another double-success day, that is to say in regard to (1) *UB*-70 and (2) *U*-32. Four submarines destroyed in a week!

As regards the former, *UB*-70 had left Germany on April 15 and a fortnight later was passing down the Western Mediterranean at the time when a destroyer was escorting a convoy some 80 miles north of Algiers. It was half past five in the afternoon when the track of a torpedo was seen crossing and destined to strike the steamer *Ingleside* which foundered with the loss of 11 lives. The *Basilisk*, however, went full speed and following up that track reckoned the position of the submarine and dropped three depth-charges over the enemy's estimated position, with the result that a large brown patch of oil appeared some 150 feet long, and 40 seconds later strong vibrations were felt on the bridge as if something were bumping along the hull. The United States Ship *Lydonia*, who was helping to escort, also dropped three depth-charges and it was thus that *UB*-70 was destroeyd.

I have not felt it necessary to relate how such losses were later confirmed, nor how on this day also in the Western Mediterranean H.M. Sloop *Wallflower* sank *U*-32. Some say it was by means of gunfire, some by depth-charges, but what matters is that the enemy could now be wiped off the list on the way from Alexandria to Gibraltar. There comes into our narrative such a speedy succession of sinkings at such narrow intervals that the mind can scarce keep up with events.

Those were the days when we were busy hurrying troops across the Channel to France. Early on the morning of May 9, 1918, the transport *Queen Alexandria* was transporting soldiers from Southampton towards Cherbourg escorted by H.M.S. *P*-33 when the transport saw a submarine 40 yards away. This *Queen Alexandra* with excellent seamanship made a quick attack travelling at 20 knots; ramming the enemy just abaft the conning-tower. The steamer, of course, damaged her stem yet she managed to hobble into Cherbourg under her own power while the P-boat went back into the English Channel finding a large track of oil and acid with small pieces of wreckage extending over a line seven miles long. Thus whilst not one of these soldiers was lost, *UB*-78 had been sent to the bottom with the loss of all hands.

Next day (May 10) H.M. Submarine *E*-34 whilst in the southern part of the North Sea at 7.15 in the evening espied *UB*-16 on the surface and stalked the German with deadly skill, firing both torpedo-tubes at 400 yards' range. Both hit: one under the conning-tower, the other striking the extreme forward end though not exploding. However, *UB*-16 became a complete casualty and only one human being could be picked up. His name was Luhe, but this surprised prisoner happened to be the distressed German commanding officer.

We have noted how comparatively easy during that last year did we sink German submarines. We saw just now that one of the converted mercantile class, heavily armed and disguised though they might be, nevertheless these were known for their weaknesses; such, for instance, as their slowness in diving and getting out of their own way. The following true story shows British and German submarines at their best. In the one case we see Commander Gercke in command of the big submarine-cruiser *U-154*, an officer of great experience, ruthlessness and of high ambition who thought nothing of wandering down to the west coast of Africa, shelling Monrovia wireless station and sinking our Atlantic shipping with impunity. But against him was now pitted Commander D'Oyly-Hughes, whose prowess, daring and skill are still remembered in the Royal Navy. When Dunbar Nasmith was winning the V.C. and fame up the Dardanelles, D'Oyly-Hughes was with him as second-in-command until the latter became Captain of E-35 and from the western end of the Mediterranean he was attracted out into the Atlantic on a lone and daring adventure requiring both cool nerve and utter skill.

The position was Lat. 35.24 N., Long. 12 W. on May 11 when he sighted a long low-lying object about three miles away. It was *U-154* coming up from the coast of Africa, an ultra-modern submarine displacing 1870 tons submerged, well armed with two torpedo-tubes and powerful deck guns; but though possessing great surface endurance of more than 13,000 miles could not exceed the speed of five knots while submerged. One visited such craft at Armistice to find ample space and quite a number of small cabins, and replete with many engineering gadgets dear to the mechanic's heart. A clever box of tricks but neither one thing nor another. Something of a marine monstrosity.

D'Oyly-Hughes now altered course to verify the stranger's nature and before 4.30 p.m. from a depth of 26 feet noticed that this large enemy was heading north. Course was altered to cut the Hun off, but by 6.17 p.m. *U-154* was coming down E-35's starboard side distant 250 yards. Perhaps rather too close for attack, and indeed the torpedo missed. But about 6.25 p.m. both tubes were fired at the enemy's fore turret and after turret, hitting where aimed. When the smoke and water had cleared away there was nothing more to be seen except a quickly expanding calm area with some wreckage. Three survivors were observed, but before these could be picked up *E*-35 sighted another German submarine two and a half miles off and had to dive. It is regrettable that in the Second World War which began in 1939, D'Oyly Hughes whilst in command of a surface vessel was destined to end his days through enemy action, and thus the sea lost a brilliant practitioner.

But by May 12 the enemy had in six days lost no fewer than nine submarines. How this eighth was accounted for on May 12 is a rather remarkable yarn.

The White Star S.S. *Olympic* was coming along full of American soldiers and marines approaching the Lizard early this morning when *U-103* lay across her track. At 3.50 a.m. the *Olympic* suddenly fired one of her bow guns but the liner already had by her weight and impetus charged so heavily into this submarine that the enemy was quickly left astern as a mass of tangled machinery.* Four U.S. destroyers at the time were escorting, and 31 Germans were rescued including Claus Rucker, the unpopular commanding officer. There were missing one officer and a handful of men, but luckily for the terrified Huns it was through the carefulness and good treatment of the U.S.S. *Davis* that so many were brought ashore for imprisonment. The rescued prisoners were landed at Queenstown as further proof of defeated Germany. The carelessness and negligence of these German submariners has been emphasized more than once, but here is a clear instance of the caution which separated life from death. The date was yet another instance of a submarine being sunk on May 12, and of the smart way in which British submarines could beat the enemy at his own cunning.

It was 4.30 in the early morning of the English Channel with a nearly calm sea, a clear atmosphere and bad light when H.M. Submarine *D*-4 sighted *UB*-72 to starboard going ahead slowly about two and a half miles away. After some slight manœuvring *D*-4 fired her upper fore tube which missed, but it was the second shot from the lower foremost tube which created a loud explosion. When *D*-4 came to the surface, only three Germans were espied swimming and picked up. Such, very baldly, is the tale of *UB*-72's destruction, but there is much more than this. She had left Heligoland on April 27, her departure being delayed by the presence of mines. Proceeding via the North Sea, Fair Isle Channel and down the Irish Sea, she had passed on May 9 between the Scillies and the mainland.

Her progress had not been easy. To begin with, she had to be escorted by five trawlers on leaving Heligoland to clear the minefields, but having reached British waters she was harassed by destroyers, trawlers and aircraft. During two hours on one night off the entrance to St. George's Channel she was pursued by a destroyer, during which period no fewer than 23 depth-charges were heard to explode, shaking the crew considerably and causing a leak in the port ballast tank which they filled presently with oil though it left a trail behind. The submarine was having a lively time and on another occasion about 20 depth-charges were heard exploding, extinguishing about half a dozen lamps.

The Germans had sent to the Mediterranean *UC*-35 which carried 18 mines and 12 she had laid off Villefranche on the evening of May 7, plus 6 off Cannes next day. But about eight o'clock on the morning of May 16 she caught sight of two sailing vessels and apparently a small steamer. The submarine opened fire, but the small steamer was actually the patrol vessel *Ailly*. The latter replied with her shells, at once tearing open the hull of the enemy, killing or wounding the captain and several men. Orders were then given for the Germans to abandon ship. Half jumped into the water and five were rescued by the *Ailly*, but the rest were lost.

Spain had become a familiar asylum for U-boats damaged in a fight. Besides those already mentioned was *U*-39 who managed to creep into Cartagena. This was on May 18, though on May 23 *UB*-52 kept up the reputation for negligence and was sunk by H.M. Submarine *H*-4's torpedoes, only two men being picked up. The incident occurred in the Eastern Mediterranean. Of course we can well understand again how German slackness led to their undoing. For *UB*-52 was just about to

*A detailed account of this incident by survivors will be found in Chapter XXVII of my volume *Danger Zone*.

reach her base at Cattaro after a month's cruise, and Lieut. Launburg, her captain, was down below making preparations for going ashore. Petty Officer Wehr happened to be on watch when two torpedoes from *H*-4 utterly surprised her, as Wehr did not keep a smart lookout. In fact all her people were far too interested in the pleasures that awaited them ashore, and only two lived to enjoy them after the war. And once again was Spain the home for damaged U-boats, for on May 24 *UB*-56 came into Santander after receiving damage in action. Why? How? Three days previously she had been attacked by the U.S.S. *Christabel* on May 21 in the Bay of Biscay. The *Christabel* was a 300-tons American steam yacht, which at that time was escorting a northbound coastal convoy and sighted the submarine's wake. It is true that an enemy was not sunk, but after depth-charges were dropped up came heavy black oil, large air bubbles and bits of splintered wood.

Curiously the next submarine to be sunk was by an English steam yacht on patrol—the 484 tons *Lorna* on May 26. A photograph will be seen on another page. On the night of May 26 H.M. Yacht *Lorna* was patrolling in Lyme Bay west of Portland Bill when she sighted a periscope about 50 yards from the bow and when 10 feet off a distinct jar was felt, caused presumably by passing over the conning-tower. The *Lorna* dropped a depth-charge and then a second. Whilst circling to pass again over the spot, four objects were noticed among the disturbed water of the depth-charges and the figures of four survivors shaped themselves. Shouts of '*Kamerad!*' and 'Help!' arose, and in the middle was seen a disturbance caused by the rush of air escaping from the submarine. Then another depth-charge was let go and it killed three of the Germans, but the remaining one when picked up was covered with a thick oil. He died three hours later. A German bluejacket's cap marked '*Unterseeboots Abteilung*' was also recovered and this was the final drama in sinking *UB*-74.

Certain submarine commanders were more successful than others, though one could not say definitely that even the most successful would never do a silly thing. There was an officer named Schmitz who was captain of *UC*-75 and had the reputation for being a success. Was it not he who in the Channel had sunk H.M. Sloop *Lavender* at the beginning of this month? *UC*-75 left Bruges afterwards on May 22 about 7 p.m. to operate off the east coast of England as soon as possible, having previously landed her mines. She must concentrate on torpedoing trading ships. So she arrived off Flamborough Head, cruised about there looking for shipping—getting a clear idea of what was going on hereabouts—and was soon able to ascertain that convoys might usually be expected off that white promontory about two or three o'clock in the morning. Such news was valuable and worthy of the trip, but on May 28 Schmitz about 3 a.m. succeeded in torpedoing one steamer—leader of the convoy bound south from the headland. The submarine, however, was spotted by H.M. Destroyer *Ouse* which dropped depth-charges. It is true that *UC*-75 was damaged and oozed much oil, but she was less seriously injured than apparent; and at 3 a.m. on May 31, when about 12 miles south of Flamborough in fine weather but low visibility, was just coming to the surface before attacking another convoy when she was rammed good and heartily by the S.S. *Blaydonian* which Schmitz had believed to be much

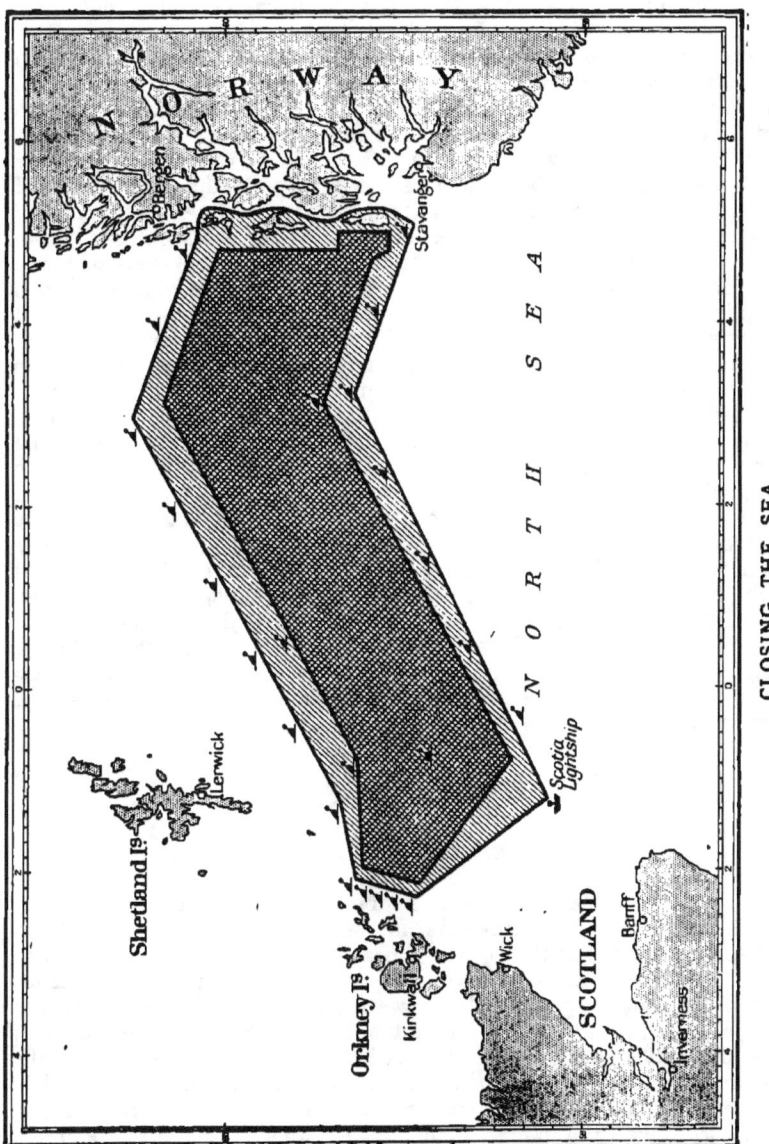

CLOSING THE SEA

How the Anglo-American minefields by the end of 1918 finally closed the North Sea against the German U-boats. Altogether 72,900 mines were laid between the Orkneys and Norway.

further away: yet it was a severe blow, the conning-tower had been struck and the hatch so badly damaged that a considerable volume of water penetrated into the conning-tower and thence into the control-room. Schmitz had made a miscalculation despite his normal successfulness.

And now he decided to blow all the tanks and rise to the surface. Today Schmitz was not at his luckiest, for he was also rammed or bumped by two other steamers of the convoy, viz. the S.S. *Tronda* and the S.S. *Peter Pan*. Even the most experienced U-boat commanders used to admit that when once they became mixed up among the stems of a convoy, panic to them was something real. *UC*-75 thought it advisable to rise above the surface, but just as he was doing so H.M.S. *Fairy* pounced upon him. Now in order to visualize such activities we must recollect that a submarine of moderate size returning to the surface needed from 30 to 84 seconds. During this interval after the *Fairy*—old-fashioned though she was—rammed her aft, the destroyer swung round and rammed her again. Then the *Fairy* opened a rapid fire with her 8-pounder; and Schmitz giving orders to flood the tanks and to his crew for abandoning ship really knew when he saw his men struggling in the water that he was not so fortunate. The total complement on leaving Germany had been 31. Of these there were rescued by the destroyer and a trawler 14 officers and men: but here comes the difficulty. The poor old *Fairy* by having rammed the enemy began to leak quite seriously and—like *UC*-75—to sink rapidly. So British and German crew were now transferred to the trawler, and an hour later to another destroyer. Certainly the *Fairy* had created desperation in the submarine, but it was the inrush of water caused by the *Blaydonian* which was the decisive factor on May 31.

On the same day *UC*-49 was definitely sunk, though there has been some confusion between this Flamborough area and the very different spot off Berry Head. *UB*-119 which had been sent to operate in the North Sea likewise disappeared. She may have perished on a British mine off Germany, or there might have been an accident; but anyway she just vanished mysteriously during May.

CHAPTER XXV

WAYLAYING THE LINER

It was the last summer of Germany's submarine campaign.

Although such a prophecy was not publicized, there were plenty of signs and portents that the U-boat was at least not far from the finishing point. The enemy at his most ingenious did not achieve much. Even when *U*-20 and *UC*-73 this June were being employed as transports between Austria and the Tripolitanian coast, bringing back from the latter such articles as saddles and other leather goods, their efforts hardly made any effect. And although the smartest submarine officers used to say that the smoke from the convoys used to be of great assistance to the U-boats, they were not impressed by our camouflage. But all were united in their respect for depth-charges which when least effective left them all nervous and jumpy.

Those converted mercantile submarines were still somewhat of a failure, and though armed with two 5.9-inch and two 4.1-inch guns still needed one and a half minutes to dive from normal surface conditions to periscope draught. Perhaps we startled Germany when we decided to turn the North Sea into a huge lake: for those mines in the Dover defile had pretty thoroughly corked up the southern end, and now the northern end between the Orkneys and Norway began to be laid by a barrage of 73,000 mines. It was a huge undertaking, largely assisted by the Americans, and this northern barrier finally accounted for six German submarines. Even during early June there had been two German submarines damaged though they did manage to reach Germany. It was not long, however, before U-boats were alarmed seriously. Whether they entered the 'lake' from the north or south, the submarines were to run terrible perils. Death seemed to stalk them as inevitable.

The Mediterranean strongly appealed to the captains of German submarines, who appreciated the space and freedom and the fine weather as compared with the Narrow Seas: yet Moraht in *U-64* (though admittedly extremely able) was another instance of being foolish in the presence of zigzagging stems proceeding in convoys. In an earlier chapter we saw her sinking with impunity the French battleship *Danton*. Eventually he sank 170,000 tons and received the coveted order 'Pour le Mérite', yet on June 17, 1918, Moraht like most of these fellows at last seemingly lost his prudence, his boat (*U-64*) and very nearly his life though forfeiting his liberty for some time. He was one of five prisoners saved and taken from the complement of 41. Not to be confused with his craft was *UC-64* which on June 20, like so many others, dived stumbling into the Dover minefields, her wreck being located afterwards by divers.

How Germany's submarine fleet, once so efficient and daring, bullying and confident yet now so much of a back number, was passing soon to its close we were soon to learn. Long ago we had learned the enemy's tricks, but ours he either could not understand or was too conceited to learn: so death or imprisonment had to be his lot.

Here is an instance of the 'know-all-about-it' type of young German who had been sent over here to plaster the neighbourhood with mines but managed to slip up badly. Lieut. Kurt Utke was aged 25, yet he was commanding officer of *UC-11* which carried 12 mines, and he left Zeebrugge at five o'clock on the evening of June 24, but about nine o'clock in the forenoon of the 26th when just E. of the Shipwash Shoal he got a fix and estimated that he was about four miles N.E. of the Sunk Lightship. It was then he steered at periscope depth to pass round the south end of the Shipwash; the tide at that time setting strongly to the S.S.W. Suddenly at 9.45 a.m., without any previous warning, there burst a heavy explosion which wrecked the after part of UC-11 and caused her to sink.

Utke was alone in the conning-tower and the force hurled him from one side to the other, rendering him unconscious; but an uprush of water restored him to consciousness and he had the presence of mind at once to open the conning-tower hatch and escape. Now the water rising in the boat had compressed the air sufficiently to make it easier for opening the hatch and he rose to the surface in a bubble of air. Simultaneously the lifeboat *Patrick* which happened to be 400 yards N.W. of the Sunk Lightship observed the heavy explosion one and a half miles from her position; wherefore the skipper proceeded in the direction indicated and found a large patch of oil. A man was picked up who said that he was from the German submarine who had laid mines in the War Channel and *UC*-11 was on her way home when she struck a mine and sank. The others had all gone and he swam with his clothes and boots on, letting himself drift with the strong tidal stream and tried to make for a dark-coloured buoy, but he soon found that after a quarter of an hour this would not support him. When nearly exhausted he was picked up by the lifeboat who eventually brought the Hun ashore. The young man had been as lucky as he was stupid. The cause of the disaster (though he did not know it) was quite simple. The Zeebrugge submarines had been laying their cargo of mines with regularity off the lightships near Harwich. Normally these explosives were duly swept up, but purposely and intentionally we had left one German mine, and it had not dawned on him that the English could be so simple.

But then it is so impossible for a young German to imagine that we could rival the other Huns at sea in ways and habits. For only a few hours before the lifeboat was rescuing Utke from death, another German submarine captain was committing an act of murder on the high seas. It was Ober-Leutnant Zur-See Helmut Patzig, whose name will continue to stink in the nostrils of any honest sailor.

On June 25 when captain of *U*-86 this loathsome creature sank the S.S. *Ailantian* when 110 miles north of Eagle Island. I do not object to his having taken prisoners therefrom the Chief Officer and Wireless Operator, but then Patzig took U-86 south and on the 27th when 116 miles W. of the Fastnet torpedoed and sank the S.S. *Landovery Castle* with the loss of 146 lives. She was a vessel of 11,423 tons—a hospital ship which was painted with the prominent Red Cross—coming across the Atlantic with no patients but all the above numbers including nurses and crew. And it was night, a hundred miles from land. Patzig's behaviour was that of a bully and cad. For his scandalous conduct he was afterwards numbered among the war criminals. When peace came and this Hun reflected on the trial which would presently convict him, this 'gentleman' bravely fled to Danzig. Perhaps Utke, on the contrary, felt a great deal of gratitude was owed to the Royal National Lifeboat Institution? I wonder if a Hun could feel anything except pain.

By July 1918 the German Submarine Flotillas were based respectively at Brunsbüttel, Heligoland, Wilhelmshaven, and Emden. At these four centres were stationed respectively 14, 18, 13, and 12 submarines or a total of 57, whilst several more were being built. In addition to these 57 were 10 more at Kiel, 20 more of the U.B. and U.C. types in Flanders, whilst the Mediterranean Flotilla based on Pola and Cattaro numbered 33. In other words a grand total of 120 U-boats were in commission just before the end of the war, though *UB*-8 had already been handed over to Bulgaria.

It should be explained that *UB*-128 and *UC*-73 were both employed as transports across the Mediterranean and *UC*-20 had been specially fitted for running as transport from Austria to the African coast, having first removed all mine-tubes. Thus on the outward voyage they had plenty of room for the carriage of rifles, small arms ammunition and shells; whilst they fetched back chiefly skins or passengers.

When German submarines came south from Europe the crews were at Pola accommodated in two ancient men-of-war, a sailing vessel and an Austrian-Lloyd liner; whilst at Cattaro they were put up in barracks which the men rarely left, for there were few social attractions. Neither in Pola nor Cattaro was there any fraternizing between German and Austrian ratings or officers. In fact with haughty disdain the German ratings despised the Austrians as mere 'paint-scrubbers'.

On an earlier page we mentioned with regard to that brush with H.M.Y. *Narcissus*, how discreditably von Mellenthin behaved in September 1917 after entering and subsequently escaping from Cadiz. After having given his word of honour in writing not to attempt this, he wounded the Spanish Navy's *amour propre*. Previously he had commanded *U-49*.

It may be convenient to anticipate what was revealed to the General National Assembly Committee of Inquiry in Germany on November 11, 1919, that Admiral von Capelle (Tirpitz's successor as Minister of Marine from March 1916) made the following statements concerning Germany's submarine position:

1. It was the Battle of Jutland which largely caused so few U-boats to be built in 1916; for the damage inflicted on the German Fleet necessitated taking workmen away from submarine work to do repairs on the High Sea Fleet.

2. The laying down of British minefields in the North Sea from 1916 caused the building of so many minesweepers to clear the exits from German harbours that workmen could not be employed building submarines.

Although before the war Tirpitz ordered 45 submarines and 186 subsequently, and Capelle had come into office in 1916, ordering 90 between March and the end of 1916, besides during 1917 ordering a further 220, these numbers existed only on paper. So the Submarine Flotillas were destined not to become as numerically big as prophesied.

3. Although the larger-displacement submarines took three years to build, and the smaller ones one year, Germany had not well calculated her position. Unrestricted submarine warfare had begun on February with 109 and during the following 19 months had averaged 127: but actually on service at sea at any moment there wer' not more than 47. Thus when spread over the north of Russia, the North Sea, English Channel, the Atlantic, and the Mediterranean, allowing also for the days spent on passage to and from their areas or in dockyard hands, there was very little strength available. Take the year 1917. During February the minimum number of submarines on service amounted to somewhere between 25 and 44; March between 32 and 57, June between 49 and 76. In detail it worked out thus: out of every five submarines there would always be one of her station at work, a second on her way home, a third coming out, and two being overhauled in dockyard hands.

This allowed nothing for accidents, injuries through war action and the moral effect on inexperienced ratings, since the latter having once been subjected to the depth-charge attacks would be rendered quite useless for some time after. We have seen so many complete or partial instances throughout the above chapters that we need not stress that point any further.

Some of these comparatively recent additions to German submarine officers were still weakening their national cause. One was Kapitan-

Leutnant Martin Schelle in charge of *UB*-65. Long before July 10, 1918, submarines of the American Navy were operating off Ireland against the enemy and the following incident this day occurred about 15 miles south of the Fastnet when the United States submarine *A.L.*-2 sighted something resembling a buoy three miles off. The American altered course to investigate. Actually there were no buoys thereabouts, but a severe explosion shook the American and a large column of water cast up in the air was preceded by the sight of a periscope.

Then *A.L.*-2 dived and tried to ram but the stranger passed very close though audible. Two submarines could be heard on the hydrophone: one to the north and one to the south. It was the one to the north whose periscope had been just seen and whose engines could be heard running at high speed. The other was running at low speed. When *A.L.*-2 stopped, the second submarine began calling up his friend but could get no answer. This went on for about an hour and it was finally reckoned that the first—and missing—submarine had evidently sunk by an accident and was definitely lost. She was *UB*-65, but the German historians who alleged that *UB*-65 perished at the hands of one of our decoys may be dismissed as quite unreliable.

On that same day in the Dover area *UC*-77 was at last to end her adventures. She had long been working the east coast of England dodging difficulties; but July 10 saw her blunder into the Dover minefield and then be depth-charged by drifters which rained such destruction that the thick oil continued to rise for two days after she had been sunk.

It almost seems as if some persons were anxious to crowd the last ounce of adventure into life before losing their ship, and we now chronicle the first but the last cruise of *UB*-110; a craft of 1000 tons submerged: rather slow at diving (45 seconds), carrying 3 officers and 36 men. Under the command of Kapitan-Leutnant Fürbringer, after she had done her trials at Kiel on June 18, she proceeded next day to Ostend, thence *via* the Bruges canal to Bruges where she arrived on June 27. The Zeebrugge entrance, as we saw, was fouled by the blockships though not wholly, since by careful seamanship and using high tide it was just possible for a submarine to wangle her exit. On the whole, bigger types such as *UB*-110 found it safer to use the Bruges-Ostend canal.

Having once got out to sea, Fürbringer made for the east coast of England, cruising up and down the War Channel between Flamborough Head and Hartlepool, keeping a sharp lookout for convoys, as Fürbringer wished to make out a time-table of their sailings; and we learned from her log that from July 6 to July 15 she patrolled between the Yorkshire coast and Dogger Bank. On July 19 an armed yacht was seen to seaward, which one of his officers (Sub-Leutnant of Reserve Tietze) recognized as the yacht which accompanied convoys. He resolved to torpedo, but Fürbringer intervened as not worth while, seeing that their principal duty was to reduce mercantile tonnage.

About 2.30 p.m., when some three miles south of Hartlepool, a south-going convoy of 29 steamers was sighted. Fürbringer was all for attacking a big vessel in the van, but a large number of escorts prevented him from getting into a suitable position, and he therefore turned his attention to a 3000-tons steamer in the rear. While carrying out this attack H.M. *M.L.*-263 was seen heading straight for the submarine.

Fürbringer sang out his order:
"Quick to 17 metres!"
He intended diving to 55 feet, but before he had reached that depth the charge had exploded under the bows, forcing her bodily up and jamming the forward hydroplanes to 'rise'; and another depth-charge exploded near the stern about the same time. The port main motor short-circuited, the No. 2 fuel-tank on the starboard side was damaged also. In order to force the bows down, the crew were rushed forward, but about this time of anxiety and panic *UB*-110 was rammed by H.M. Destroyer *Garry* which struck her conning-tower on the port side, causing the submarine to develop a list to starboard.

Immediately afterwards came another depth-charge right underneath so that this submarine was forced to the surface and all efforts to dive the boat were unavailing. Finally the captain ordered them to blow the tanks and abandon the ship. Meanwhile the British vessel had opened fire, hit the conning-tower three times and the crew managed to prize open the conning-tower hatch and then to escape. There had developed a panic amid all this confusion. Many tried escaping simultaneously through the hatches but got stuck and lost their lives, so as *UB*-110 rose to the surface, *Garry* again rammed her till she capsized and sank. There were saved all three commissioned officers and 10 men out of a total of 36. It was *M.L.*-263 who on sighting the periscope dropped a couple of depth-charges and *M.L.*-49 astern of her who also dropped a depth-charge; that were primarily responsible for destroying the enemy. Then in addition to the *Garry* came the assistance of H.M. Trawler *Strathclunie*. The sinking of *UB*-110 was yet another tribute to the *wasser·boms*.

The *Garry* was commanded by Lieut.-Commander C. H. Lightoller, D.S.C., R.D., R.N.R., who distinguished himself by ramming the submarine several times. He sustained considerable damage, though by effective shoring up of decks and bulkheads the *Garry* managed to make harbour. It was during the historic withdrawl from Dunkirk in the spring of 1940 that this officer again did excellent work though as a gallant volunteer. His name is still remembered in connection with the foundering of the *Titanic*.

CHAPTER XXVI

GERMANY BEATEN

The N.E. English coast, past which went so much traffic, was wonderfully attractive to the submarines, for there were many colliers and other kinds of steamers always on the move, though generally in convoy. On the other hand the coast is so exposed to stress of weather with few harbours for small craft to run for shelter. Torpedoings were unfortunately frequent, escorts were kept busy, but the enemy kept commissioning new U-boats with fresh but inexperienced crews. And so the contest continued till the end. Hydrophones were being used by our patrols more and more for listening to the submarines, but when these led to the quick deposit of depth-charges one realized that the enemy approached danger no matter when he dived. Robin Hood's Bay was a busy concentration for trawlers, M.L.s, and enemy efforts alike.

The clue to victory was the depth-charge, as so thoroughly it had demonstrated. Thus when on July 27 it was known to the patrols that a submarine was off the Yorkshire coast somewhere near Robin Hood's Bay, it would be certain that the enemy twisting and turning in different directions would ultimately show his periscope, reveal his hull, and come up to breathe. The great thing therefore was for the patrols to keep alert and be ready with a shower of depth-charges. For instance, despite the foul weather the trawler *Calvia* needed no shelter, waited till *UB*-107 broke surface, summoned others to drop their explosives across the tide and meanwhile use eyes and ears. They had not long to wait.

Then H.M. Yacht *Vanessa* was signalled and she let go her depth-charges. The result seemed as automatic as deadly. The releasing of depth-charges was followed by oil, bubbles and wreckage, and next morning the *Calvia* noticed a headless body in naval uniform floating by. No need to explain that *UB*-107 was destroyed. Very rarely these inadequately trained Germans would just disappear—perhaps it was through bad seamanship, forgetfulness, panic, or too much self-confidence. But now and again they just vanished and no one will ever be able to explain why. It was thus that *UB*-108 was never seen again though she lies somewhere in the English Channel just a rusty steel coffin. The Germans continued to have alarming losses even in their own waters by the minesweepers; but even in the Mediterranean we had made the Otranto barrage so effective that it had become most difficult for U-boats to go in and out of Pola and Cattaro. In Zeebrugge the submarines through continual dredging could use the harbour past our blockships only from three hours before till three hours after high water, so little detailed information was known exactly concerning the Dover area that the English Channel was regarded by the Germans as one huge danger. Yet it seemed extraordinary even in these final weeks that the enemy could not learn in the final chapter. *UB*-12, for example, set out from Flanders on August 19 for her minelaying voyage, and her capacity for carrying was eight only. She would therefore be used for short trips. But something went wrong either in her navigation or her internal economy, and she likewise simply disappeared leaving behind no record.

There remained to the foe after all these months of vicissitudes only August, September and a few days in October of 1918 before the submarine menace would come to a dead stop and in these final attempts we see just a few spurts to keep active, though the hand of fate was about to squeeze all life out of the Huns.

In August 1918 the steam yacht *James Fletcher* and the drifter *J. Burn* were patrolling the Dover area, and time being about 8 p.m. *UB*-103 was outward bound on the usual ruthless sinking projects. Her commanding officer, Kapitan-Leutnant Hundius, chanced to be one of our very greatest enemies: he actually destroyed nearly 80 ships of one sort or another. Tonight these two vessels shook him up properly with depth-charges, though did not wipe him out, and he wended his way to complete his nefarious cruising. But neither German officer nor German crew, having once been subjected to these explosions around, ever forgot the unnerving effect. Even if the hull received no serious damage, the moral result of sudden darkness when every electric globe was immediately smashed, and men stumbled about in darkness with unpleasant ominous leaks seeping through rivet-holes and hydroplanes developed awkward defects was such that all hands became jittery. They dreaded the thought of another narrow escape.

Thus, Hundius towards the end of his month's marauding, on the way up Channel hoped to give every patrol the widest berth. On September 16 he knew nothing about the Folkestone–Grisnez minefield, thought he would fool our surface vessels nicely, and avoid their *wasser boms*. But the British airship *SSZ*-1 saw him; so also did no less than six eager drifters—*Young Crow, Calceolaria, East Holme, East Anglia, Fertility* and *Pleasants*. Hundius didn't want any more depth-charges. So he took a dive below surface, and made himself invisible.

That turned out to be the biggest mistake of his career, for he submerged into our hidden trap, and the hidden minefield did the rest. His was the last U-boat to be sunk in the Dover Straits during the first German war.

That the Otranto barrage had at last proved extremely efficacious against submarines was well demonstrated on August 3, 1918. There had left Pola *UB*-53 (Lieut.-Commander Sprenger) on August 1 and two days later she was trying, submerged, to pass the barrage, but about 5 p.m. fouled the mined nets, having dived at 2.30 that morning being submerged between 98 and 131 feet at a speed of three and a quarter knots. Two mines had exploded, and damaged her badly, water flooded the stern tube, some of the electric lights went out, the boat lost trim and finally *U*-53 was running slowly on the surface when an investigation proved that things were indeed serious. Escape was useless, so Sprenger placed four explosive charges in the engine-room, threw overboard all secret papers, and about 5.30 p.m. she sank as the crew took to the water.

About 9 p.m. the engine-room warrant officer sighted and swam alongside H.M. Destroyer *Martin*. Being an old Mercantile Marine man he was able to shout in English that 35 men from a German submarine were swimming about so the *Martin* switched on her searchlight and picked up 27: the rest were drowned. Second Class Petty Officer Erich Reich was a former member of the crew from the *Emden* which had joined the schooner *Ayesha* in the Cocos Islands at the beginning of the war.

Our well-tried methods were still being repeated in the North Sea. Depth-charges, trawlers and yachts repeated their proof of superiority to the enemy with almost monotonous success. But Hunnish carelessness could not be cured so the Germans must remain in ignorance. The incident on August 13 became a free-for-all fight. It began at noon with *UB*-30 turning her periscope so that the mirror was turned on a convoy three and a half miles away but proceeding south. H.M. Trawler *John Gilman* in approaching the submarine was therefore unobserved till suddenly the periscope dipped and a few seconds later shot up, whereupon the trawler dropped a couple of depth-charges, followed presently by another pair. Oil and air bubbles came to the surface, but as the reader well knows this is not always a conclusive indication.

But when H.M. Steam Yacht *Miranda II* (a twin-screw yacht of 792 tons owned by Lord Leith of Fyvie) arrived on the scene she also depth-charged it. Two other trawlers were watching and listening on their hydrophones when they were startled by noticing the submarine break surface and each fired two rounds at her. But at 2.30 p.m. arrived still another trawler and further depth-charges were released. Still one more trawler depth-charged the position at slack water. The attack was strenuous. Minesweepers and divers, too, examined the place and the obstruction could not be denied. The Tyne area could thus boast that *UB*-30 had been definitely destroyed. Next day *UB*-57 foundered on one of our mines laid off Zeebrugge.

Events have a curious habit of soon recurring in the same district, but the following reads more after the manner of the present war with Germany than the first. It had not yet struck 3.30 on the afternoon of August 28 when Pilot Lieut. Waring, R.A.F., on anti-submarine patrol caught sight from his aeroplane of *UC*-70 off Whitby. The submarine was lying on the sea-bed leaking a long track of oil. Waring now dropped a 500-pound bomb sending up more oil, and H.M. Destroyer *Ouse* hearing the explosion rushed up and released six depth-charges, so that after the position had been buoyed divers were sent down who after a fortnight located the wreck as of *UC*-70 finally destroyed. On the following day *UB*-109 got on the Folkestone minefields and was destroyed on her way back from the Azores.

In accordance with the German sense of honour, the commanding officer was the first to leave this damaged boat, but when the Navigating Warrant Officer and one of the ratings competed with the commanding officer for this privilege, all three got stuck in the conning-tower hatch but the captain freed himself with difficulty. He and seven others were rescued from the water by a trawler suffering from deafness due to excessive air pressure. But the rest perished. And the Anglo-American Northern Mine Barrage across the sea from Scotland to Norway was not instituted till September 1918 though it soon began to account for six German submarines bound home. *U*-92 on September 9 crossing the western end of this huge minefield thus blew herself up. *UB*-127 also was blown up in this part of the barrage, and *U*-102 had set out from Germany only in September and a week later was destroyed in this Northern barrier and it is surmised that *UB*-113 which left Germany on September 14 was similarly disposed of, though nobody can exactly say either how *UB*-123 or how *UB*-104 perished, though it is to these Anglo-American efforts that their loss has been reputed. And the same remark applies to *U*-156.

It seems as if the submarines were resolved to finish up this war by wholesale immolation, for during the final days the list of their sinkings is remarkable. *UB*-83 was sunk off the Orkneys by H.M. Destroyer *Ophelia* towing through the sky a balloon. The destroyer released four depth-charges with great effect and then another four.

We have already referred to the sinking of *UB*-103 on September 16 by the *James Fletcher* though directly due to a mine; and she was the last submarine to be sunk in the Dover area before Armistice. Events were happening quickly, the setting forth of a submarine being followed generally by explosion and death. Thus though *UB*-115 left Germany on September 18 for her cruise she was depth-charged to destruction off the N.E. English coast by destroyers and trawlers.

So, then, we come to the final month of those hostilities—October 1918. The enemy was about to make a great offensive with cruiser submarines, ocean-going minelayers, U-boats and UB-boats. Such efforts actually were postponed for a generation until 1939, and only about a dozen boats were destroyed before the Armistice. It was interesting to note how this 1914-1918 period fizzled out. On October 4, 1918, *UB*-68 tried to attack one of our convoys in the Mediterranean, but H.M. sloop *Snapdragon* sank her with the fourth shell, and 12 days later H.M. Submarine *L*-12 stalked *UB*-90 on the Skageraak leaving no survivors. The cracking of the German system had most patently begun when on October 17 Ostend was retaken by the Allies. At the evacuation of Flanders the enemy himself destroyed *UB*-10, *UB*-40, *UB*-59 and *UC*-4. By October 23 German submarines had been recalled from the Atlantic and three days afterwards the outward-bound Atlantic traffic from Liverpool were authorized to proceed independently without escort. What a change had come over the sea! Of course there were a few isolated events during these closing days. On October 28 H.M. Submarine *G*-2 torpedoed *U*-78 with no survivors. It was a dark night with practically no moonlight and the scene at the eastern side of the North Sea. It was the same day that *UB*-116 bravely but foolishly tried to enter Scapa Flow: for a crew of German officer desperadoes wanted to sink our flagship. By daylight on October 29 nothing of this submarine remained except oil, air bubbles and a German naval watch-coat. It was the enemy's absolutely final effort in time of war. In the Mediterranean German U-boats were preparing to leave Pola and Cattaro for their return home through the Mediterranean, but at these two places the Huns destroyed *U*-47, *U*-65, *U*-72, *U*-73; *UB*-48 and *UB*-129; *UC*-25, *UC*-34, *UC*-53 and *UC*-54. On the night of November 8-9 off Almina Point in the Gibraltar area *U*-34 was sunk by the efforts of H.M.*M.L.*-155 and the Q-Ship *Privet*. Although the Armistice was signed on November 11, there were still several submarines which remained to be sunk before the Grand Surrender of these German pests yielded up their might to the British Navy.

It has been stated that 200 German submarines from all causes were lost by shells, depth-charges, mines, internment, torpedoes or any other cause: the two hundredth occurring off Almina Point as above. A slight difference in the grand total is given by another authority who makes the losses to have been 203. But I find from the German Memorial Column erected at Kiel in 1930 that the Germans claimed 199 U-boats and 5132 Germans were lost during the war. There were also seven Austrian submarines sunk.

The greatest number of German submarines had been sunk by depth-charges and practically the same amount by mines. By Armistice about 3714 auxiliary ships were employed against mines or submarines and the losses to our personnel had amounted to less than 2500 officers and men. The enemy laid during the war about 10,000 mines and by his submarines sank nearly seven million tons of British merchant ships.

APPENDIX

THE CAPABILITIES OF A U-BOAT

DURING the year 1917 German submarines began frequently to take as prisoners the Master, together with the Chief Engineer (in some cases), from the mercantile ships sunk. The intention was part of their scheme for crippling our Merchant Navy and thus depriving us of imports. By adopting such prisoners-of-war the enemy with curious lack of foresight was the means of disclosing much information not otherwise easily ascertained. For the British mariner is naturally an extremely observant individual, who acquires much knowledge from his immediate surroundings: indeed it would be impossible to find any class of visitors so critically disposed when suddenly bereft of their normal sea abode. Comparisons though noted silently are none the less real and such officers do not fail to mark many things which by the German were considered scarcely noticeable. So limited is the space available on board even the largest submarine that the admission of these people into the intimate seafaring life of U-boat crews cannot be done without creating certain clear and definite impressions.

For instance, I remember one Master Mariner being captured off our coast by a UB-boat on the latter's maiden voyage round the British Isles during her way to the Adriatic. The British Master told me how as an unwilling guest he voyaged three adventurous weeks, finally passing through the Gibraltar Straits and Otranto Straits till landed at Cattaro, whence our compatriot was sent overland for many months' internment at a German camp. He told me of the German captain's typical arrogant bearing, his callous determination and cool courage, though not even the heartless Hunnish grin presently could prevent the U-boat officer from being driven to episodes of panic. The same Mercantile prisoner-of-war related how when this submarine was attacked by depth-charges the boat was badly shaken up, the interior turned into darkness through the smashing of electric globes till the emergency lights were again set going. The water was washing about unpleasantly, but such attacks often meant that the hull started leaking at the rivets, followed also by further explosive bombs that might finally burst apertures into the hull, smashing down watertight doors, or jamming the hydroplanes so that the submarine could no longer rise from the sea's depths. On January 5 and 8, 1917, Kapitan-Leutnant Lothar von Arnauld de la Periere, the German submarine 'ace of aces'—the only man that ever sank in the last war 400,000 tons of shipping—who crowned his distinguished career by rising to the rank of Admiral in Hitler's Navy till one day he was killed in France while our 'planes were making an air raid, also took captive two of our shipmasters after sinking their vessels in the Mediterranean. These he confined to the after part of *U*-35. They noticed that this submarine passed the Otranto patrol line on the surface about 10 p.m. on January 12 during a westerly gale: and U-boat commanders would always choose (if they could) such a dark and dirty night for making up the Adriatic.

The Masters likewise observed that whilst on patrol the submarine was in wireless communication every day about 1 a.m. Arnauld admitted in conversation that he had been in London on German Secret Service just before the outbreak of the last war. Now this same expert U-commander used occasionally to come outside the Mediterranean and on April 14, 1917, passed Gibraltar on the surface about midnight, taking up his position roughly 100 miles to the westward. He had a busy time here sinking by gunfire the British S.S. *Patagonier* and sank that same day another vessel some 35 miles further west of the Straits. The deed was committed by gunfire, since Arnauld believed strongly in such technique, for which purpose he carried one of the gunlayers from the High Sea Fleet. This permitted him much greater scope since his four torpedo-tubes were more expensive to use than shells.

It is wonderful how very complete a record may be built up from a series of observations made by these Master Mariners who (despite their being on board as prisoners) kept their eyes open and their brains at work. For instance, Captain W. Mudd (Master of the S.S. *Maplewood* who was captured whilst that vessel was still in the Mediterranean) noticed that when U-35 was returning through Gibraltar Straits and was passing abreast of the Spanish lighthouse, Las Hormigas, she signalled to that lighthouse. So also this U-boat whilst passing Cape Palos on April 28 was observed by Captain Cundy to hoist her German Ensign. Captain Cundy had been Master of the S.S. *Trekieve* which Arnauld had sunk on April 18. These seafarers did not omit to notice that the Straits of Gibraltar were negotiated at night and Captain M. Hunter who had been captured from the *Patagonier* related that a professional cinema operator was being carried during this cruise aboard U-35, so that whenever possible moving pictures were taken as the submarine sank shipping. I myself was present afterwards when this film was privately shown in London.

The behaviour of these U-boats was, of course, subject to personal eccentricities. For example, the second pair of submarines to reach the Mediterranean from Germany consisted of U-39 (Lieut.-Commander Forstmann) and U-33 (Lieut.-Commander Gansser). Now when Forstmann in the early morning of December 6, 1915, sank the Greek steamer *L. G. Goulandris* north-west of Alexandria, he presented the Master with a signed certificate; but when Forstmann, also off Alexandria, sank the S.S. *Garfield* on January 15, 1917, he took the Master prisoner. Both U-35 and U-39 were careful to demonstrate from the chart that they knew exactly the tracks assigned to these merchant ships.

In general details (such as the nightly use of wireless, the confining in a small space aft of the captured Masters) there was much the same routine in all these Mediterranean U-boats. It was by some commanders recognized that these captive mariners on board such crowded submarines —U-35, for example, carried a crew of 30—were somewhat of an embarrassment. When Otto Schulze was operating in U-63 during March 1917 he put into Beyrouth (Syria) for water. Already during that cruise he had sunk so many ships that he carried a number of British prisoners, so these he now landed, whence they were taken to Constantinople and Germany.

By piecing together various incidents it becomes possible to obtain more than a sidelight on the habits of German submarines and to confirm certain suspicions. Thus we learned that when U-52 (Lieut.-Commander Hans Rose) was bound back home in April 1917 from the Mediterranean she spoke to several local Spanish craft on the voyage and received German newspapers. One cannot merely confirm the reports of the Spaniards usually extending sympathy towards the Germans, but by comparing dates we can obtain a fairly accurate idea of the U-boat's progress. Thus on April 14 U-52 passed Gibraltar, nine days later had reached the Irish coast, was steering between the Orkneys and Shetlands on April 25, and two days later crossed the North Sea to Heligoland.

Ruthless both in the Narrow Seas and the Mediterranean, Lieut.-Commander Rucker was operating in *U-34* on May 9, 1917, off the approaches to Marseilles. So much shipping was always going in and out that he could be well sure of at least one victim. Beyond the Ile de Planier, that low flat island which lies several miles from the shore near Marseilles and has a conspicuous lighthouse, Rucker sighted and torpedoed the British S.S. *Harpagus* (5866 tons). From her he took as prisoner Captain W. E. Pope, and besides this Master he selected also the Chief Engineer, whom he confined to the after end of the submarine near the stern torpedo-tube. Now the second-in-command of *U-34* was really a Mercantile Officer who had been serving as Chief Officer in the Hamburg-Amerika Line. German naval officers were wont to have very little to do with these shipmates whom they carried chiefly for navigation duties. But between the Mercantile officers of the two nations thus thrown into the close proximity of a little ship, naturally there was reason for much fraternizing. It was thus learned that *U-34* when off the Spanish coast frequently welcomed Spanish fishermen in their boats alongside. We have therefore plenty of evidence that throughout hostilities German U-boats and Spain's seafarers used to co-operate very closely.

These reluctant guests, landed eventually at Cattaro, usually were able to note that when U-boats on passage were attacked by our depth-charges the German crews were inclined to become panicky. All German U-boats could dive to a depth of 200–300 feet. It was not unusual for an attacked German submarine to plunge so deeply that the steel plates showed signs of bulging, creaking and cracking. There were instances, too, when the U-boat having foolishly dived into a minefield was suddenly startled by an explosion which blew a wide hole in the hull and admitted so much water that the craft sank to the bottom where air was compressed as if by an hydraulic ram. Men breathed with the greatest difficulty and died in violent agony. Well-established instances of such deaths occurred in the Dover Straits when two or three survivors managed to float up to the surface and narrate their terrible experiences.

Usually when a German submarine was compelled to dive this was done in about 45 seconds. The engine having been shut off and the batteries switched on with the tanks fully blown, she left behind for about a minute the swirl from the conning-tower. In such clear waters as the Mediterranean the shape of a U-boat could be visible over 70 feet, but in the North Sea and English Channel it was not easy to sight her under the surface. When the sulphuric acid from the batteries gets in contact with sea-water there is generated that very deadly chlorine gas. And I remember one German submarine at dead of night off the N.E. Irish coast surrendering to our patrols without firing a single shot. Why?

The German commanding officer frankly admitted that his men already were 'fed up' with the chlorine and tired of being hunted, so they were only too pleased to become captives. Many have been the instances of a submarine leaving a patch of oil behind after having dived. It may have been only a thin trace, but this followed the direction taken; for after diving there was always a certain amount of oil from hydroplane bearings and periscope—not amounting to much—but enough to leave a clear streak of evidence. Nevertheless it was not always a sure and certain proof of a submarine that the oozing up of oil could be accepted as evidence unless air bubbles also appeared and the oil continued for a considerable time. In fact U-boats later on were fitted with means for ejecting oil and bits of old chairs or gratings; pieces of ships' panelling would also be allowed to float up from a torpedo-tube to simulate a wreck caused by depth-charges. The claim to have sunk the enemy therefore required more than ordinary confirmation. Even the continuous leaking of oil towards the surface might be caused by a damaged external tank.

A patrol vessel coming upon a widening, welling slice of oil near the coast would sometimes puzzle our crews. I have known cases where the British ship even stopped engines to lower a bucket and take a sample of the oil, only to realize in the end that this had come from the wreck of some oil-tanker. Tides, a shift of wind, or commotion along the sea-bed have been known to make an area highly suspect.

When after some months of successful submarine warfare Germany in the year 1918 completed the building of what were known as cruiser submarines, including some converted mercantile *Deutschlands* which had shown what they could do in carrying cargo across the Western Ocean, she was really making an interesting but costly failure. True they measured 300 feet long, could keep the sea for three months motoring down to the Azores and even the West Coast of Africa. But their speed on the surface was not more than nine knots, they were disappointingly slow in submerging and they could only proceed at five knots when below water. Some critics had foretold that the submarine would eventually become a battleship below the surface, but in thus working out their idea they had followed a somewhat fantastic conception. Handiness, with readiness to hide beneath the waves in less than a minute, a surface speed of 17 knots and a submerged speed about nine knots, have been proved the best-tested desiderata. And the war of 1939 has established that the standard type of U-boat in the 1914–1918 period was not far wrong. These boats in the Kaiser's days measured about 220 feet long and about one-tenth that amount in breadth. But UB-boats, which varied from 180–190 feet in length, had a maximum surface speed of $13\frac{1}{2}$ knots with submerged speed of eight knots for one hour. The UC-boats were built originally for laying mines off our East and S.E. coasts. Their length later was about 162 feet and originally they carried 18 mines which were placed vertically in tubes forward—three mines to the tube.

These craft were slow: they could travel along the surface at 12 knots, but under water they could do only seven knots for one hour. When the UC-class first came out they were smaller—111 feet long and carrying only a dozen mines. These craft were employed in running across from Zeebrugge, depositing their black 'eggs' off such places as Lowestoft, the lightships around Harwich, near the entrance to Havre, and the Dover approaches. But the bigger type used to carry their dangerous cargoes to be laid off such areas as the entrance to Queenstown Harbour and sufficiently seaward of the Old Head of Kinsale to entrap shipping coming along from across the Atlantic. At the bows was a zig-zag-shaped net-cutter useful for breaking through such obstructions as the Dover Straits barrage.

We have given instances in *Fighting the U-Boats* of how a German submarine usually when negotiating Dover Straits would pass down Channel at night on the surface with the first of the west-going tide. Bound back to Germany or Zeebrugge she was fond of coming along past Folkestone and Dover on the surface in the early hours of morning with the east-going tide. Not infrequently perhaps two, or even three, U-boats would work together; but would fire their torpedoes at a range of about 400 yards, though when attacking a convoy the distance might be even as great as 1000 yards.

Just about the most difficult conditions under which a submarine attacked were when there was neither wind nor sea but a long swell running. With these circumstances the lookout in the steamer ought to espy at least part of the hull if not the periscope making a feather as it moves through the water. That is why the enemy might wait till an oncoming shower, or night, or early dawn, might be suitable. Bad weather with suitable waves might afford all the protection required, but really heavy weather might be considered so inconvenient for gunnery with the risk of men being washed overboard that a submarine might dive deep and await some other target.

The minelaying submarines found that an ideal time for fouling a channel would be on a dark night about high tide with facilities—such as a lighthouse's flashes—for fixing the position. High water was preferred since it meant greater depth for manœuvring: yet I know of some instances where one UC-boat appeared on a spot that had not been swept up since the visit of her predecessor. Thus it happened that the second carrier of mines blew up on those laid by the firstcomer. A really clever and observant UC-boat would make a note at what hour of the day the channel was given its routine sweep. Then the submarine, having followed some distance astern of the trawlers, would lay her 'eggs' and scurry away. An inaccurate chart, or careless navigation, not infrequently brought it about that mines had been laid so carelessly that daylight revealed at low water the horns of this spherical object bobbing up and down with the swell. Under such conditions it was never very easy to fire at the target—now above the surface, now hidden by the seas—but at least the area could be regarded as dangerous and merchantmen be warned to give it a wide berth. In the Mediterranean these mines were painted blue or green and laid even at over 100 fathoms.

The practice of German submarines using a dummy funnel or setting a mizzen sail aft was very common. At a distance it was fairly easy so to disguise herself that the U-boat might be taken for a drifter or trawler. Smoke could be allowed to emerge from the funnel and the sail was quite useful if the U-boat wished to heave-to and stop her engines whilst waiting in the swell for some cargo ship to come along. But the feigning needed to be done with seamanlike sense. For instance, whilst a German submarine might readily be unnoticed among a number of scattered trawlers working their gear in the neighbourhood, yet I have also known of a U-boat who foolishly went into a bay with her mizzen flapping wildly against a head wind. She was at once noted from the shore as an intruder who threw away all disguise beyond the limits of prudence.

Especially towards the close of 1918, when German commanding officers were becoming scarce and ill-selected, was such unseamanlike procedure noticeable. Yet in reading the pages of this book we shall do well always to bear in mind that the German crews putting to sea from Zeebrugge were usually about to experience a most nerve-racking time. Indeed by reaction when they got back to Wilhelmshaven or Zeebrugge or found themselves again safe at Bruges, such were the wild drunken orgies by these submarine Huns that even now the Belgians have not forgotten.

Briefly, then, we can picture the submarine after starting out from Bruges and passing through Zeebrugge skirting the sandy coast towards the eastern end of the English Channel. Being ahead of tide and sunset, the U-boat would decide to dive somewhere near where the Sandettie Lightship lay, sit on the sea-bed, have a meal and sleep before the tide was due to run west. A nerve-racking time would begin as the U-boat returned to surface. Buoys, nets, fast-moving patrol-boats, all seemed to spring up everywhere. Our anti-submarine barrage was certainly a source of anxiety, but later on those deep-laid minefields which had to be negotiated when passing through the Straits were to the enemy a veritable nightmare—when he began to suspect.

Nor must we forget that our aircraft, our submarines and all sorts of wide-awake vessels such as trawlers and drifters, destroyers and motor-craft, were ready instantly to pounce on the German with a shower of depth-charges which might persuade him to panic into quick submergence of the mines.

If perchance the U-boat should rush the Straits below water, he would use up so much 'juice' that he must be glad at the first opportunity to regain the surface and begin recharging his batteries. And in those anxious moments of becoming once more a ship on the surface any attack might await him.

Having cleared the Dover defile he might sight a merchantman approaching, spend some time in gaining a suitable position for torpedo assault . . . only to be put off at the last by the steamer's alteration of course and the creation of a smoke-screen. Mines were laid complete with sinkers and mooring gear. Hydrophones were developed during this last war and a listener learned to discriminate at several miles' distance between the noise of a ship with turbines and one with reciprocating engines.

Three mines in each vertical tube meant a cargo of 18, but some special U-boats were fitted to lay 34 mines from the stern. Sometimes our patrols on sighting submarines used to marvel that the enemy was at trouble to avoid action. It was, however, quite natural that the Germans should avoid warships until the explosive mines had been got rid of. Submarine commanders on either side used to exercise their ingenuity in some strange methods. One was to take the place of a buoy, trim at a convenient depth and torpedo the passing U-boat. Contrariwise German U-boats have been known to conceal their periscope ingeniously. On May 23, 1917, the armed merchant cruiser *Moldavia* (9500 tons) was sunk in the English Channel whilst American troops were being brought across. All that the lookouts descried was an apparently innocent soap-box; but it was discovered too late that this object floating *against* the tide concealed a U-boat's periscope. Similarly one of our British submarines had painted over it also the replica of a steamer, the funnel coinciding with the conning-tower. Thus in normal weather, such as the North Sea is wont to provide, this object provided the appearance of a small collier.

By the spring of 1918 practically all the German submarines were fitted with at least two, though frequently three, periscopes. One of these was specially made for searching the skies if aircraft were suspected. Most U-boats were double-hulled, the space between outer and inner hull being occupied by water ballast and oil fuel in narrow tanks. Compensating tanks allowed for the expenditure of stores, oil, and torpedoes. Often enough when attacked by the light guns of an armed merchant ship or perhaps a Q-ship, only the U-boat's outer hull had been punctured. At the beginning of that war when some of our patrols got near enough to a German submarine that rifles and revolvers were fired, it was hardly realized that our people were acting with excessive optimism. A more realistic appreciation would have shown the folly of wasting such small ammunition.

The greatest of all deterrents to a submarine was always the depth-charge; but the second most panicky occasion for any U-boat captain was to find himself in the middle of one of our convoys. Even the bravest and most skilful of Germany's U-boat captains have admitted that for a submarine to find herself diving amid the steel stems of oncoming steamers is a terrifying experience never again to be undergone willingly.

As a typical example of the problems with which our patrols used to be confronted let me relate the episode which happened on January 7, 1917, to a couple of the Portsmouth trawlers, whose duties took them to watch the trade and transport routes along one part of the English Channel. That morning H.M. Trawler *Sitvel* (Lieut. J. T. Rowe, R.N.R.) was at her work patrolling with H.M. Trawler *Alaska* about 10 miles N.N.E. of Cape Barfleur when *Sitvel* sighted a curious object about five miles to the north-eastward. The time was 9.30 and the weather fine and clear, so course was altered and at full speed the trawlers proceeded to investigate. After 20 minutes Rowe through his glass could see that the object was a submarine but he could discern also her conning-tower with a small mizzen sail aft, attached to a small mast. He could likewise see the enemy's gun.

The submarine now spotted the trawlers and at 9.55 began to go below the surface. At once *Sitvel* opened fire with her 6-pounder and 12-pounder so that 14 shots were loosed off before the German had disappeared out of sight. The *Sitvel* then altered course E.S.E. and at 10.20 a.m. reached the position of submergence where a streak of oil was visible stretching half a mile from N.W. to S.E. Along this line *Sitvel* followed and after five minutes when on the edge of the oil streak dropped a depth-charge and buoyed the spot. He searched the neighbourhood in case the submarine came up but no more was ever seen.

It was an unsatisfactory sequel, but if the German knew his business, doubtless he had in the meantime shut off his engines and was lying near the bottom till the trawlers had moved away.

INDEX

A

A.L.-2, 148
Abdiel, H.M., 43
Aberdeen, 9, 10, 33, 46, 59, 63, 70, 82
Active, H.M.S., 75
Aden, 20
Admirals, retired, war service of, 10
Admiralty, 8
Admiralty, awards of, 118, 129, 130, 133, 135
Admiralty House, Queenstown, 60
Admiralty, "Special Construction Section", 50
Adriatic, 44, 55, 59, 85, 104, 154
Aegean, 48, 58
Aegusa, H.M. Yacht, 58
Aerial torpedoes, use at sea, 64
Aeroplanes, German, sink shipping, 67
Aeroplane raids by Germans, 70
Africa, North, 146
Africa, North-West coast, 95, 140, 157
Africa, South, 21
Agatha, H.M. Yacht, 10
Ailly, patrol vessel, 141
Alaska, H.M. Trawler, 160
Albrecht, Kapitän-Leutnant K. (*U*-32), 131
Alderney, 19
Alexandra, steam trawler, 24
Alexandria, 9, 104, 131, 139, 155
Alexandrian, S.S., 46, 63
Algiers, 130
Allen, Lieutenant C. (*E*-41), 107, 108
Almina Point, 153
Alyssum, H.M. Sloop, 50
Amazon, Royal Mail liner, 123
American submarines, 148
American troops, first arrival of, 75
Americans' help in minelaying, 145
Amsterdam, 86
Anchor Line, The, 90
Anglo-American sea traffic, 8, 152
Annan, S.S., 43
Anti-submarine measures, British, 8, 29, 59, 110
Antillian, S.S., 88
Arab, H.M. Destroyer, 94
Aracataca, S.S., 40
Archangel, 50, 83, 84, 108
Arctic Ocean, 23, 84, 97
Arctic Ocean, gales in, 21, 23
Ariadne, H.M. Cruiser, 97
Arius, Riga, 17
Armed trawlers, British 68
Armed trawlers, German, 63
Armistice, 140, 152, 153
Arnauld de la Perière, Lothar von, 43, 49, 154
   death of, 50

Arnold, Ober-Leutnant E. A. (*UC*-33), 93
Ashwold, steam trawler, 38
Ativern, H.M. Drifter, 37
Atlantic convoys, 70, 83
Atlantic, North, 9, 13, 46, 50, 70, 71, 73, 77, 78, 89, 95, 133, 140, 147, 148, 153, 157
Atlantian, S.S., 146
Aubrietia, H.M. Sloop, 11, 12, 13, 34, 73
Audacious, H.M.S., 21, 22
Aurania, S.S., Cunard, 121
Auskerry Island, 59
Australia, 20
Austria, 144, 146
Austrian Captains, chivalry of, 68
Austrian submarines, 153
Auxiliary Patrol, the, 22, 86
Aurora, 94
Ayesha, sailing vessel, 104, 151
Azores, 69, 93, 152, 157

B

Babcock, Commander, U.S.N. ("Mr. J. V. Richardson"), 55
Bailey Light, 99
Baltic, 29
Bar Lightship, 43
Baralong, Q-ship, 59
Bard Head, 95
Barfleur, 29, 62
Barfleur, Cape, 43, 105, 160
Barnstaple, 32
Barra Head Light, 88
Barten, Ober-Leutnant, 45
Basilisk (*Q*-13), 139
Batavia, 21
Bauer, Commander H., 69
Bawdsey Banks, 33
Bayard, sailing lugger, 32
Bayly, Admiral Sir Lewis, 41, 60, 67, 112
Bayonne, French sailing ship, 51
Beating the U-Boats, 7
Beaton, Lieutenant, W. D., R.N.R., 52, 54
Beaumaris, 13
B.E.F., 1940, 85
Belfast, 121
Belgian barrage, 117
Belgian Prince, S.S., 77
Belgium, 76, 79, 116
Bell, Lieutenant Joseph S., D.S.C., R.N.V.R. (*ML*-413), 133
Belle Ile, 61
Belvoir Castle, steam trawler, 38

INDEX

Benguela, S.S., 70
Berehaven, 39, 40, 51, 93
Bernis, Kapitän-Leutnant J. K. (*U*-104), 111, 113
Berry, Skipper A. E., D.S.C., 119
Berry Head, 15, 33, 144
Bersay, Brough of, 101
Berwick-on-Tweed, 40, 138
Beryl III, H.M. Drifter, 118, 120, 121
Beyrouth, 155
Biscay, Bay of, 13, 17, 27, 44, 79, 96, 97, 102, 142
Bizerta, convoy off, 116
Black deep, The, 59
Blackwood, Commander M. B. R., R.N., 93
Blanche, H.M. Destroyer, 45, 62
Blanc Nez, 77
Blankenberghe, 63
Blaydonian, S.S., 142, 144
Bleeck, Petty Officer, 109
Blind steering by submarines, 44
Boer farmers find a sea mine, 21
Bombay, 20
Bonetta, H.M. Destroyer, 82
Bonifacio, Straits of, 49
Borkum Roads, 46
Boston, 55
Boulogne, 77
Boutefeu, French Destroyer, 69
Boy Alfred, armed smack, 28, 29
Bracondale, collier (*Chagford*), 78
Braeneil, S.S., 54, 114
Braun, Lieutenant, 139
Bremen, 130
Bremen, trans-oceanic *U*-boat, 70
Bremse, German light cruiser, 101
Brest, 16, 84, 114
Breyer, Lieutenant-Commander, 23, 25, 26
Brindisi, 69
Brine (*Q*-9), 14
Bristol Channel, 16
Bristol, H.M.S., 69
British Isles, 154
British Transport, S.S., 84
Brixham, 14, 32
Brixham trawlers, 32
Broadstairs, 41, 42
Broke, H.M.S., 58
Brown Mouse, yacht, 32
Brownstone, 93
Bruges, 23, 63, 97, 99, 134, 142, 148, 158
Brummer, German light cruiser, 101
Brunsbüttel, 71, 91, 101, 146
Buch, Commanding Officer (*U*-48), 101
Buchan Ness, 38
Buchanan, Lieutenant, R.N., 73
Bulgaria, 146
Bull Rocks, 63
Bullock, Skipper J. H., D.S.C., 118
Buncrana (N. Ireland), 22, 78
Buoys, Knoll, 41

Buoys—
No. 1, 43
No. 2, 43
No. 2A, 58
No. 7A, 62
No. 11A, 36, 41
No. 12, 134
No. 15, 129
Buoys, our tricks with, 33
Burford Buoy, 99
Burney, Commander Sir D., 37
Butt of Lewis, 54
Buttercup, H.M. Sloop, 39

C

C-class submarines, British, 7, 56, 97, 99
C-7, 56
C-15, 97, 99
Cadiz, 85, 147
Caen, 60
Calceolaria, drifter, 151
Calgarian, Canadian Pacific Steamship, 122
Calvia, trawler, 150
Campanula, H.M. Sloop, 116
Campbell, Captain Gordon, V.C., R.N., 32, 39, 51, 56, 71, 74, 75, 104
Campbell, Commander V. L. A., D.S.O., R.N., 62
Canadian, S.S., 50
Cancalais, 17
Candia, 9
Cannes, 141
Capabilities of a *U*-Boat, the, 153
Cape Bon, 72
Cape Clear, 9, 10, 56
Cape Colony, H.M. Drifter, 10
Capelle, Admiral von, 147
Cape of Good Hope, 20
Cape Palos, 155
Cape Verde Islands, 83
Carnation, H.M. Sloop, 59
Carrickfergus, 13
Cartagena, 141
Casquets, 10, 19
Cattaro, 44, 54, 55, 58, 68, 69, 72, 85, 130, 142, 146, 147, 150, 153, 154, 156
Celebes, 21
Cette, 14
Chagford (*Bracondale*), 78
Chalutiers, French, 45
Channel Islands, 10, 14, 19, 34
Chapman, Captain, 86, 87
Château Renault, cruiser, French, 109
Chatham, 32
Cherbourg, 35, 60, 64, 66, 139
Chikara, trawler, 82
Christabel, U.S.S. Steam Yacht, 131, 142
Christopher, H.M. Destroyer, 75
Church Bay, 98
Circe, French submarine, 69
Clover Bank, drifter, 116

INDEX

Clover Bank II, drifter, 116, 117, 118, 120
Clyde, 68, 78
Coastal motor-boats, British, 63
Cocos Islands, 151
Colombo, 20
Combined Operations, 96
Commander Fullerton, armed trawler, 106
Confidential documents, disposal of, 33
Coninbeg Lighthouse, 93
Constantinople, 155
Converted mercantile submarines, 144
Converted submarines, *U*-151–157, 104
Convoys, 59
Convoys, American, success of, 59
Convoys, Coastal, 64
Convoys, Ocean, 64
Convoys, N. Atlantic, 64, 99, 104
Convoys, Scandinavian, 104, 105, 106
Convoy system, 64
Conyngham, U.S. Destroyer, 59
Coreopsis, H.M. Drifter (Lieut. P. S. Peat, R.N.R.), 136, 137
Corfu, 44
Corsican Prince, S.S., 29, 30
Corsewall Light, 98
Corunna, 77
Crisp, Skipper T. S., 28, 80, 81
Crisp, Tom (junior), 80, 81
Cromarty Firth, 40
Cromer, 8
Cross-Channel drifters, 70
Cruisers, Austrian, 68
Cruiser submarines, 157
Cummings, U.S. Destroyer, 75
Cundy, Captain (master of *Trekieve*, S.S.), 155
Cyclamen, H.M. Sloop, 115, 116
Cygnet, H.M. Trawler, 10

D

D-class submarines, British, 60
D-4, 114, 115, 138, 141
D-7, 85, 86
Dakar, 83
Dale, steam trawler, 32, 38
Danton, French battleship, 44, 45, 72, 145
Danzig, 146
Dardanelles, 60, 130, 134, 140
Dargle, brigantine, 32
Dartmouth, 15, 21
Dartmouth, H.M.S., 69
Daunt's Rock Lightship, 84, 99
"Davidson, Mr. S. W." (Rear-Admiral Sims, U.S.N.), 55
Davis, U.S. Destroyer, 59, 141
Deal, 36
Decoy ships, 32, 39, 65, 66
"Defensively Armed Merchant Ships" (D.A.M.S.), 64, 110
Degetau, Ober-Leutnant, 47, 56
Deliverer, H.M. Drifter, 99

Denmark, 111
Depth-charges, 30, 31, 32, 65, 68, 125, 150
Destroyers—
 British, 31, 36
 Italian, 69
 German, 31
 U.S., 55, 59, 61, 68
Deutschland (*U*-155), 55, 69
"*Deutschland*" Class, German cruiser submarines, 157
Devonport, 27, 51, 71, 74, 84
Devonshire coast, 33
Dietrich, Engineer Sub-Lieutenant F., 134
Dingle Bay, 72
Divers, work of, 26
Dixon, Lieut. J., R.N.R., 29
Dogger Bank, 106, 148
Doon, H.M.S., 30
Dorset, 48
Dover approaches, 157
Dover area, 9, 31, 43, 64, 119, 129, 145, 148, 150, 151, 152
Dover defile, 159
Dover minefield, 118
Dover Narrows, 62
Dover, net barrage, 27, 31, 36, 42, 58, 70, 104, 132, 157
Dover Patrol, 36
Dover, Straits of, 29, 36, 40, 41, 44, 47, 61, 65, 68, 71, 79, 97, 98, 100, 101, 109, 110, 120, 129, 134, 139, 156, 158
Dover Straits, raid on, 127
Dover Straits, secret minefields of, 117
Downs, the, 36, 41, 59
D'Oyly-Hughes, Commander, 140
Drake, H.M.S., armoured cruiser, 68, 98
Drammen (Christiania), 106
Drier, Leutnant, 87
Drifters, 32, 36, 65, 102, 117
Drifters, British in Adriatic and Aegean, 48, 68
Drifters, steam, 8, 48
Drifters, anti-*U*-boat work of, 48
Druridge Bay, 82
Dublin Bay, 98
Dunbar-Nasmith, Captain, V.C., R.N., 60, 134, 140
Dundee, 82
Dungeness, 31, 43, 127
Dunkirk, 64, 85, 149
Dunnose, 104
Dunois, French destroyer, 35
Dunraven, Fleet collier (*Q*-ship), 74, 75, 104
Durham, 29

E

E-class submarines, British, 60
E-1, 108
E-34, 138, 139

L*

INDEX

E-35, 140
E-38, 92
E-42, 107, 108
E-45, 96, 97
E-50, 56
E-52, 97, 98
E-54, 60, 83
E-55, 70
Eagle Island, 146
East Anglia, drifter, 151
East Anglian coast, 67
East Coast, 27, 76
East Coast, dummy lightships on, 71
East Holme, drifter, 151
Eastbourne, 61
Eddystone, 61
Eider (Q-ship), 17
Elands Bay, 21
Elbe, River, 91, 111, 129
Elie Ness, 40
Else, sailing schooner, renamed *Prize* (later Q-21; see *First Prize*), 51, 52, 54
Elysian, H.M. Trawler, 118
Emden, 44, 52, 67, 146
Emden, raider, 102
Emden, new light cruiser, 105, 151
Ems, River, 46
England, East coast of, 148
English Channel, 13, 17, 27, 40, 50, 64, 75, 76, 81, 95, 96, 97, 114, 128, 129, 133, 134, 138, 139, 141, 142, 147, 150, 151, 156, 158, 159
English coast, N.E. of, 149, 152
Eschenberg, Engine-room Petty Officer Karl, 113
Europe, Northern, 95

F

Fair Isle, 33, 38
Fair Isle Channel, 112, 141
Fairy, H.M. Destroyer, 61, 144
Falmouth, 13, 14, 15, 51, 72, 115
Fanad Head, 22, 87
Fanning, U.S. Destroyer, 100
Farnborough, S.S. (Q-ship), 32, 51, 71
Faroes, 46
Fastnet, 54, 60, 65, 146, 148
Feasible, H.M. Drifter, 102
Ferrol, 130
Fertility, drifter, 151
Fife Ness, 132
Fifth Light Cruiser Squadron, 130
Fighting the U-Boats, 7, 27, 34, 97, 158
Firedrake, H.M. Destroyer, 97
Firks, Kapitän-Leutnant von (U-59), 46,
First Prize (Q-21; see *Else* and *Prize*), 52
Fishermen, backbone of coastal patrols, 116
Fishermen, British, as fighters, 28, 69, 80, 102
Fishing-smacks, sunk by U-boats, 41
Flamborough, 21, 29, 37, 43, 61, 96, 99, 144

Flamborough Head, 9, 40, 101, 142, 148
Flamborough Head minefields, 105
Flanders, 29, 33, 79, 96, 99, 118, 146, 150
Flanders, Evacuation of, 153
Flanders, U-boats based on (The "Flanders Flotilla"), 32, 76
Flare Patrol, 117, 120
Flemish coast, 63
Flemish Flotilla, 47
Flotillas, German submarine, 146
"Flower"-class sloops, H.M.S., 63
Flying Falcon, H.M. Tug, 88, 89
Folkestone, 70, 101, 117, 118, 151, 152, 158
Forstmann, Lieut.-Commander (U-39), 155
Fort George, Q-ship trawler, 87, 121
Forth, Firth of, 40, 46, 76, 87
France, 75, 76, 139
Frank, Lieutenant F. A., R.N.R., 34, 35
Frankfurter Zeitung, 76
Frascati, trawler, 119
Fremantle, Rear-Admiral Sir Sydney, 56
French coal trade, 64
Fresh Hope, sailing Q-ship, 76
Frisian Islands, 119
Fronda, S.S., 144
Fulda, German minesweeper, 46, 63
Fürbringer, Kapitän-Leutnant (UB-110), 148

G

G-Y-60 (*Alexandra*, steam trawler, Skipper J. A. Ives), 24
G-2, H.M. Submarine, 153
G-13, 36, 37
Gaelic, 75
Galley Head, 75
Gallipoli, 130
Galloper, 98
Gamma, S.S. Dutch, 86
Gansser, Lieut.-Commander (U-33), 155
Garfield, S.S., 155
Garry, H.M. Destroyer, 149
Geary-Hill, Commander S. A., D.S.O., R.N., (H.M.S. *Jessamine*), 113
Gebeschus, von, 86
Gena, S.S. (British), 64
Genista, H.M.S., 46, 63
Gercke, Commander (U-154), 140
German Fleet mutiny, 78, 79
German High Seas Fleet, 29
German-laid mines, 79, 80, 132
German morale, 80
German Secret Service, 154
German submarine officers, despondency of, 97
Germany, 79, 83, 93, 96, 149, 152, 155, 158
Ghurka, H.M.S., 31
Gibraltar, 48, 49, 54, 55, 59, 64, 131, 139, 153, 155
Gibraltar, Straits of, 83, 133, 154, 155

INDEX 165

Gipsy, H.M. Destroyer, 102, 109
Girdleness, 46
Glasgow, 121
Glen, auxiliary schooner, 65, 66, 67, 69, 75
Glenart Castle, S.S., hospital ship, 131
Goeben, 108
Gold for New York, loss of, 22
Golden Grain, 47
Goodwins, 13, 27, 97, 102, 117, 118
Goodwins Lightship, South, 79
Goodwins net barrage fouled, North, 101
Goodwins-Snouw barrage, 59, 77
Grand Fleet, 36, 132
Grand Fleet Kite-Balloon's destroyers, 76
Grand Harbour (Malta), 58
Granton, 76
Gravelines, 77
Great Skellings, 72
Great Yarmouth, 42
Green Head, 22
Grenfell,' Commander F. H., R.N. (Retd.), 19, 20, 42, 50, 56, 94
Greyhound, H.M. Destroyer, 129
Greypoint, S.S., 41, 42
Grimsby, 24, 27
Gris Nez, 77
Gris Nez barrage, 101
Gris Nez, Cape, 117, 118, 119
Gris Nez minefield, 151
Grive (Narcissus), 85
Guernsey, 19, 114
Gull Lightship, 42, 102
Guy, Lieut.-Commander J. D. B., 48

H

H-class, British submarines, 48, 60
H-4, 138, 141
Haack, Warrant-Officer Bernard, 23, 25, 26
Haaks Lightships (Texel), 119
Halcyon, H.M.S., 77
Half-Flotillas, 3rd and 4th, 106
Halifax, 73, 76, 121
Hall, Skipper, 38
Hallifax, Lieut. O. E., R.N., 86
Hallwright, Lieut.-Com. W. W., R.N.R., 56
Hamburg-Amerika Line, 9, 62, 68
Hammerfest, 23
Hampshire, H.M.S., 108, 109
Hampton Roads, 70
Hanna Larsen, S.S., 31
Hannah, Lieut., 53
Hansa Line, 68
Hansen, Lieut.-Com., 58
Harpagus, S.S., 156
Hartlepool, 47, 107, 111, 129, 148
Hartnoll, Lieut.-Com. H. J., 128
Harwich, 9, 10, 17, 36, 40, 97, 108, 110, 146, 157
Harwich Harbour, Shipwash Shoal, 33
Hashagen, Commander (*UB-21*), 111

Havre, 43, 60, 61, 62, 64, 77, 157
Headlands, 95
Heather, H.M.S., converted sloop, 56
Hebrides, 87, 123
Heinecke, Captain, 119
Helgoland, Austrian cruiser, 68
Heligoland, 23, 26, 32, 33, 38, 45, 47, 63, 72, 91, 111, 113, 129, 131, 141, 146
Heligoland Bight, 45, 107, 116, 119
Herbert, Commander Geoffrey, D.S.O., R.N., 72, 73
Herock, Petty-officer, 114
Hersing, 35, 36
Hewett, Lieut.-Comm., R.N., 67
High Seas Fleet, German, 107, 108
Hillebrand, Captain, 67
Hinder Ribbon, 40
Hipper, Admiral von, 107
Hitler, 7, 49
Holland, 82
Holland, compensation by Germany, 35, 36
Hollenden, Lord, 131
Hollesley Bay, 59
Holyhead, 86, 111
Horn's Reef, 23, 26, 45, 63, 84
Hospital ships, 37
Hull, 22
Humber, 8, 25, 46, 110, 138
Hundius, Kap.-Lt. (*UB-103*), 150, 151
Hunter, Captain M., 155
Hydrophone, 33, 41, 48, 77

I

Ile de Planier, 156
Ile de Reé, 61
I'll Try, 28
Immingham, 64
Ingleside, S.S., 130, 139
Inishtrahull, 22, 121, 137
Iolanda, H.M. Yacht, 49
Ireland, 27, 32, 38, 41, 50, 52, 54, 63, 64, 70, 74, 79, 91, 93, 95, 99, 110, 148
Iris, H.M.S., 9
Irish Channel, 132
 coast, 52, 64, 126, 155, 156
 Sea, 32, 51, 111, 113, 120, 141
Islay, 87, 89
Isle of Wight, 19, 66, 97
Italian cruisers, 69
 destroyers, 69
 Navy, 58
Italy, 48, 49
Itea, 109
Ives, Skipper J. A. (*Alexandra*), 24
Ivy, 134

J

J. Burn, drifter, 150
Jacinth, H.M. Trawler, 82
Jade, River, 46, 108

INDEX

James Fletcher, steam yacht, 150, 152
James Johnson, H.M. Trawler, 100
James Pond, trawler, 119
Jeannette, converted yacht, 14, 85
Jellicoe, Admiral of the Fleet Lord, 55, 108
Jessamine, H.M. Sloop, 112, 113
John Gilman, H.M. Trawler, 151
John Lincoln, 36
Jones, Engr.-Lieut. E., 132
Justicia, S.S. (*Statendam*), 90, 91, 92
Jutland, 7, 8, 43, 107, 108

K

Kai, Danish steamer, 10, 12, 13
Kaiser, Wilhelm II, 49, 50
Kaiserin, German battleship, 78
Kandy, S.S., 72
Kattegat, 111, 129
Kent, 70
Kentish cliffs, 127
Kerr, Sub.-Lieut. J., R.N.R., 14, 15
Kessingland, drifter, 47
Ketches, 17
Keyes, Vice-Admiral Sir Roger, 120
Kiel, 55, 91, 103, 104, 111, 129, 146
Kiesewetter, Kap.-Leut., 131
Killybegs, 41
King Alfred, steam trawler, 33, 38
King, Lieut.-Com. P. W. S., R.N., 31, 32
Kingston valves, 23
Kinnaird Head, 64
Kinsale, Old Head of, 9, 53, 56, 80, 157
Kirkabister Lighthouse, 10
Kirkwall, 10, 40, 95
Kitchener, Lord, 108
Kitson, Lieut., J. F. B., R.N., 109
Kitty, H.M. Trawler, 61
König Albert, German battleship, 78
Königin Luise, minelayer, 8
Kola Inlet, 50
Kophamel, Commander (*U*-151), 83
Krech, Lieut.-Com. G., 137, 138
Kroll, Korvetten-Kapitän K. (*U*-110), 123, 124
Kustner, Lieut., 66
Kynance Cove, 73

L

L-class, British submarines, 125, 153
L-2, 125
L-12 153,
Laburnum, H.M. Sloop, 39
Lady Olive, 34, 35
Lady Patricia (*Q*-25), 67
Laforey, H.M.S., 42
Lafrenz, Lieut.-Com. Claus, 99
La Houle, 14, 17
Lambart, Captain the Hon. L., D.S.O., R.N., 85
La Pallice, 131
Lansquenet, French destroyer, 109

Larne, 133, 136, 137
Las Hormigas, 155
Launburg, Leut., 42
Laurentic, H.M. Armed Cruiser, 22
Lavender, H.M. Sloop, 61, 142
Laverock, H.M. Destroyer, 36
Lawrie, Lieut. J., R.N.R., 14, 15, 16, 17
Leer, 54
Leith of Fyvie, Lord, 151
Lemnos, 9
Lerwick, 10, 40, 42, 64, 86, 95
Les Pierres Lighthouse, 16
Leven, H.M. Destroyer, 118, 121
Lewis guns, 13
L. G. Goulandris, Greek steamer, 155
Liberty, H.M. Destroyer, 30
Lightoller, Lieut.-Com. R. D., D.S.C., R.N., 149
Lightships, 9, 10
Lilienstern, Ober-Leut. Ruhle von, 68, 95
Liners, attacks on, 144
Livingstone, armed trawler, 106
Liverpool, 55, 59, 78, 84, 121, 153
Lizard, 14, 64, 73, 77, 100, 115, 140
Llandovery Castle, hospital ship, 146
Llewellyn, H.M. Destroyer, 42
Lloyd's Register of Shipping, 10, 16
Lodorer, S.S., (*Q*-5), 39
Logischen, Leut. Frieherr von Teichmann und (*UB*-54), 130
Longstone Lighthouse, 26, 61
Lord Alverstone, armed trawler, 106
Lorna, converted steam yacht, 85, 131, 142
Lough Swilly, 88
Louw, Abraham, 21
Louw, Girt, 21
Lowestoft, 9, 27, 32, 40, 42, 63, 64, 77, 79, 100
Lowestoft, bombardment of, 110
Loyal, H.M. Destroyer, 115, 130
Luhe, Commander (*UB*-16), 140
Lusitania, S.S. Cunarder, 83
Lychnis, H.M. Sloop, 72
Lydonia, U.S. armed yacht, 130, 139
Lyme Bay, 142
Lynas Point, 43

M

M.L.s, H.M.S.—
  M.L.-12, 119
  M.L.-29, 64
  M.L.-49, 149
  M.L.-201, 86
  M.L.-263, 148
  M.L.-357, 108
  M.L.-461, 33
  M.L.-476, 98
Maas, 40
Madeira, 83
McDougal, U.S. Destroyer, 59, 61
McLeod, Lieut., R.N.R., 56
McNabb, Lieut. (*M.L.*-201), 86

INDEX

Mainland, 113
Majesty, drifter, 102
Malin Head, 123
Malta, 9, 48, 58
Mameluck, French destroyer, 109
Manchester Commerce, S.S., 21
Maori, H.M.S., 31
Maplewood, 85, 155
Margate, 36
Margit, 48
Marguerite, H.M. Sloop, 58
Marie Thérèse, 14
Marlborough, H.M.S., 96
Marne, H.M. Destroyer, 92
Marsal, German Petty Officer Fritz, 97
Marseilles, 156
Martin, H.M. Destroyer, 151
Marx, Admiral J. L., 10, 12, 13
Mary B. Mitchell, 13, 14, 15, 16, 17, 18, 19, 75
Mary Bell, 33, 38
Mary Rose, H.M. Escort Destroyer, 100
Mary Y. José, 14
Massue, French destroyer, 44, 45
Matapan, Cape, 49
Maxim guns, 39
Mayfly, 25
May Island, 87, 112
Mead, Skipper, R.N.R., 52
Medea, H.M.S., 39
Mediterranean, 9, 27, 29, 36, 38, 45, 47, 48, 49, 50, 72, 85, 95, 109, 133, 140, 141, 145, 147, 150, 153, 154, 156, 158
Melampus, H.M. Destroyer, 96
Mellenthin, Lieut.-Commander H. von, 85, 131, 147
Mercantile Marine, British, 9, 120
Mercantile Marine, German, 9
Merops, decoy brigantine, 76
Mersey, 43
Mersey Bar Lightship, 55
Messina, 49
Michael, H.M. Destroyer, 123, 124
Milewater, H.M. Tug, 88
Milford, 14, 48, 52, 53, 75
Millbrook, H.M. Destroyer, 92
Mill Cove, 39
Mills grenades, 13
Milne, H.M. Destroyer, 62
Minch, 112
Minelayers, German *UC*-boats, new developments, 79, 80
Minelaying, 8, 9, 10, 20, 21, 33, 36, 37, 40, 45, 48, 59, 63, 79, 86, 119, 133, 149
Minesweeping, 8, 9, 29, 50, 59, 117
Miranda, H.M. Destroyer, 62
Miranda II, H.M. Steam Yacht, 151
Mizzen head, 9
Moltke, German battleship, 107, 108
Mongolia, S.S., P. & O., 20
Monitors, 36
Monrovia, 104

Monsa, 94
Montrose, 38
Moraht, Lieut.-Commander Robert, 43, 44, 45, 72, 145
Moravia, minesweeping trawler, 94, 95
Moresby, H.M. Destroyer, 123, 124
Morlaix, 18, 76
Motor drifters, Scottish, 8, 59
Möwe, 8
Muckle Flugga, 36, 38, 91
Mudd, Captain W., 155
Mudros, 48
Mull of Galloway, 121, 137
Mull of Kintyre, 87
Mutinous conduct in German Fleet, 78, 79
Mystery or *Q*-ships (general), 52, 125

N

Nairn, H.M. Yacht, 10
Narcissus, converted steam yacht (see *Grieve*), 85, 147
Narrow Seas, the, 145, 156
Navigating Warrant-Officers German, 9
Nelson, sailing smack (Skipper T. Crisp, V.C.) 80, 81
Neptun (*Q*-9, see *Eider*), 14
Nerger, Captain, commanding German raider *Wolf*, 20
Nestorian, S.S., 9
Net-barrage, 117
New York, city of, 55, 86
New York, S.S., 55
New Zealand, 20, 52, 74
Newbury, ex-pleasure paddle-steamer, 119
Newcastle, 76
Nicholson, U.S. Destroyer, 100
Nith, H.M.S., 30
Nitrates, imports, 105
Norderney, 119
North Cape, 23
North Carr Lightship, 10
North Channel, 77, 95, 98, 112, 121, 137
North Foreland, 36, 43, 94
North German Lloyd, 68
North Goodwin, 36
North of Ireland, 78
North Hinder Lightship, 101
North Passage, 85
North Sand Head, 41
North Sea, 24, 25, 26, 30, 32, 64, 65, 71, 77, 78, 79, 83, 101, 105, 111, 130, 132, 133, 139, 141, 144, 145, 147, 151, 155, 156, 160
Northern Russia, munitions for, 1917 and 1943, 22, 23
Northumberland, 29
Norton, Captain (S.S. *Laurentic*), 22
Norway, 21, 70, 145, 152
Novara, 68
Nubian, H.M. Destroyer, 127

INDEX

O

Oban, 59, 78
Ocean Roamer, drifter, 139
Old Head of Kinsale, 9, 40, 56, 80, 157
Oldenburg, German battleship, 107
Olive Branch, S.S., 83
Olympic, S.S., White Star liner, 140
Onslow, H.M. destroyer, 129
Ophele, H.M. Destroyer, 152
Oracle, H.M.S., 78
Orkneys, 10, 32, 38, 40, 44, 59, 94, 145, 152, 155
Osprey, H.M.S., 41
Ostend, 62, 63, 79, 135, 148, 153
Otranto, 58, 59, 68, 104, 150, 151, 154
"Otter-gear", 8, 37
Ouse, H.M. Destroyer, 142, 152
Outer Gabbard, 98
Outer Hebrides, 87, 88
Outer Ruytingen Shoal, 117
Oversay Light, 88
Owers Lightship, 9

P

P-class ships, British, generally, 132
    P.12, 128
    P.24, 129
    P.32, 105
    P.33, 139
    P.51, 132
    P.57, 101
    P.60, 77
P.C. Class—
    P.C. boat, 110
    P.C.61, 94
    P.C.62, 51, 120
Paddlers, 8, 117
"Panic-Parties", 52, 53
Paper-pulp imports, 106
Paragon, H.M.S., 42
Paramount, H.M. Drifter, 41, 42, 102
Paravane, 8, 37, 40, 59
Pargust, Q-ship (*Vittoria*), 71, 72, 74
Parthian, H.M. Destroyer, 40
Partridge, Auxiliary, 72, 106
Patagonier, S.S. (British), 154, 155
Patrick, lifeboat, 145
Patriot, H.M.S., 76
Patrol Motor-boats (P.M.B.s), German, 63
Patrols, sea, 65
Patzig, Ober-Leutnant zur See Helmut, 146
Paxton (Q.25), 67
Pecklesheim, Lt.-Com. Freiherr Spiegel, von und zu (Spiegel), 52
Pelleur, destroyer, 106
Penshurst, Q-ship, 19, 20, 34, 42, 50, 51, 94
Periscopes, multiple in *U*-boats, 160
Peter Pan, S.S., 144
Peterhead, 63, 91
Petersen, Heinrich, Sub-Lt. of Reserve, 62

Petrel, trawler, 25
Phelan, Captain, 63
Pickles, Temporary-Surgeon P. D., R.N.V.R., 58
Pigeon, H.M. Trawler, 29, 30, 92
Pilot Me, drifter, 81, 133
Pilotage, German ignorance of, 9
Pit-props, imports of, 106
Platypus, H.M.S., 41
Plymouth, 75, 115
Pleasants, drifter, 151
Pohl, Admiral von, 49
Pola, 146, 147, 150, 151, 153
Poole, 48
Pope, Capt. W. E., 156
Port Ellen, 88
Port Said, 9, 49, 104
Portland, 9, 21, 61, 64, 114, 142
Portsmouth, 27
Potsdam, 52
Pour Le Mérite, Order of, 43
Primrose, H.M. Sloop, 88
Primula, H.M.S., 49
Privet (Q-19), 40, 153
Prize (Q-21), three-masted schooner (see *First Prize* and *Else*), 32, 51, 53, 54, 55, 65, 69, 115
Probus, brigantine, 75, 76
Protected convoys, 100

Q

"Q" ships generally, 11, 12, 13, 17, 19, 34, 40, 48, 49, 50, 64, 65, 66, 67, 75, 76, 93, 125
"Q" sailing ships, 76
Q-5 (*Lodorer*), 39
Q-7, 19
Q-9 (*Mary B. Mitchell*, etc), 13, 14, 15, 16, 17
Q-12, 56
Q-13, 11, 13, 37
Q-18 (*Lady Olive*), 33, 34
Q-19 (*Privet*), 40
Q-21 (*Prize, First Prize, Else*), 51, 54
Q-22, 18
Q-25 (*Lady Patricia, Paxton*), 67
Q-30, 18
Quail, H.M.S., 31
Queen Alexandra, transport, 139
Queen Louise, transport, 42, 43
Queenstown, 27, 40, 55, 59, 61, 67, 70, 75, 80, 99, 100, 122, 141, 157

R

Rafts, adventures on, 34
Raikes, Lieut.-Com. R. H. T., 60
Ramming, 30, 148
Ramsay, S.S. (Captain J. A. McLean), 138
Ramsgate, 36, 41, 42, 104
Ranter, fishing trawler, 82
Rathlin Island, 122
Rathmullen, 92
Rawlings, Skipper Alfred, 46

INDEX

Reay, Lieut. Marshall, D.S.C., R.N.R., 112
Redwald, H.M. Drifter, 42
Reich, Erich, bo'sun's mate, *UB*-53, 102
Remy, Kap.-Leut. J. (*UB*-70), 130
Result, topsail schooner, 32
Retriever, H.M.S., 130
"Richardson, Mr. J. V." (Commander Babcock), 55
Ries, Leut. C. (*UC*-77), 65
Riga, 13
Robin Hood's Bay, 149, 150
Rockpool, S.S., 111
Rohr, Leut.-Com. (*U*-84), 50, 51
Roker Pier Lighthouse, 26
Rolleston, Rear-Admiral J. P., D.S.O., 85
Ronaldshay, 38
Rovenska, H.M. Yacht, 37
Rowanmore, S.S., 63
Rowe, Lieut. J. T., R.N.R. (*Sitvel*), 160
Roxburgh, H.M., Armed Cruiser (Capt. G. W. Vivian), 12, 64, 70, 121, 122
Royalist, H.M. Destroyer, M.L., 45, 63
Royal Sovereign, Eastbourne, 61
Rucker, Lieut.-Com. Claus (*U*-103), 140, 141, 156
Russell, H.M.S., 58

S

Safa-el-Bahr, H.M. Yacht, 58
Saida, 68
Sailing ships, 65
St. Abb's Head, 61, 132
St. Catherine's Point, 66
St. George's Channel, 112, 114
St. Kilda, 91, 111, 122
St. Malo, 14, 17
St. Mary's, 15
St. Minian, S.S., 29, 30
Salonika, 9
Salvage, 10
Salvia, 74
Salzwedel (*UC*-71, *UB*-81), 104, 105
San Urbino, S.S., 60
Sanders, Lieut. W. A., V.C., R.N.R., 52, 54, 55
Sandettie, 117, 119, 159
Santander, 131, 142
Santaren, S.S., 86
Sapphire, steam yacht, 85
Sarah Colebrooke, ketch, 32
Sarba, H.M. Trawler, 100
Sardinia, S.S., 15
Scandinavian convoys, 65, 95, 100, 110, 138
Scapa, 7, 108, 153
Scarborough, 96
Scheer, Admiral, 29, 51, 101
Schelle, Kap.-Leut. Martin (*UB*-65), 148
Schmettow, Graf von, 62
Schmitz (*UC*-75), 142, 144
Schouen Bank Buoy, 101
Schoute, Captain (*UC*-75), 142
Schouwen Lightship, 83

Schrader, Ober-Leut. von (*UB*-64), 90, 93
Schulze, Otto, 155
Schwieger (*U*-20), 83, 84, 94
Scillies, 36, 113, 141
Scotland, 33, 48, 68, 69, 78, 83, 87, 110, 152
Sea-bottles, 20, 29
Seaflower, drifter, 134
Seaham, 23
Sea King, H.M. Trawler, 72, 73
Seaplanes, 33, 64, 67, 70, 131
Sea Singer, H.M. Trawler, 73
Seevers, Leut. G., 91
Seuffer, Captain, 128
Shackleton, Sir Ernest, 94
Shambles, 61
Shapinsay Sound, 10
Shetlands, 44, 95, 155
Shields, 32, 38
Shipmates, drifter, 134
Ships' boats, adventures of, 34
Shipwash, 33, 145
Sicily, 49, 131
Siebs, Leut.-Com. G. (*U*-41), 58
Sierra Leone, 132
Silvel, H.M. Trawler (Lieut. J. T. Rowe), 160
Sims, U.S. Admiral ("W. S. Davidson"') 55
Sinkings, 1917, 35
Sixth Flotilla, 36
Skageraak, 153
Skaw, 91, 111
Skerryvore, 90, 92
Skoldulf, S.S., 14
Sloops, 9
Smalls, 34, 51, 120
Smithwick, Lieut.-Com. A. R., D.S.O., R.N., 121
Smith's Knoll, 33, 77
Smoke-screens, 40, 73, 116
Snapdragon, H.M. Sloop, 153
Souter Point, 23
South China Sea, 20
South Arklow Lightship, 43
South-east coast, 76
Southampton, 64
Southwold, 29, 64
South Falls, 101
Spain, 12, 141, 155
Spar Buoy, 77
Speedwell, H.M. Trawler, 24
Spiegel, 52, 54
Spies, German, 19
Spiess, Kap.-Leut., 107, 122
Spurn Head, 31
Start Point, 61, 100
Statendam, S.S., Holland-Amerika Line (see *Justicia*), 89
Stavanger, 107
Steam trawlers, 38
Steam yachts, 38
Steinbrinck, 32

INDEX

Steinhauer, Lieut.-Com. (*UB*-48), 54
Stenhouse, Lieut. J.R., D.S.C., R.N.R., 49
Stirling S.S., 24
Stonecrop (*Glenfoyle*), 93
Stonehaven, 132
Stornoway, 42, 64
Strathclunie, H.M. Trawler, 149.
Strongbow, H.M. Destroyer, 100
Stuart, Lieut. R. N., D.S.O., R.N., 72
Sturgeon, H.M., Destroyer, 130
Stuttgart, 8
Submarines, generally (see *U*-boats, passim.), 8, 29, 36, 40, 44, 60, 69, 83, 97, 109, 110, 114, 135, 144, 157, 158, 160
Submarines, British, 97
Submarine warfare, unrestricted, 32
Sunderland, 9, 21, 23, 26
Sunk Light, 23, 33, 40, 93, 145
Surf, H.M. Yacht, 22
Suvla, 130
Swallow, H.M. Trawler, 29, 30
Swanmore, 54
Sweden, 111
Swedish steamers, 23
Swilly, Lough, 21, 22, 40, 88
Swift, H.M.S., 58
Sylvia, H.M. Destroyer, 94, 95

T

Taranto, 48
Tarbet Ness, 10
Tay, 9, 82
Tebbenjohanns, 32, 33, 38, 39
Tees, 21
Teichmann and Logischen, Leut. Freiherr von (*UB*-54), 130
Teredo worm, 48
Thames, 63, 76
Thirza, 18
Thistle, trawler, 25
Thomas Young, H.M. Trawler, 82
Thorbecke, Captain (*König Albert*), 78
Thornhill, S.S., 48
Thrasher, H.M.S., 31
Tietze, Sub-Lieut, 148
Timber, 106
Titanic, S.S., 149
Tirpitz, Admiral von, 147
T.N.T., 21, 65
Tokio, armed trawler, 106
Toli-Toli, 21
Tongue Lightship, 40
Tor Head, 133
Torpedo-boat 4 (British), 41, 42, 46, 63
Torpedo-boat, 78 (German), 21, 77, 78, 90
Torr Head, 81
Tottenham, Lieut.-Com. C. L., D.S.O., R.N.R., 131
Tory Island, 15, 21, 90
Toulon, 44
Trager, Kap.-Leut., 113, 114

"Trap" Ships (see "*Q*"-boats), 53
Trawlers, 8, 40, 54, 117
Trerieve, S.S. (Captain Cundy), 155
Trevose Head, 42
Tripel, S.S., 44
Tripolitanian coast, 144
Tronda, S.S., 144
Tucker, U.S. ship, 74
Tulip, H.M. Sloop, 56
Turnbull, Lieut. R. J., R.N.R., 65, 66
Tuscania, S.S. (Anchor Line), 121
Tuskar, 32, 51, 120
Tyne, 9, 21, 23, 64, 110, 152

U

U-boats generally, 27, 43, 51, 64, 65, 99, 102, 107, 118, 120, 125, 144, 157, 158
U-8, 31
U-19, 107, 122
U-20, 83, 144
U-21, 35
U-26, 45, 60
U-28, 83
U-32 (Albrecht), 131, 139
U-33, 155
U-34, 153, 156
U-35, 49, 155
U-38, 122
U-39, 65, 141, 155
U-41 (Siehs), 58
U-43, 53, 54, 93, 121, 125
U-44, 77, 78
U-45, 85, 86
U-46, 67, 96
U-47, 152
U-48 (Buck), 101, 102
U-49, 65, 85, 147
U-50, 96
U-52 (Hans Rose), 155
U-53, 151
U-54, 86, 92, 121
U-58, 99, 100, 123, 129
U-59, 46, 63
U-61, 132
U-62, 56, 111
U-63, 155
U-64 (Moraht), 43, 44, 45, 72, 145
U-65, 153
U-66, 96
U-67, 53
U-68, 32
U-69, 76
U-72, 153
U-73, 56, 58, 153
U-75, 108, 109
U-76, 23, 31
U-78 (mine-layer), 56, 153
U-81, 60
U-83, 32, 40
U-84 (Rohr), 50, 51, 120, 126
U-86, 46, 106
U-88, 83, 93

INDEX

U-89, 122
U-92, 121, 152
U-93, 52, 54, 55, 115
U-94, 111
U-95, 121
U-96, 105
U-99, 74
U-102, 152
U-103 (Rucker), 140, 141
U-104 (Bernis), 111, 112, 113
U-106, 96
U-109, 118, 119, 121
U-110 (Korvetten-Kap. Kroll), 123, 124
U-151 (Kophamel), 83, 93
U-154 (Gercke), 70, 138, 140
U-155, 70
U-156, 70, 152
U-157, 70, 132
U-293 (*UB*-49), 85
UB-boats, generally, 7, 23, 24, 79, 84, 157
UB-6, 40
UB-8, 146
UB-10, 153
UB-12, 150
UB-16 (Luhe), 138, 139
UB-17, 129
UB-18, 100
UB-19, 19, 34, 50
UB-20, 79
UB-21 (Hashagen), 111, 129
UB-22, 116
UB-23 (Voigt), 12, 77
UB-27, 77
UB-30, 151, 152
UB-31, 139
UB-32, 81
UB-33, 132
UB-35, 118, 119, 121
UB-36, 19, 75
UB-37, 20, 31, 50
UB-38, 119, 129
UB-39, 66
UB-40, 153
UB-41, 96
UB-48 (Steinhauer), 54, 55, 153
UB-49 (*U*-293), 85
UB-52, 138, 141
UB-53 (Sprenger), 103, 151
UB-54 (Logischen), 130
UB-55 (Wenniger), 134, 135
UB-56, 110, 119, 141
UB-57, 152
UB-58, 130
UB-59, 153
UB-61, 102
UB-63, 86, 87, 121
UB-64 (Schrader), 90, 93
UB-65 (Schelle), 148
UB-66, 116
UB-68, 153
UB-69, 116
UB-70 (Remy), 130, 139
UB-71, 133
UB-72 (Traeger), 113, 114, 115, 133, 138, 141
UB-74, 132, 142
UB-75, 96, 105, 108
UB-78, 139
UB-81 (Salzwedel) 99, 104, 105
UB-82, 81, 133
UB-83, 121, 152
UB-85 (Krech), 137, 138
UB-90, 121, 153
UB-103, 152
UB-104, 152
UB-107, 150
UB-108, 150
UB-109, 152
UB-110 (Fürbringer), 148, 149
UB-113, 152
UB-115, 152
UB-119, 144
UB-123, 152
UB-124 (Wutzdorff), 91, 92
UB-126, 121
UB-127, 152
UB-128, 146
UB-129, 153
UC, Types of, 7, 79, 99, 157
UC-1, 76
UC-4, 153
UC-6, 94
UC-11 (Utke), 79, 145, 146
UC-14, 96
UC-16, 79, 96
UC-17, 27, 40, 43
UC-18, 40
UC-20, 146
UC-21 (Zerboni de Sposetti), 94
UC-24, 69
UC-25, 153
UC-26, 61, 62
UC-29, 71
UC-30, 48, 56
UC-33 (Arnold), 93, 94
UC-34, 153
UC-35, 141
UC-36, 67
UC-38 (Wenlandt), 109
UC-39, 31
UC-41, 81, 82
UC-42 (Muller), 61, 84, 93
UC-43, 9, 36, 37
UC-44, 32, 38, 39, 84, 93
UC-45, 32
UC-46, 32, 61
UC-47, 101
UC-48, 130
UC-49, 144
UC-50, 119, 128
UC-51, 97
UC-53, 153
UC-54, 153
UC-55, 40, 65, 68, 95
UC-56, 131
UC-57, 101
UC-61, 76

UC-62, 96, 97
UC-64, 145
UC-65, 32, 99
UC-66, 73
UC-68, 32, 47, 56
UC-69, 105
UC-70, 151
UC-71 (Salzwedel), 104
UC-72, 93
UC-73, 144, 146
UC-75 (Schmitz), 61, 142, 145
UC-76, 45, 63
UC-77 (Ries), 46, 47, 65, 70, 148
UC-78, 139
UC-79, 96
Udsire, 106
Unterseeboots Abteilung, 131, 142
Unterseeboots Flotilla, 81
Unterseeboots Flotilla IV, 133
Unterseeboots Flotilla V, 133
U.S.A., entry into war, 55
U.S. Destroyers, 100
Ushant, 14, 15, 16, 18, 74, 75
Utke, Leut. Kurt (UC-11), 145

V

Valentia, 65
Valentiner, Max, 43
Valeria, S.S., Cunarder, 73, 74
Valorous, H.M. Drifter, 136
Vane Shoal, 134
Vanessa, H.M. Yacht, 150
Varne Lightship, 129, 133
Vaterland, ex-German liner, 90, 91
Vedette, H.M. Armed Trawler, 82
Vigo, 14
Villefranche, 141
Virgilia, trawler, 46
Virginia, 70
Vittoria, collier, Q-ship (see *Pargust*), 71
Vivian, Capt. Q. W., R.N. (H.M.S. *Roxburgh*, armed cruiser), 121
Voight, Lieut.-Com., 12, 13
Vulcan, H.M.S. (submarine mother-ship), 40, 41, 60

W

Wadsworth, U.S. destroyer, 59, 110
Wagenfuhr, Leut.-Com., 77, 78
Wainwright, U.S. Destroyer, 59, 61
Walker, A., Skipper, 81
Wallflower, H.M. Sloop, 58, 131, 139
War Channel, the, 29, 59, 146
Waring, Pilot Lieut., R.A.F., 152
Warrant-officers, German, as navigators, 23
Waterford, 38, 84, 93, 94
Waveney, H.M.S., 30
Webster, Lieut. D. T., R.N.R., 116
Weekly sinkings, 138
Wehr, German Petty Officer (UB-52), 142

Wellholme (see *Wonganella*, *Werribee*, Q-ship), 48
Welsh coast, 110
Wenlandt (UC-38), 109
Wenninger, Leut.-Com. Ralph (UB-55), 134
Werribee (see *Wellholme*, *Wonganella*, Q-ship), 48
Weser, 111
West Bay, 34, 131
West Hinder Lightship, 67
Westego, U.S. tanker, 86
Westerbrock, 54
Western Approaches, 51, 64
Western Mediterranean, 115, 139
Westward Ho! H.M. Trawler, 41
Weymouth, 19
Whale explodes mine, 20, 21
Whalebone-pattern minelaying, 63
Wharton, Skipper W. S., D.S.C., R.N.R., 28, 29
Whistle Buoy, 40
Whitby, 9, 21, 29, 30, 37, 61, 152
White, Lieut.-Com. John, R.N., 46
White, Skipper (*Aegusa*), 58
White Sea, minesweeping in, 50
Wick, 40
Wilhelmshaven, 26, 36, 46, 78, 100, 101, 111, 123, 146, 159
William Tennant, drifter, 96
Williams, Captain W. H., 54, 55
Williams, Seaman W., R.N.R., 72
Wireless, U-boats use of, 65
Wissant Shoal, 77, 120
Wolf, German raider, 8, 20, 21
Wonganella, Q-ship, (see *Wellholme* and *Werribee*), 48, 49, 73, 74
Worsley, Lieut.-Com. F. H., D.S.O., 94
W. S. Bailey of Granton, Q-ship trawler, 87, 121
Wutsdorff, Ober-Leut. (UB-124), 91

Y

Yachts, armed, 10
Yorkshire coast, 29, 37, 59, 61, 96, 148, 150
Young Crow, drifter, 81, 151
Young Fred, drifter, 133

Z

Z-1, British airship, 151
Zan Zeferino, S.S., 94
Zeebrugge, 13, 58, 63, 77, 79, 96, 97, 104, 118, 127, 128, 135, 145, 146, 150, 152, 158, 159
Zeebrugge Mole, 117
Zeebrugge as submarine base, 101
Zerboni di Sposetti, Com. (UC-21), 94
Ziegler, Sub.-Lt., 54
Zylpha, S.S., Q-ship, 72, 74
Zubian, H.M.S. (Q-ship), 124, 127, 128
Zulu, H.M. Destroyer, 127

www.ingramcontent.com/pod-product-compliance
Lightning Source LLC
Chambersburg PA
CBHW071820230426
43670CB00013B/2515